MW00444318

Infractions

Infractions

Rule Violations, Unethical Conduct,
and Enforcement in the NCAA

JERRY PARKINSON

University of Nebraska Press
Lincoln

Portions of this book have previously appeared in
"Scoundrels: An Inside Look at the NCAA Infractions and
Enforcement Processes," *Wyoming Law Review* 12, no. 1
(2012): 215–36; and "The Impact of Social Media on NCAA
Infractions Cases," *Mississippi Sports Law Review* 1, no. 1
(2011): 37–69.

Library of Congress Cataloging-in-Publication Data
Names: Parkinson, Jerry, 1954– author.
Title: Infractions: rule violations, unethical conduct, and
enforcement in the NCAA / Jerry Parkinson.
Description: Lincoln: University of Nebraska Press, [2019] |
Includes bibliographical references and index.
Identifiers: LCCN 2018049386
ISBN 9781496205476 (cloth: alk. paper)
ISBN 9781496216922 (epub)
ISBN 9781496216939 (mobi)
ISBN 9781496216946 (pdf)
Subjects: LCSH: National Collegiate Athletic
Association—Rules and practice. | College sports—
Administration—United States. | College sports—Corrupt
practices—United States. | College sports—Moral and
ethical aspects—United States.
Classification: LCC GV351 .P37 2019 |
DDC 796.04/30973—dc23
LC record available at https://lccn.loc.gov/2018049386

Set in Questa by E. Cuddy.

To Deb, my beautiful life partner and soul mate . . .

Thanks for all the wonderful memories and
for all your sacrifices.

Contents

Acknowledgments

I owe a great debt to my son, Josh, who helped to research and write some of the chapters. His creativity helped the book immensely, and he deserves considerable credit for keeping me on task and for providing an honest, critical eye. Josh's name probably deserves to be alongside mine on the cover of this book.

Other family members provided immense support throughout the project, particularly my wife, Deb, who kept things afloat whenever I holed up in our basement office to write. Many thanks to my daughter, Angela; her husband, Gary; and their beautiful daughters, Maya and Zoe; to my daughter-in-law, Paige, and young Whit and Dylan; to my father-in-law, Harry Simmons; and to my brothers, Dave and Larry, who read early chapters and provided encouragement.

I'm deeply grateful to three dear friends who also read earlier drafts and provided helpful comments and encouragement: Garth Massey, Alyson Hagy, and Jill Higham. All are superb writers; just having them in my corner meant a lot.

Much of my writing occurred during a time when I was employed at the University of Wyoming College of Law. Thank you to deans Steve Easton, Jacquelyn Bridgeman, and Klint Alexander for supporting my work with summer research support. Thanks to David Swank and Phil Dubois for making it possible for me to serve on the Committee on Infractions in the first place. And deepest thanks to the Schwartz family—particularly Bill and Cheryl Schwartz and Sally and

Jim Belcher. For several years, I was privileged to serve as the William T. Schwartz Professor at the College of Law, and that endowed professorship also provided support, both financially and otherwise. The biggest benefit of the professorship was to know the Schwartz/Belcher clan; I count them among my dearest friends.

I'm grateful to Rob Taylor and his colleagues at the University of Nebraska Press. Rob's eagerness to publish the book was heartening. My project editor at the press, Sara Springsteen, was terrific, as was copy editor Jeremy Hall. The design crew, marketing staff, and others at the press are simply first-rate. Special thanks to Jackson Adams and Rosemary Sekora.

This work germinated in a presentation I made at the University of Wyoming College of Law in September 2011. The presentation resulted in the publication of an essay in the *Wyoming Law Review*, and I am grateful to the law review editors for allowing me to use in this book some of the same material that appears in the journal. Other portions of the book appeared in the inaugural issue of the *Mississippi Sports Law Review*, and I thank those editors as well for permission to use that material.

Finally, I'm indebted to the many colleagues with whom I worked on the NCAA Committee on Infractions. I have never worked with a more talented, more dedicated group of individuals. To consider what they have contributed, many on a volunteer basis, to the goal of keeping college athletics fair and clean is simply mind-boggling.

Infractions

Introduction

Nathan Darrell Ford sent an email message to me and other members of the NCAA's Division I Committee on Infractions in December 2000, shortly after the committee had released its public report in a major infractions case involving Southern Methodist University (SMU).

> How can you people impose such a stupid penalty on a major university that you have already KILLED before with your decisions, just to set an example? Why haven't you all checked into the larger, richer programs that are committing far worse violations than these? Why have you chosen SMU to KILL? You must be getting an awful lot of compensation for looking the other way. This school tried to do what's right and conduct an inhouse investigation, and impose sanctions on itself, yet you still have to bury a hatchet in our spine with probation. How can you live with yourselves? You will be held accountable some day [sic], if not judgement day, for your actions. This will go down in history, just as the death penalty did, as the most unfair, hiddeous [sic] thing in the world. I sure hope you enjoy your little power now while you have it, because GOD will deal with you ALL for your part in ruining a good ! institution. Thanks For Nothing, Nathan Darrell Ford.

The case involved violations in SMU's football program related to recruiting, "extra benefits" to student athletes, academic fraud, and unethical conduct by an assistant coach. The infractions committee imposed several penalties on the institution, including a two-year period of probation, a vacation of records in games in which a student athlete competed while ineligible, and a reduction in the number of expense-paid recruiting visits for prospects. None of these sanctions was the least bit extraordinary, particularly the two-year probation that Mr. Ford likened to a "hatchet in [the] spine."

Unless you're a graduate of SMU or are particularly attuned to this school's athletic fortunes for some other reason, you're likely never to have heard of this infractions case—and for good reason: it's simply one of dozens of major infractions cases to have been decided since 2000, and it certainly did not garner the attention from the media and sports fans that many other cases have. Mr. Ford's email message, though, raises several themes that permeate discussions of NCAA rules enforcement:

> The unbridled passion many people have for college sports generally and for their favorite teams in particular. Many fans are simply incapable of viewing their teams' troubles with any semblance of objectivity; when sanctions are imposed, these superfans believe *in their souls* that the NCAA has wronged them. It is not surprising, then, that people like Mr. Ford seek to call down the wrath of GOD upon those responsible.

> Assumptions about what NCAA sanctions mean and the impact of those sanctions. Probation, for example, is almost meaningless, except in public perception. Of course, many readers know that SMU is the only Division I school on which the "death penalty" has been imposed, so Mr. Ford's fear of sanctions "killing" a program may be more justified than the fears of others.

> A perception that schools receive differential treatment in the imposition of sanctions based on status, conference affiliation, or some other characteristic. Mr. Ford's suggestion that rule enforcers would take money "for looking

the other way" is a bit extreme, but it highlights the depth of the perception.

Mitigation of penalties. What kind of "credit" should be given to a school that cooperates fully with the NCAA, including conducting a thorough internal investigation and imposing meaningful sanctions on itself? Was sufficient credit given to Penn State in 2012, for example, for hiring former FBI director Louis Freeh to investigate allegations of child sexual abuse and then accepting the Freeh report without a hint of dissent?

The legitimacy of NCAA sanctions. Mr. Ford, for example, seems to assume that penalties are improper if they are "just to set an example." But isn't deterrence of misconduct by others a legitimate objective of the sanctioning process? What about other objectives? To use Penn State again, is it legitimate to use sanctions as a means of changing campus *culture*?

I address all these themes, and many more, in this book. One of my objectives is to shine some light on a process that receives substantial attention from media and sports fans across the nation. Try Googling any major infractions case to get an idea of the level of interest in these matters. A recent search for "Louisville infractions case," for example, yielded "about 147,000 results" in a half second. Head to the Southeastern Conference, where college sports are *really* taken seriously, and expect to find much more.

When it comes to major infractions cases, everyone has an opinion, but it has become increasingly clear to me over the years that even knowledgeable college sports fans know very little about how an NCAA infractions case *really* is processed. I hope this book helps to fill an informational void, even for (or perhaps particularly for) those who reserve their harshest criticism for the NCAA itself.

Let's face it—some readers have picked up this book because they are looking for an exposé on NCAA scoundrels who selectively enforce the rules, conduct poor investigations, impose ridiculous penalties, and engage in a variety of nefarious deeds that undermine the fair administration of intercollegiate athletics. Sorry, no such exposé is forthcoming. I might as well be clear at the outset that I consider the real scoundrels in this arena to be the rule violators, not the rule enforcers. That is not to say that NCAA officials don't screw up occasionally. They do, and the book addresses some of these screwups. The fiasco that developed in the investigation of the University of Miami is a good example. Improprieties in that case led to the firing of the NCAA's vice president of enforcement and one of her directors of enforcement. But true misconduct by rule enforcers is rare.

Of course, I'm biased. I spent much of the first decade of the twenty-first century immersed in NCAA infractions cases. In April 2000 I was appointed to the Division I Committee on Infractions as the committee's first coordinator of appeals. I argued my last appeal in January 2010, officially ending my service on the committee after nearly ten years. I did fill in occasionally after that time as a substitute on the committee when it was shorthanded for a particular hearing. In addition to participating in over one hundred infractions cases, I handled twenty-eight appeals on behalf of the committee, including twenty-two oral arguments at appeal hearings.

During that time, I had the unique opportunity to observe firsthand the NCAA enforcement staff, the infractions committee, and others involved in the rules-enforcement process. I know of instances, in addition to the Miami case, in which investigators' conduct appeared to be out-of-bounds. I also can recall committee-imposed penalties that have seemed, in retrospect, to be either heavy-handed or too lenient. And as the committee's former appeals coordinator, I certainly can take issue with decisions of the Infractions Appeals Committee that reversed penalties I tried mightily to defend on appeal. But for the most part, these isolated incidents represent disagreements over the exercise of professional judgment, and rarely could I question the integrity or personal motives of those making such judgments. Overwhelmingly, the individuals tasked with enforcing NCAA rules are dedicated, hardworking people acting in good faith to try to get things right.

My intent in writing this book is not to defend the NCAA. It is a high-profile organization, and criticism of its actions comes with the territory. When the NCAA gets it wrong, critics have every right to point out the NCAA's shortcomings. Again, the Miami case provides a good example; the NCAA certainly invites scorn when it shoots itself in the foot. But I do believe that a more balanced perspective is in order. In recent years, it seems to have become almost fashionable to bash the NCAA in the most disparaging terms:

> Pulitzer Prize–winning civil rights historian Taylor Branch blasts the NCAA in *The Atlantic* in an article titled "The Shame of College Sports." Branch's shrill tone overshadows what might otherwise be compelling arguments about exploitation of student athletes. And when he tackles the infractions process, using a Florida State case as his example, he mischaracterizes the process badly and descends into the kind of critique one would expect from a superfan: "Cruelly, but typically, the NCAA concentrated public censure on powerless scapegoats."

> *New York Times* columnist Joe Nocera decides to use his regular column in one of the country's foremost newspapers to tell, for weeks on end, one-sided stories of NCAA "abuses." Nocera's attacks are stunning in their lack of objectivity and ignorance of basic components of the NCAA rules-enforcement process. ("I stand corrected. Contrary to my assertion last Saturday, the N.C.A.A. does allow college athletes to engage a lawyer if they are accused of violating its rules.")

> Buzz Bissinger, another Pulitzer Prize winner and the author of *Friday Night Lights*, likens the NCAA to the Mafia in the wake of the Cam Newton controversy: "Like the Mafia, the

National Collegiate Athletic Association, ostensibly there to sanction college sports and keep the game clean, is really in the business of finding fall guys to protect the multimillion-dollar empire."

U.S. congressman Bobby Rush of Illinois also uses the Mafia comparison ("I think you would compare the NCAA to Al Capone and to the Mafia") but then ups the ante: the NCAA is "just one of the most vicious, most ruthless organizations ever created by mankind."

Award-winning journalist Frank Deford characterizes the NCAA on National Public Radio as "an incredibly hypocritical and autocratic cartel . . . [that] peddl[es] sanctimonious claptrap about how it really cares about academics."

My, oh my. It's a miracle this nasty leviathan hasn't been shut down completely by now. But wait . . . would that jeopardize the Big Dance? The NCAA is such an easy target, of course, because of our age-old tendency to look beyond the *people* involved in administering organizations—associations such as the NCAA, corporations, and government agencies—and to view the organizations as faceless, monolithic entities without a heart or a conscience.

The IRS comes to mind—another entity that's easy to bash. Not long ago, I read an interesting column from a tax blogger with a startling approach to the agency: "It's easy to cast the IRS as the villain, a heartless entity seeking to punish honest hardworking people, but at the end of the day, the IRS is concerned about one thing: generating revenue. They don't make the tax laws; they simply enforce and collect on them. With all the political talk about debts and deficits, you'd think more politicians would laud the IRS for their efforts to more accurately collect tax revenue." How refreshing—a straightforward, unemotional, and practical view that implicitly recognizes the hard work and admirable motives of the people behind the scenes.

Part of my effort in this book is to shine a similar light on the people involved in the conduct of infractions cases. The NCAA, after all, does not exist in a vacuum; it is the embodiment of thousands of people who represent NCAA member institutions, some of whom are often among the association's most vocal critics, and hundreds of people who actually work at NCAA headquarters or who volunteer to serve on NCAA committees. My hope is that an appreciation for the jobs these people do will help to temper some of the more outlandish criticism. Even Rick Neuheisel (formerly head football coach at Colorado, Washington, and UCLA), who won a $2.5 million settlement with the NCAA as a result of one infractions case, has been quoted as saying this about NCAA investigators: "At first I thought they were out to get me. But you start to learn who the people are and spend more time with the people. A lot are just trying to do their job."

My last appellate case provides a good example of NCAA rule enforcers just trying to do their job, in the face of withering criticism. The case involved the University of Memphis men's basketball team, which made it to the national championship game in 2008. Leading their team that year was a freshman point guard named Derrick Rose, who moved on to the Chicago Bulls as the year's number-one draft pick and later became both NBA Rookie of the Year and the youngest MVP in NBA history.

(Note: The NCAA's public infractions reports do not name student athletes or even coaches involved in rule violations, even though virtually all major cases are the subject of local or national media reports and those news accounts do name names. The Memphis case, because of its high-profile nature, was discussed at length in the national media, and all observers were aware that Derrick Rose was at the heart of the case. In some cases, it seems almost quaint that the NCAA continues its practice of anonymity, particularly with respect to coaches and other nonstudents who are involved in rule violations. In 2009–10 I chaired a penalty subcommittee of the infractions committee, and that subcommittee recommended a policy change to permit the use of nonstudent names in public infractions reports. In this book, I occasionally use widely known names but generally do not use names of student athletes, particularly in more obscure cases.)

One of the allegations in the Memphis case was that Derrick Rose had been ineligible to compete because someone else had taken his SAT, upon which his admission to the University of Memphis was based. Following a hearing, the infractions committee determined that Rose was indeed ineligible because the Educational Testing Service (ETS), which administers the SAT, had concluded that there was evidence of impropriety in the taking of Rose's exam, which thus invalidated his score. Contrary to popular belief, the Committee on Infractions did not make its own finding of cheating; it based Rose's ineligibility on the invalidation by the ETS of Rose's test score. The infractions committee then determined that the University of Memphis, as a consequence of competing with an ineligible player, would have to vacate its record thirty-eight-win season achieved with the help of Rose.

The University of Memphis appealed, and the Infractions Appeals Committee upheld the penalty, with straightforward reasoning: the ETS's invalidation of Rose's SAT score rendered him academically ineligible, and vacating or forfeiting wins is common at all levels of athletic competition when a team competes with an ineligible player. Not surprisingly, though, the NCAA became the target of online venom from Memphis fans: "crooks," "absolute crap," "arrogant and self-serving," the "NCAA is corrupt and everyone knows it."

One comment on ESPN *Conversations* following the Memphis appeals decision was particularly interesting: "Total bull from the NCAA. A self-protecting ruling which ignores any form of logic, *even Vitale logic*. The NCAA has no credibility left after this decision." The italicized reference, of course, is to Dick Vitale, who had been quoted in *USA Today* as saying, "My feeling is Memphis' appeal of the decision has merit. The NCAA Clearinghouse indicated on several occasions that Derrick Rose was eligible to play. Why have a clearinghouse if its word is meaningless?"

With all due respect to Mr. Vitale, who certainly has earned his status as a college basketball guru, that analysis is awfully simplistic. The NCAA Clearinghouse (now the Eligibility Center) is responsible for certifying student athletes as eligible to compete. But of course, the clearinghouse can act only on information that is available to it. If the clearinghouse, for example, has no information that a student athlete's standardized test scores are anything but legitimate, it reasonably will certify the student athlete as eligible to compete. In the Memphis case, as the public infractions report makes clear, *the university* had information in the fall of 2007, as the basketball season was just beginning, that Rose's test scores were in question. After interviewing Rose, who denied any impropriety, university officials chose to allow him to compete. The NCAA Clearinghouse, however, first learned about the SAT irregularities in a May 2008 communication from the ETS, after Rose had competed for the entire season.

There's nothing special about the criticism in the Memphis case; indeed, most high-profile infractions cases engender equally passionate criticism of the NCAA, sometimes from observers who think the enforcers were too *lenient* on rule breakers. But the Memphis case does illustrate how misperceptions about infractions cases are formed; sometimes if commentators and other observers would scratch just below the surface, they might develop a deeper understanding of how infractions decisions are made. It is my hope that this book will encourage readers to do just that.

One place to start would be the NCAA website (ncaa.org). The website provides explanations of the enforcement and infractions processes, and it also includes a copy of the NCAA *Division I Manual* (the rule book) so that observers can see for themselves what is required or prohibited by the rules. More importantly, the website also contains full reports of every major infractions case ever decided. (After accessing the website, click on "Division I," then "Compliance" and "Legislative Services Database." Click "Search" and go to "Major Infractions," which will take one to an interactive database on major infractions cases.)

My focus in this book is strictly on the rules-enforcement process. I leave it to others to examine NCAA policies relating to compensation or exploitation of student athletes, use of student-athlete likenesses in video games and other commercial ventures, concussion prevention and treatment, status of student athletes as "employees" for purposes of labor relations or workers compensation, or a myriad of other current hot topics on the agenda of both the NCAA and its critics.

Finally, my goal with this book is to entertain as well as to educate. There are some remarkable stories here—tales from the dark side of college athletics. I present this information from the perspective of an insider, based on my experience with the Committee on Infractions. I speak only for myself, however, not the NCAA or the infractions committee. I've also done my best not to breach confidences. Nearly everything in this book relating to particular cases is information that is readily available, either in public media accounts or in public infractions reports found on the NCAA website. I urge those with a deeper interest in particular infractions cases to access the public reports; many provide compelling tales that need no embellishment in this or any other book.

1

The Fallout

Nose in but fingers out.

BILL SWAN

The kid could play ball. He was six feet eight, a force in the paint as a junior college center, and a fearsome shot blocker. From all indications, this was a guy who could make the transition from junior college to Division I ball. Consequently, several D1 schools took a serious look at him . . . until they discovered the problem.

NCAA bylaws permit student athletes from two-year colleges to transfer to NCAA Division I institutions and become immediately eligible to compete *if* they "receive an associate or equivalent degree in an academic or technical, rather than a vocational, curriculum." This particular prospect attended Coastal Georgia Community College and was enrolled in the junior college's welding-technology curriculum. That curriculum, described in the junior college's course catalog as vocational, led to a certificate of welding.

One can imagine the one-minute conversations occurring in spring 2002 on several college campuses around the country:

Coach: We have a strong juco prospect out of Georgia—can shoot, rebound, block shots; runs the floor well; 6'8" but plays even bigger than that. Problem is, he's going to get a certificate of welding.

Director of athletics: A *what?*

Coach: A welding certificate.

Director of athletics: Nice try, Coach. Come back when you have a real prospect.

St. Bonaventure, however, was undeterred. The men's basketball coaching staff had had its eye on this kid since January, and he was the real deal. They invited him to make an official recruiting visit to the campus in upstate New York in early April, and shortly afterward, he signed a National Letter of Intent to play ball for the Bonnies.

Yes, there was some concern about the student athlete's eligibility. The university's senior woman athletics administrator, who had oversight responsibility for rules compliance, sent an email to the Atlantic 10 Conference's assistant commissioner for compliance, seeking a definition of a degree that was "equivalent" to an associate degree. The Atlantic 10 representative responded that the two-year college awarding the degree must consider it to be equivalent to an associate degree. Thus, exercising due diligence, the university's assistant athletics director for student services and compliance, at the direction of athletics director Gothard Lane, faxed a letter to the registrar at Coastal Georgia, asking for an interpretation of the certificate in welding. The registrar responded promptly with a letter explaining that "the certificate programs are not considered equivalents to the associate's degree program."

End of discussion. Lane delivered the bad news to the head coach of the men's basketball team, Jan van Breda Kolff: sorry, the kid is ineligible. But van Breda Kolff *wanted* him . . . and he had an ace in the hole.

Robert Wickenheiser was president of St. Bonaventure. He was also a big basketball fan and, just the year before, had strongly supported the hiring of van Breda Kolff as head coach at St. Bonaventure. The hiring was considered a coup: van Breda Kolff not only had had a successful professional career as a player, but he also came with a superb bloodline as the son of former college and NBA coaching great Butch van Breda

Kolff. Jan was coming off a 47-18 two-year record at Pepperdine, after successful head coaching stints at Vanderbilt and Cornell. His hiring would elevate the profile of St. Bonaventure instantly. Naturally, Wickenheiser would be inclined to support van Breda Kolff's efforts to bring St. Bonaventure back to national prominence. (The university made it to the Final Four in 1970, led by future Hall of Famer Bob Lanier.) This would be a particularly natural instinct for the president since van Breda Kolff, shortly after his hiring, named Kort Wickenheiser, the president's son, as an assistant coach.

So when van Breda Kolff received the bad news from his athletics director, he knew it was not the end of the story. He spoke to Kort, who relayed to his father van Breda Kolff's concerns about declaring the student athlete ineligible. Next came a meeting with President Wickenheiser, Director Lane, and Coach van Breda Kolff. Lane reiterated his position that the student athlete was ineligible, citing the letter from the Coastal Georgia registrar. Wickenheiser, of course, had the last word. Not only was he the boss, but NCAA bylaws also make presidents and chancellors ultimately responsible for intercollegiate athletics at their institutions. The meeting ended with the president's declaration that the student athlete was eligible, based on Wickenheiser's personal assessment that the student athlete had earned a technical, rather than vocational, degree.

Lane was determined that *this* would not be the end of the story. In June he expressed his concern about the student athlete's eligibility to James Gould, chair of the university board of trustees' athletics committee. Gould suggested that Lane reiterate his concerns to President Wickenheiser in writing. Lane did just that, in a very direct email message to the president:

> I believe we have a problem. . . . The more I think about the student-athlete's eligibility situation the more I am convinced that we cannot unilaterally declare him eligible. . . . [The junior college] has stated that under their academic

structure his "Certificate" is not equivalent to an associate's degree. In my opinion, if we declare him eligible, we leave ourselves open to a possible NCAA violation. I do not believe that we can ignore their institutional stance without putting ourselves into possible jeopardy. . . . I do not believe that we can declare him eligible without taking a major risk. . . . In my opinion we have to either "red shirt" [the student athlete] or petition the NCAA for a review of his status. Why do we want to put ourselves into a situation where we can be challenged at any time during the next two years about this and not be able to truly justify our position in relation to NCAA rules?

Lane's logic seemed irrefutable, but Wickenheiser was not deterred. He responded with a lengthy email laying out an argument that the student athlete was eligible—an argument, as it turns out, that was drafted two days earlier by his son Kort. At a subsequent face-to-face meeting, the president informed Lane that he was growing weary of Lane's objections and that Lane "needed to accept" the president's decision.

At significant personal risk, Lane again contacted Gould, the university trustee who chaired the athletics committee, to express his concern about President Wickenheiser's decision. Gould said he would discuss the matter with Bill Swan, the chairman of the board of trustees. According to Swan's account,

> Lane, still with some reservations about the athlete's eligibility, raised the issue casually with James Gould, . . . who in turn discussed it with me in a very brief conversation. Gould showed me Wickenheiser's e-mail, and we concluded that the university's chief executive had investigated the matter and had reached what seemed a well-reasoned position.
>
> We had confidence in the president and, based on the information presented, believed it would be inappropriate for trustees to become further involved in an administrative matter.

Swan said that he "had long adhered to the policy of keeping one's 'nose in but fingers out' when it comes to board involvement in day-to-day university operations." He there-fore informed Lane that Wickenheiser's decision would stand, noting that the president would be "accountable" if it turned out he was wrong. Seeing no reason to pursue the matter fur-ther, Lane signed the student athlete's eligibility certification form. The student athlete competed on the men's basketball team during most of the 2002–3 season.

Most of the 2002–3 season. In mid-February 2003 the board of trustees learned of another problem involving the student athlete. He had been informed in December by Kort Wicken-heiser that he was being withdrawn involuntarily, by the bas-ketball coaching staff, from one of his fall courses due to poor academic performance. The student athlete was upset by this decision, because he believed he was capable of doing well on the final exam and could pass the course; nonetheless, he acceded to the coach's request that he not take the final exam.

Unfortunately, that did not solve the problem. University policy established a deadline of November 15 as the last date on which students could withdraw from fall courses. The stu-dent athlete's withdrawal in December was well beyond the deadline, which triggered a very undesirable consequence. If the student athlete could not withdraw, the only way he could avoid a failing grade would be to take an incomplete in the course. That course of action, however, would place the stu-dent athlete into the university's Academic Restoration Pro-gram, which, under institutional policy, would prevent him from traveling with the basketball team to away games during the spring 2003 semester.

When the student athlete failed to take the final exam, the course instructor gave him a grade of incomplete. The men's basketball coaching staff was unwilling to lose the student ath-lete for away games, so Kort Wickenheiser asked his father to intervene. President Wickenheiser spoke with the vice pres-ident for academic affairs, who agreed to change the student athlete's grade from an incomplete to a withdrawal.

The day would have been saved but for the pesky Lane,

who reported what had happened to James Gould, the trustee who remained chair of the board's athletics committee. Gould passed along this new information to other members of the board. Under pressure from the board, President Wickenheiser directed Lane, at long last, to report the student athlete's eligibility issues to the Atlantic 10 Conference office. Conference officials then referred the matter to the NCAA, which concluded on February 27, 2003, that the student athlete had never been eligible to compete.

The fallout was swift. On March 3 the university announced that it was forfeiting six conference victories that season. The same day, the members of the Atlantic 10 Conference voted to disqualify St. Bonaventure from the conference's postseason tournament. In protest, the remaining members of the men's basketball team announced on March 4 that they would boycott the remainder of the season. The university informed conference officials that it would not play its remaining two regular-season games.

Five days later, on Sunday, March 9, the board of trustees held an emergency meeting that lasted nearly seven hours. Following the meeting, the board asked for and received President Wickenheiser's resignation and placed Kort Wickenheiser, Director Lane, and Coach van Breda Kolff on paid administrative leave pending an investigation into the basketball program. The board appointed a special review committee to investigate and report back to the board. The committee submitted its report to the board on April 16, with findings that led to the resignations of Lane and Kort Wickenheiser and the firing of van Breda Kolff. Van Breda Kolff claimed that he was unaware of any discussions about the athlete's eligibility status after the meeting in which President Wickenheiser declared him eligible. He later sued the university for wrongful termination and reached a settlement in 2005.

If that were the end of the story, the case would be remarkable enough. As the NCAA Committee on Infractions later stated in its public report (from which most of the facts are derived), the "devastating" consequences "ruined careers and rocked the foundation of a venerable and well-respected . . . institution." Indeed, the penalties ultimately imposed by the committee, in February 2004, seem almost inconsequential, even though they included a three-year probationary period, a one-year ban on postseason competition, significant scholarship and recruiting restrictions, a vacation of records, and a financial penalty.

The last chapter of the story is the most devastating and tragic of them all—and not mentioned in the infractions report. The special review committee report in April 2003 included references to Lane's communications with board member Gould—and Gould's communications with Swan—back in June 2002, when the eligibility concerns first surfaced. After reading the report, St. Bonaventure supporters wondered aloud why Gould and Swan did not step in to question President Wickenheiser's initial decision to declare the student athlete initially eligible based on his welding certificate. A sports columnist for the *Buffalo News* called for Swan's resignation from the board.

Swan, by all accounts, was the consummate St. Bonaventure backer, dating back to his time as a student, when he proudly served as "the Brown Indian," the athletics mascot until 1992 (surely a story in itself). After graduating from college, he remained in the Buffalo area, roughly an hour from St. Bonaventure, where he had a very successful career in banking, becoming president and CEO of First Niagra Financial Group. More than anything, Swan loved St. Bonaventure and its Franciscan values. He relished his role as chairman of its board of trustees.

The public criticism of Swan's inaction in June 2002 took its toll on this man who had dedicated much of his life to the betterment of his alma mater. Yet the criticism subsided by summer, and in June 2003 Swan was reelected board chair. Swan and the university seemed poised to move forward, leaving the scandal behind . . . until Swan decided to write an article for *Trusteeship*, the magazine of the Association of Governing Boards, which supports boards of trustees at American universities. The article was titled "The Real March Madness: Anatomy of an Athletics Scandal," and it chronicled both the scandal and the board of trustees' response. Who knows who came up with the subtitle and tagline—"After a basketball recruiting violation made national headlines, the board of St. Bonaventure University came up big"—but in retrospect, it probably was not the best choice of words. Nor was the article's timing, published in the July–August 2003 issue, when the wounds were still wide open.

Bill Swan stated early in the article that he did not mean "to engage in institutional self-congratulation but to drive home a point: Appropriate, decisive, and substantive actions by boards of trustees can place an institution back on track after it faces a momentous challenge to its integrity, reputation, and existence." His point is on the mark; unfortunately, the tone of the article was too self-congratulatory for many St. Bonaventure supporters who viewed Swan's actions at the outset of the scandal as inappropriate, indecisive, and lacking substance.

Publication of the *Trusteeship* article led to vicious social media attacks, including one in mid-August reported by his wife Ann: "Every time Bill Swan opens his mouth, he hangs himself." The following week, on August 20, 2003, Bill Swan ended his life at the age of fifty-five by hanging himself in the basement of his home. He left a suicide note: "I am so sorry for the pain I have caused St. Bonaventure University, my family, friends, my colleagues at First Niagra and my beloved wife, Ann."

I begin with the St. Bonaventure case because I am often asked about the worst infractions cases I've seen. This one always comes to mind first—not because of the nature or scope of the violations but because of the human tragedy that could have been averted at so many points along the way. Plenty of infractions cases result in damaged careers or weakened athletic programs, but rarely do rule violations have deadly consequences. The fallout, in my mind, is what defines a truly horrendous case, and in no case has the fallout been more tragic than at St. Bonaventure.

The case also highlights core issues at the heart of institutional governance and responsibility. As noted earlier, NCAA bylaws make university presidents and chancellors ultimately responsible for the conduct of intercollegiate athletics at their institutions. At every major infractions hearing, the president is expected to be sitting in the first chair of the university delegation. Typically that president begins and ends the testimony in the hearing by delivering opening and closing statements.

So we want university presidents overseeing athletics programs on their campuses. What we do not want are university presidents becoming so close to those programs that they lose the perspective and reasoned judgment of a leader. Clearly, President Wickenheiser had no business overruling his director of athletics in determining the initial eligibility of the basketball prospect, *particularly* when his son was a member of the coaching staff.

To his credit, President Wickenheiser accepted full responsibility, noting that he "gave in because [Coach van Breda Kolff] wanted the student-athlete." He also acknowledged a "fractured relationship between the men's basketball coaching staff and the athletics administration." But by stepping in as he did, Wickenheiser exacerbated that fractured relationship by permitting the coaches to bypass the chain of command.

President Wickenheiser breached the line between oversight and interference. That line, however, is not always clear. One of the most interesting aspects of the St. Bonaventure case was the role of the university's board of trustees. In truth, the tagline of Bill Swan's article in the *Trusteeship* magazine was on target: "*After* a basketball recruiting violation made national headlines, the board of St. Bonaventure University came up big." Surely the board of trustees deserves praise for its swift and decisive actions that led to the resignation or termination of the president, athletics director, and two basketball coaches. Indeed, the board acted responsibly even before the story made national headlines by pressuring Wickenheiser to report the student athlete's eligibility issues to the Atlantic 10 Conference and the NCAA following questions about his course withdrawal.

But what about the trustees' failure to act more forcefully when the student athlete's initial eligibility was raised? *That* inaction, after all, is what led ultimately to Bill Swan's death. Did he deserve the internet beatdown for not stepping in and overruling the president? Swan himself engaged in considerable self-reflection in his article about whether he should have done more: "This decision point, frankly, is the one that troubles me the most. Had I decided to intervene at that time, the unfortunate chain of events leading to this spring's controversy might have been avoided. But I had long adhered to the policy of keeping one's 'nose in but fingers out' when it comes to board involvement in day-to-day university operations. Still a firm backer of that policy, I now believe there needs to be more discussion about what constitutes appropriate assessment and support of the chief executive in today's complex and highly charged governance environment."

Perhaps in some instances, the question is not whether university trustees should second-guess decisions of the president but simply whether more questions should be asked. The St. Bonaventure scenario surely suggested some dysfunction on campus if the athletics director felt it imperative to go directly to a trustee, defying a presidential directive. Presumably, in the relatively small St. Bonaventure community, trustees knew that the president's son was on the basketball coaching staff. Even if they did not, one of the first questions to present itself should have been why on earth the *president* of the university would be making a student-athlete eligibility determination. As the Committee on Infractions put it in its public report, "the inappropriateness of such action is staggering."

Oddly enough, the NCAA *Division I Manual* does not mention the role of university boards of trustees. Its governing principle on accountability is clear: "The institution's president or chancellor is responsible for the administration of all aspects of the athletics program." But those of us on campus know very well that presidents answer to boards. Is it time that governing boards exercise more authority and control in matters involving intercollegiate athletics?

In August 2011, Tom McMillen, a former U.S. representative and University of Maryland and NBA basketball star, wrote in an opinion piece in the *New York Times* that "there is just too much money involved in the multibillion-dollar industry that is college athletics to expect the participants to police themselves." At least part of the solution, according to McMillen, a regent of the University System of Maryland, is for university boards of trustees to "take control" of intercollegiate athletics. McMillen's proposal may have merit, but I don't see it happening on a widespread scale. On too many campuses, trustees are as eager as any well-heeled fan to have prime seats at athletic events and perhaps a ride on the team plane to the bowl game.

To truly change campus *culture* and reprioritize, boards of trustees must buy in and be involved. The Penn State case had the potential to change the landscape. I address the Penn State matter in depth in the final chapter of this book, but I trust most readers are generally familiar with the case, including the fact that Penn State retained former FBI director Louis Freeh to investigate, following allegations of child sexual abuse by former assistant football coach Jerry Sandusky. The Freeh report took the Penn State trustees to task for their failure even to insist on regular reports of what was happening in the investigations of Jerry Sandusky. According to Anne D. Neal, president of the American Council of Trustees and Alumni, "This really should be a clarion call to trustees across the country to ask questions, to demand answers, to insist that the president is responsible to them, not the other way around. For too long, the boards have been viewed more as boosters than as legal fiduciaries. And where athletics are involved, I think there is an urgent question whether some institutions have lost touch with their purpose."

Yet there were two striking aspects of the NCAA announcement of the sanctions against Penn State. The first was the pronouncement by President Edward Ray of Oregon State University, who also served at the time as chair of the NCAA Executive Committee (later renamed the NCAA Board of Governors). President Ray insisted that one of the lessons of the Penn State sanctions was that "presidents and chancellors are in charge," without a mention of the governing boards to whom those presidents and chancellors report.

Second was the realization that Penn State's new president, Rodney Erickson, had signed a consent decree accepting the unprecedented sanctions without consulting or seeking the consent of the full board of trustees. Within two weeks of the announcement of the sanctions, one of the trustees formally challenged every one of the sanctions imposed on Penn State on the ground that "the President of the University lacked the legal authority to agree to the entry of the consent decree." Astonishingly, the trustee contended that "the Board was not informed or consulted about this matter, nor did it grant approval to the President to take the questioned action."

In an ESPN: The Magazine article in August 2012, one of the Penn State trustees was quoted as saying he was completely surprised by the announcement of the harsh sanctions against the university: "I can't believe this shit. No one told me a damn thing." Apparently only the board chair and her executive committee were informed of the impending sanctions, while a majority of the board was kept in the dark—ostensibly because Penn State may have been handed a multiyear death penalty (i.e., eliminating its football program for a period of time) if the proposed penalties had been leaked to the media prior to the NCAA's Monday morning announcement.

In contrast, Bill Swan, as chair of the St. Bonaventure Board of Trustees, insisted that all board members be apprised of the matter, at least in the spring of 2003, when the student athlete's eligibility issues reared their head for a second time. As Swan put it in his *Trusteeship* article, "I knew it was essential that every trustee be given the same information the executive committee had considered over the previous days and that everyone had an opportunity to voice an opinion."

Swan's approach seems to be a sound one, recognizing that ultimate authority over university affairs, including intercollegiate athletics, rests with the full board, not a segment of the board or the president. At the very least, Swan was correct in asserting that "there needs to be more discussion" about the appropriate oversight role of boards of trustees in matters relating to athletics.

The St. Bonaventure case presents another interesting lesson in accountability. The athletics director, Gothard Lane, was doggedly persistent, asserting from the outset that the prospect from Georgia was academically ineligible to compete. Not only did he press his position with both the president and the head basketball coach, but he twice went directly to a member of the board of trustees to complain about the president's decision.

Months later, after learning that the men's basketball coaching staff, the president, and the vice president for academic affairs manipulated institutional policy on course withdrawals, Lane again contacted James Gould, the trustee chairing the board's athletics committee, to apprise him of the suspected impropriety. Without this action by Lane, the infractions may never have come to light; only at the insistence of the board did President Wickenheiser agree to refer the matter to the Atlantic 10 Conference and the NCAA.

In some respects, Lane could be considered something of a heroic figure, bucking his superior (the president) to do what's right. Yet not only did he lose his job along with the others, but the Committee on Infractions cited him specifically for failure to report the student athlete's improper eligibility certification to either the conference office or the NCAA.

That result may seem harsh, but a strong ethic exists in the NCAA rules-enforcement process that *everyone* associated with an intercollegiate athletics program is responsible for rules compliance—and that responsibility includes a duty to report suspected violations. In 2001 the Committee on Infractions had considered another case involving a university president who overstepped appropriate bounds and an athletics director at odds with the president. In its report in that case, involving Jacksonville University, the committee stated that the athletics director "had an affirmative obligation under NCAA legislation to 'go above the president's head' and report his knowledge of possible NCAA violations directly to either the conference office or the NCAA."

In the St. Bonaventure case, the committee recognized that Lane had gone above Wickenheiser's head by reporting his concerns to the trustee and that he may have feared for his job if he had reported those concerns outside the university. Nonetheless, the committee held Lane to a high reporting standard: "The committee . . . firmly believes that in situations similar to what occurred at St. Bonaventure in 2002 and at Jacksonville several years earlier, directors of athletics should 'take the extra step' and report their concerns to appropriate officials at the respective conference office and/or the NCAA."

Similar standards of accountability apply to coaches of intercollegiate athletics teams. In a particularly strong statement regarding responsibilities of head coaches, the NCAA Infractions Appeals Committee in 2001 stated that "the responsibility of a head coach is not based on a chain of command; it arises from the fact that he is one of those who are responsible for the integrity of the program and, specifically, for the welfare of student-athletes in the program."

The case in which the appeals committee made this statement involved extensive academic fraud in the men's basketball program at the University of Minnesota. It was my first appellate case, and former head basketball coach Clem Haskins had contended that he did not have actual knowledge of the fraud and therefore could not be found to have engaged in unethical conduct. The appeals committee seized the opportunity to clarify the scope of a head coach's responsibility:

> The head coach of an athletics program . . . is expected to know what those in the program are doing. To conclude otherwise would be to encourage coaches or others in similarly responsible positions to close their eyes and ears to what is happening in areas for which they are accountable. It would be irresponsible for this committee, the NCAA, or any member institution to tolerate, let alone encourage, such intentional ignorance.
>
> A head coach's responsibility goes beyond merely acting upon academic fraud that comes to his attention. A coach should take reasonable steps to see that it does not happen in the first place. This is not to say that he is absolutely liable for every instance of academic fraud that might occur; it is to say, however, that his accountability should be measured by more than what he actually knew. It should be measured by what a reasonably vigilant, observant, and diligent person in his position should have known.

The appeals committee's statement, of course, extends well beyond the context of academic fraud. Regardless of the nature of the violations, head coaches are on notice that they will be held accountable for major infractions that occur in their programs. If a reasonably diligent person in the coach's position would have known the violations were occurring, the coach will not be insulated by ignorance.

An analogy could be made to the treatment of Joe Paterno in the Penn State case, even though that case did not involve the kinds of rule violations that are found in a typical infractions case. Coach Paterno reportedly informed his nominal superior, athletics director Tim Curley, of what Mike McQueary had observed in the showers of the football complex. I use the word "nominal," of course, because many people understood football to be king on campus and head coach Paterno to be king of kings, answerable to no one. Many have decried Joe-Pa's treatment, including (at least initially) the stripping of fourteen years of wins from his record, because he did what any employee would be expected to do: report the incident to his superiors and let them handle it. But should the accountability of the head coach, particularly in a matter as serious as potential child abuse, be defined by chain of command or instead by some higher measure of responsibility?

Head coach responsibility also was addressed in structural reforms that took effect in August 2013. The reforms resulted from a year-long study by an NCAA enforcement working group, following an August 2011 retreat of university presidents who called for more effective means of deterring rule violators. In the past, head coaches often could escape penalties by disavowing knowledge of misconduct by "rogue" assistant coaches; the new legislation *presumes* head coach responsibility for rule violations that occur in their programs. Head coaches will be able to overcome that presumption only with evidence that they "promoted an atmosphere of compliance" within their programs (presumably by properly training and educating their assistants in rules compliance) and properly monitored the activities of their assistants. Penalties for head coaches who cannot provide such evidence include suspensions that can range from 10 to 100 percent of a season.

In 2015 the new standard got its first major test. The Committee on Infractions leveled a nine-game suspension on legendary coach Jim Boeheim of Syracuse for failing to monitor adequately the activities of subordinates who, among other things, committed academic fraud in an effort to keep a star player eligible. No evidence existed that Boeheim knew about the misconduct; nonetheless, he bore responsibility for the actions of his subordinates.

2

Hangin' Offenses

The remarkable words above are attributed to Bill Clements, speaking to Donald Shields, president of SMU, on two separate occasions—in the fall of 1983, on the very day Clements was introduced as the new chair of the SMU Board of Governors, and again six months later, in May 1984. Clements, who had served as governor of Texas from 1979 to 1983, was addressing President Shields's concerns about the nature of SMU football recruiting. Shields was just beginning to learn of a years-long scheme of boosters providing cash to football players and their families, all with the knowledge and active participation of coaches and other athletics department personnel.

In essence, Clements was telling the president of the university that cheating in the football program was none of his business; board members would handle the boosters and "take care of it." The verbal exchange is set forth in the definitive work on the SMU death penalty case, *A Payroll to Meet: A Story of Greed, Corruption, and Football at SMU*, by David Whitford. The book was first published in 1989 and had been difficult to get one's hands on until the University of Nebraska Press rereleased it in paperback in 2013. Whitford's book, which should be required reading for any student of NCAA infractions history, clearly highlights the downside of *too much* control of athletics by governing boards.

In the quote at the beginning of this book, SMU fan Nathan Darrell Ford asked why the Committee on Infractions chose SMU "to KILL" and suggested that the committee's December 2000 sanctions would "go down in history, just as the death penalty did, as the most unfair, hiddeous [sic] thing in the world." An examination of SMU's infractions history will help to explain much of Ford's anguish, as well as provide a benchmark against which all other major infractions cases are measured.

SMU leads the country with an ignominious record: the most major infractions cases—ten—since the NCAA began keeping an infractions database in 1953. As of this writing in 2018, Arizona State was runner-up with nine major infractions cases. In 2011 and 2015, respectively, Oklahoma and Wichita State closed the gap with their eighth major cases. Eleven schools followed with seven major cases each: Auburn, Baylor, Cal-Berkeley, Florida State, Georgia, Memphis, Minnesota, Texas A&M, UCLA, West Virginia, and Wisconsin.

While some schools have spread out their infractions among different sports, the first eight of SMU's cases all involved football. The tone was set early. In 1958 the NCAA found that an SMU booster had provided a football prospect a summer job that was "not legitimate in its nature and function." As the infractions report goes on to say, the player's job responsibilities and performance were "not commensurate with his pay." Similar scenarios have played out in numerous infractions cases since the 1950s—student athletes getting paid (usually by boosters) for doing little or no work. At least the student athlete in the SMU case actually was on the job . . . and SMU certainly was not alone in its wrongdoing. The same day the SMU decision was announced, Auburn was hit with a three-year ban on postseason competition and television appearances because of improper recruiting inducements. The SMU case was minor in comparison; nonetheless, it was a harbinger of what was to come, particularly in regard to booster involvement in recruiting.

A booster also was involved in SMU's next infractions case, in 1965. The Committee on Infractions found that the booster had made "offers of assistance" to a football prospect and his parents and had provided prospects transportation between Dallas and their homes on his company airplane. The violations were more serious this time; the infractions committee accepted the Southwest Conference's imposition of a two-year bowl ban.

SMU was just getting started. The university's real problems occurred during a thirteen-year stretch from 1974 to 1987, when the football program was implicated in *five* major infractions cases. No other NCAA institution has matched that record, described in the infractions committee's 1987 report as "nothing short of abysmal."

The 1974 case involved both recruiting inducements (to prospective student athletes being actively recruited to attend the university) and extra benefits (to student athletes already enrolled). The recruiting inducements were troublesome but relatively modest—cash for travel expenses not incurred, entertainment of a prospect's friend. The extra benefits were more creative and generated more heat—cash rewards to players involved in outstanding plays during competition or to those who volunteered for the scout team in drills conducted after regular practice sessions ended. The head football coach also paid cash to student athletes in lieu of providing them complimentary tickets. It was a serious case, resulting in a two-year ban on postseason competition and television appearances. At the time, the NCAA controlled the games broadcast on TV, which made TV bans relatively easy to administer. That came to an end in 1984 when the University of Georgia and the University of Oklahoma won a U.S. Supreme Court decision allowing schools to contract with TV networks independently.

Less than a year and a half later, the SMU football program was back before the Committee on Infractions, with allegations of improper recruiting inducements, including small amounts of cash and improper meals for a prospect and his girlfriend. Boosters remained on the scene, providing improper transportation to prospects. The committee also found an assistant coach to have engaged in "unethical conduct," the most serious finding that can be made against an individual employed at an NCAA institution. Not only had the coach engaged in underlying recruiting violations, but he also had submitted a false affidavit and encouraged others to lie during the investigation to cover up his actions.

The NCAA's repeat-violator legislation did not come into existence until 1985, but the infractions committee's 1976 report makes clear that an institution's prior history with the committee will be a significant consideration in the determination of sanctions. The committee recognized that many of SMU's underlying violations were "not serious in nature" but noted forcefully that they were committed while the university was on probation from the 1974 case.

The same month the 1976 infractions report was released, SMU hired Ron Meyer as its new head football coach. Meyer had been an assistant coach at Purdue and a scout for the Dallas Cowboys and had engineered a turnaround at UNLV (University of Nevada, Las Vegas). The SMU faithful were hopeful that he could do the same for their institution, which had been in a bit of a malaise since Doak Walker had won the Heisman Trophy and led SMU to national prominence in the late 1940s. SMU had won fewer than half its games since then.

Meyer was flashy and got things done. And getting things done meant recruiting good players. Fortunately, there were a *lot* of good players in Texas, but many of them knew little about SMU. Those who did know something about the school, mostly from the Dallas area, were unimpressed by the football team's mediocrity. Meyer embraced the challenge, not only in Dallas but also in Houston. He hired Steve Endicott from the University of Miami as an assistant coach and assigned him to recruit inner-city Houston, where he often tag teamed with a local stockbroker named Robin Buddecke. Buddecke was not even an SMU alum, but he was *damn* impressed by Ron Meyer and was eager to help in any way he could.

Buddecke later would become one of David Whitford's principal sources of information on what was going down in the SMU recruiting game in the late 1970s and early 1980s. Buddecke told Whitford that he first saw money change hands in the summer of 1977—mostly in small amounts, "maybe twenty or fifty bucks or something like that" to a prospect, in the presence of Meyer, Endicott, and perhaps another coach. Buddecke began handing out cash himself in 1978 and said the group "started to get serious about this thing" on prospects' official visits to the SMU campus.

Under NCAA rules, prospects can make a maximum of five "official visits" to potential schools, beginning in the athlete's senior year of high school. The universities pay the expenses for an official visit—transportation, lodging, meals, complimentary game tickets, "entertainment"—but those expenses are limited and carefully circumscribed in the rules. SMU, undoubtedly like many other schools at the time (statements from recruited athletes certainly would suggest SMU had plenty of company), regularly would exceed those limits. As Buddecke told Whitford, "Let's face it, your official visit has got to be your close. It's got to be when you put your best foot forward, when you do what you have to do."

Soon things ratcheted up—both the money and the organization. If SMU were really going to compete, it needed a sizable slush fund, and Meyer found that numerous wealthy businessmen in Dallas were up to the task. Meyer, who left SMU to be head coach of the New England Patriots, never admitted his involvement in any wrongdoing at SMU, but the boosters who spoke with Whitford uniformly said Meyer was involved. As one put it, "Ron Meyer built the organization" for funding the football players. (Meyer died in December 2017.) When recruiters needed funds, they could stop by a Dallas office and pick up a package of $100 bills. And by 1978, says Whitford, there was sufficient funding "to have a significant impact on recruiting."

When it came to the *really good* players, funding now might take the form of serious cash up front (hundreds, if not thousands, of dollars) but more commonly, at least in Houston, direct monthly payments (typically a few hundred dollars a month) to the student athlete's *family* for as long as he played for SMU. This way, said Buddecke, "if the NCAA would come to you and say, 'Did you give this *player* money?' [and you said,] 'No,' a lightning bolt wasn't gonna come flashing down on you."

SMU was good about making promises to recruits; it also was good about *delivering* on those promises. That, in the end, would be the program's downfall, but in the interim, it made for loyal student athletes who were not about to rat out the program or even to talk to NCAA investigators when they hit campus. And hit campus they did—in 1981, just as SMU football was hitting its stride. Months earlier, SMU had beaten Texas for the first time in fourteen years, and over the next four years, the program again would become *elite*, notching more wins than any other program in Division I.

SMU fans had every right to be nervous upon learning that the NCAA enforcement staff was in Dallas in 1981. A major infractions case would be SMU's *fifth* involving the football program, including the third since 1974. Had the fans known what was *really* happening—tens of thousands of dollars being paid every year to a group of top players and their families under a program orchestrated by both boosters and coaches—they would have been terrified. And to top things off, the Committee on Infractions was headed by the esteemed Charles Alan Wright, who just happened to teach law at the University of Texas. These days, committee members automatically recuse themselves from hearings involving schools from the same athletics conference as the institution at which the member is employed.

What the fans didn't know is that the NCAA investigators were not on the trail of any smoking gun, such as a huge slush fund. Indeed, when the infractions committee announced its findings, on June 10, 1981, the violations seemed relatively minor in the grand scheme of things—mostly lodging, transportation, and meal violations during recruits' visits. The findings did, however, offer hints of more serious problems: Coach Meyer telling a recruit that he could sell the student athlete's allotment of complimentary game tickets, at a premium, and get the cash to the athlete; lodging and dinners for recruits at the home of a booster; student-athlete use of a booster's home for entertainment purposes.

The Committee on Infractions has no investigative authority; its role is to examine the evidence the enforcement staff brings to it. The school on the hot seat, of course, also has the opportunity to present its own evidence. The committee had no way of knowing that SMU's football program was rotting ethically. In the end, the program's track record was as much responsible for the sanctions as the latest violations themselves. Imposing another ban on postseason competition and TV appearances, this time for one year, the committee said it was "particularly concerned that this case represents the third time in the last seven years that the Southern Methodist University football program has been found to be in violation of significant NCAA rules."

The sanctions did not slow the momentum of the SMU Mustangs. The team finished the upcoming 1981 season with its best record in over four decades—10-1, with a 9–7 loss to Texas as the only blemish on what otherwise seemed to be nearly a perfect season. Of course, it wasn't close to perfect, because the season ended abruptly, with no opportunity to compete in a postseason bowl game. And as noted in Whitford's book, the Mustangs became known as the "Best Team Nobody Saw," due to the TV ban. The team finished fifth in the final AP rankings but was unranked in the UPI poll because teams on NCAA probation were ineligible for national ranking. A similar practice remains today for the USA Today/Amway coaches poll, which bars from its rankings teams that are subject to a ban on postseason competition.

Ten SMU players earned all-conference honors, including

running backs Eric Dickerson and Craig James, a tandem coming to be known nationally as the "Pony Express." All the while, of course, improper payments to many of the team's top players had continued, since they had not been discovered in the recent NCAA investigation.

The Mustangs soared again in 1982, crushing Texas on the way to an undefeated season, a Cotton Bowl victory, and a number-two final ranking in both major polls. The 1981 probation was only for one year, so they were not only bowl eligible but also UPI eligible in the rankings. And they did it without Ron Meyer, who had bolted in January 1982 to accept the head coaching position with the NFL's New England Patriots.

SMU hired Bobby Collins from Southern Mississippi to succeed Meyer. Collins had enjoyed remarkable success in Hattiesburg, leading the Golden Eagles to a top-twenty finish in 1981. He followed that with an incredible first-year season at SMU . . . but that success came with Meyer's recruits, and studs like Dickerson and James were off to the pros.

James headed for the fledgling USFL and was drafted number four overall in its inaugural draft in 1983. He soon migrated to the NFL, where he was a Pro Bowler in 1986 with the New England Patriots—yes, reunited at least for a short time with Coach Ron Meyer. A succession of injuries cut James's career short. Dickerson was *special*. As the number-two pick in the NFL draft, he was Rookie of the Year in 1983 and followed that up in 1984 with a single-season rushing record that still stands today—2,105 yards. In an eleven-year career, Dickerson rushed for over 13,000 yards and earned Pro Bowl selections six times. In 1999, his first year of eligibility, he was inducted into the Pro Football Hall of Fame.

Studs indeed. Collins would have to prove he could get the job done with his own recruits, and the big-time boosters funding the cash-to-players program were skeptical. Several boosters had held a "summit" meeting in February 1982, on the heels of Meyer's resignation. Robin Buddecke, the SMU program's go-to man and paymaster in Houston (and Whitford's source for what occurred), was at the meeting. Hosting the meeting was Bobby Stewart, chairman of the SMU Board of Governors and chairman and CEO of InterFirst Corp., a spinoff of the First National Bank that Stewart had headed earlier in his career. Buddecke said Stewart was his principal cash supplier for the payment program. Also in attendance were two former SMU scholarship football players and prominent Dallas business-men: Sherwood Blount and George Owen. Both had made a lot of money in real estate, and both were willing to use their money to help SMU football.

On the summit agenda was the question, now that Meyer was gone, of what would happen to the cash-payment pro-gram. According to Buddecke, Blount and Owen argued that of course the payments needed to continue—SMU had made *commitments*, and those student athletes currently on the dole could not be left high and dry. And as for new recruits, pay-ments should *increase* so that SMU could "go after the very best players in the country." Buddecke said he resisted, but in the end, Blount and Owen won out, with the acquiescence of the chairman of the SMU Board of Governors: the payment program would continue.

A year later, with the Mustangs riding high from the 1982 season, the future should have looked rosy indeed. SMU foot-ball had just attained its best season record in decades; it was off probation; and the payment program was humming along, undetected by the NCAA enforcement staff. The boost-ers funding the cash payments had a lot riding on contin-ued success of the program, but unfortunately, in the heart of the 1983 recruiting season, they were distressed by what they were seeing.

Ron Meyer had been one of them—sharply dressed, sophis-ticated, flashing a Super Bowl ring from his early seventies scouting stint with the Dallas Cowboys—and understood this was *business*. Bobby Collins? He was from a small town just down the road from Hattiesburg, Mississippi. One booster is quoted in Whitford's book putting it this way:

It doesn't take Einstein to see that these guys are just giving it more or less a lick and a promise as far as their recruiting effort. Instead of us basically picking through the best players in America to determine which ones we're going to annoint [*sic*], guys were committing elsewhere.

It's like they opened the back door and let all these guys from Mississippi in. I don't mean to be regionally bigoted, but honest to God, if you take your best banker from Laurel, Mississippi, and throw him down here in Dallas, he's gonna be eaten alive. He's gonna be absolutely picked like a chicken. These guys didn't know what it took. They *just really did not seem to want it*. The irony of it is, had they come into town six or seven years before, when it wasn't quite as hell-bent-for-leather, maybe they would have fit in better. But Ron had changed the equation. Ron had taken the damn thermostat and turned it up about fifteen degrees.

Needless to say, some of the boosters were not at all pleased at the prospect of losing their hard-won momentum. One booster in particular, according to Whitford, "was not going to leave the future in the hands of the good ol' boys." Sherwood Blount hit the road in the last few weeks of the recruiting season, taking it upon himself to do "Bobby Collins's job." The results were stunning—SMU's 1983 recruiting class was thought to be as strong as any class that had come before it, even the class with Dickerson and James.

Cash may have had something to do with Blount's success. Eight of the twenty-two recruits signed that year became participants in the payment program. One of those recruited stars was a high school linebacker from Angleton, Texas, named David Stanley. Three and a half years later, Stanley would report to NCAA investigators and to Channel 8 in Dallas that he had accepted a lucrative deal to enroll at SMU—a down payment of $25,000 and monthly installments of $750 for the time he was enrolled.

The chickens started coming home to roost before then,

however. In early March 1983, less than a month after signing day, the NCAA enforcement staff sent a letter of "preliminary inquiry" to SMU, notifying university president Donald
Shields that investigators would be looking into allegations
of improprieties within the football program. NCAA investigators are notoriously and professionally tight-lipped about
ongoing investigations. Over the next several months, though,
local media in Dallas dripped reports that several recent prospects had been promised cash or other inducements to play
at SMU—in one case, a Camaro; in another, $4,000 in cash
up front and $400 a month thereafter.

Despite the distractions, the SMU Mustangs continued to
roll on the gridiron. They ran their NCAA-leading unbeaten
streak to twenty-one games before that perennial bully from
Austin upset the apple cart. In late October, before a national TV
audience, the Texas Longhorns defeated the Mustangs 15–12.
In December SMU dropped a Sun Bowl contest to Alabama but
still finished the season at 10-2, ranked eleventh in the nation.

On the surface, then, the 1983 season seemed to be another
resounding success. But storm clouds were building. Supporters knew that yet *another* major infractions case, coming so soon on the heels of three prior cases, would be bad
news indeed.

The university hired outside counsel to conduct an internal investigation, which turned up hard evidence of wrongdoing. Two current players and at least one former player
provided details of the payment program to the university's
attorney. In addition to naming boosters who had contributed funds, they also delivered disturbing news about *institutional* responsibility: members of the football coaching staff
not only knew about the booster payments, but they served as
bagmen, delivering the illicit funds to the players. Assistant
coach Bootsie Larsen served as chief "paymaster."

The attorney reported his findings to university president
Donald Shields, who, by NCAA legislation, bore ultimate responsibility for ensuring rules compliance within his athletics pro-

grams. Reacting with "shock and outrage," Shields called on the carpet head coach Bobby Collins and athletics director Bob Hitch. Both denied knowledge of, or participation in, the scheme, though it seemed implausible to many that Larsen would have acted without the complicity of someone higher up the food chain.

The actions of university officials going forward are what make the SMU story so sordid. It is now November 1983. The NCAA enforcement staff has been conducting an investigation into the football program for the past eight months. Most of the university officials who matter are no longer in the dark, if they had been before: the president, athletics director, head coach, and university counsel now have firsthand knowledge of the booster slush fund and regular cash payments to numerous players and their families.

Who else mattered? The university's board of governors and a separate oversight body, the board of trustees. President Shields immediately took his concerns to the trustees' chairman, Ed Cox, who suggested a meeting with Bill Clements. In three days, Clements would be taking over as chairman of the university's board of governors for the second time, having chaired the board from 1967 to 1973. He left the chairmanship in 1973 to become deputy secretary of defense in the administration of President Richard Nixon and later, after Nixon's fall from grace, in the Ford administration. Upon his return to his home state, Clements successfully ran for governor of Texas, serving from 1979 until January 1983. He was defeated in the 1982 general election in his bid for a second term.

No longer in the governor's office, Clements was cajoled into reassuming his role as chairman of SMU's board of governors. He would take the reins on November 11, 1983. A couple of days earlier, two old friends, Ed Cox and Bobby Stewart, came calling. Cox and Stewart had been members of Clements's campaign finance committee during his first bid for governor in 1978. President Shields had met with Cox on November 8 to convey his distress over revelations emerging from the internal investigation of the football program. Stewart, of course, knew all about the pay-to-players program; he was one of the funders. If Clements did not know about the payments before, he certainly knew after the meeting with Cox and Stewart.

It was now time to reengage the president. On November 11, Clements and Cox met with President Shields and the university's outside attorney. According to an account in the Whitford book, Shields again expressed his outrage, but Clements "had no stomach for his moral indignation." Accusing him of being naive, Clements said, "Do you think all the nationally recognized football players found their way to SMU by accident, or did they choose SMU instead of UCLA or Oklahoma because they liked SMU's school colors? . . . We'll take care of it. You stay out of it. Go run the university."

From that moment on, President Shields knew who really ran the university.

The NCAA is a voluntary association of member institutions. Collectively, they are to govern themselves, with a rules-compliance regime that depends on self-reporting of violations and full cooperation with NCAA enforcement personnel. Compliance is the responsibility of everyone at an institution; everyone has a duty to report known violations. Sounds as naive as Clements's characterization of President Shields, doesn't it?

With as much at stake in major college athletics as there is, many participants at one time or another will be confronted with a cost-benefit analysis: What might I gain from bending or breaking the rules? What are the chances I will be caught? What will happen to me if I am caught? Are the benefits to be gained from cheating worth the risk?

SMU had already gained enormous benefits from cheating. Its payment program helped to secure blue-chip recruits, and those players helped to turn an also-ran into one of the top football programs in the country. SMU officials also had learned a valuable lesson from the 1981 infractions case: what the NCAA enforcement staff didn't know couldn't hurt them. The player slush fund and payment program were cruising along by 1981, but NCAA investigators had evidence only of relatively minor violations. The investigators' inability to put together a stronger case was attributable primarily to one major handicap: the NCAA enforcement staff has no subpoena power. While universities certainly have power over their own employees and student athletes (e.g., they can be fired or kicked off the team for failing to cooperate), NCAA investigators must obtain their information strictly from the voluntary participation of those with knowledge of infractions.

Armed with that knowledge and experience, SMU officials devised a strategy thoroughly at odds with the principles of self-disclosure and cooperation contemplated by the NCAA rules. They might not actively hinder the enforcement staff in its investigation, but neither would they be forthcoming with the knowledge they possessed. And because *institutional* culpability ultimately was what mattered, they added a familiar element to their strategy: if NCAA investigators did learn of booster involvement in payments to players, SMU would portray those boosters as *rogues*, acting on their own without the knowledge of coaches or other university personnel, despite the fact, of course, that now *everyone* of importance at SMU knew exactly what was going on.

As the NCAA investigation plodded along, through the entire calendar year of 1984, it was business as usual for the SMU football program. Sherwood Blount was back on the recruiting trail, with cash in hand. And the Mustangs again excelled on the field, finishing the 1984 season at 10-2 after a bowl victory over Notre Dame. Over the past four seasons, SMU had compiled a record of 41-5-1, the best in the country.

Toward the end of the 1984 season, in late November, the media reported that a recent recruit named Sean Stopperich was talking to NCAA investigators. Up until that time, the enforcement staff had learned of numerous violations involving a handful of other recruits, but most were modest—improper meals and transportation, free game tickets, relatively small cash payments ($20, $100, a $300 loan), improper help in finding employment for a recruit's family member. Stopperich, however, had the ability to raise the stakes significantly.

A prized recruit out of a small town in Pennsylvania, Stopperich told investigators that Sherwood Blount had come calling in February 1984 with an offer that was too good to pass up: $5,000 in cash up front, a free apartment for his family and $300 a month during Sean's enrollment at smu, and help in finding Sean's dad a job in Dallas. According to the upcoming infractions report, Stopperich's family accepted the $5,000 down payment and approximately $6,000 in additional payments from April through October. Unfortunately, a knee injury kept Sean off the field in the fall of '84, and he and his family moved back home to Pennsylvania.

The enforcement staff finally had some of the major infractions it was looking for, and it built its infractions case around the Stopperich violations. Of course, those violations were just the tip of the iceberg in terms of smu's ongoing payment program, but university officials were not about to disclose what they knew. The enforcement staff either did not know about, or at least could not prove, violations involving about a dozen other players on the team who had been recruited with sizable cash and who were continuing to receive regular payments.

The Stopperich violations, however, were enough to lower the boom on smu, particularly in light of its recent infractions history. smu's only chance to avoid crippling sanctions was to deflect institutional responsibility by portraying the boosters as rogues acting on their own initiative without the involvement of smu employees. Clements met with Blount in January 1985 and convinced him to speak to ncaa investigators and admit his participation in the Stopperich payments. Blount met with ncaa representatives in February; according to witnesses quoted by Whitford, Blount not only admitted his participation in the Stopperich payments but was "absolutely unapologetic," effectively telling investigators, "I can damn well spend my money any way I damn well please."

Blount clearly displayed the intransigence and independence

of smu boosters, but the university needed to take one more important step to implement its strategy. Clements hosted a meeting in March 1985, one month before the infractions hearing. In attendance, among others, were former board chair Bobby Stewart, athletics director Bob Hitch, smu's outside attorney, and the two most formidable of the slush fund benefactors—Sherwood Blount and George Owen. Clements delivered the bad news to the boosters: for smu to put its best foot forward in the infractions hearing, it would have to "disassociate" Blount, Owen, and several other boosters.

"Disassociation" is one of the few tools at the ncaa's disposal to deal with wayward boosters. The ncaa has no authority over the boosters themselves, because they are not employees of the member institution. The institution itself, however, can be sanctioned for failing to take appropriate steps to distance itself from boosters who engage in wrongdoing. The disassociation can be complete—essentially no contact between the university and the booster, including acceptance of donor gifts—or more focused. In the smu case, for example, the restrictions focused specifically on *recruiting*: "During the period of probation, the university shall make every reasonable effort to ensure that outside representatives of the university's athletics interests are not engaged in any activities related to the recruitment of prospective student-athletes in the sport of football on behalf of the institution, including but not limited to: in-person (on- or off-campus) contacts with prospects, their relatives or friends; contacts with prospects, their relatives or friends by telephone or by letter, or any other activity that could be construed as recruiting prospective student-athletes."

smu president Donald Shields effected the formal disassociations in letters dated April 24, just days before the infractions hearing. In total, the disassociated group numbered nine. Conspicuously absent was Bobby Stewart, who was identified later by Robin Buddecke as one of the leaders in establishing the slush fund in its early days. Of course, public disclosure of the involvement of Stewart, former chairman of the SMU's board of governors and close friend of current chairman Bill Clements, would have been a tad too embarrassing for the university.

The infractions hearing took place over three days in late April. SMU representatives stayed on script—we're sorry, but those rogue boosters got away from us. Governor Clements even made an appearance to remind the Committee on Infractions that Sherwood Blount and the other boosters had been disassociated and to provide assurance to the committee that, as board chair, he would control them in the future. The SMU delegation kept quiet about everything else they knew.

The committee released its report on August 16, 1985, finding dozens of violations. Most of the violations involved only four recruits. But the Stopperich violations were egregious, and of course, this was SMU's *fourth* major case in eleven years. Accordingly, the committee's penalties were stiff: a two-year postseason ban in 1985 and 1986, no TV appearances in 1986, and a potentially crippling scholarship reduction—the loss of *all thirty* initial scholarships in 1986–87 and fifteen more in 1987–88. These sanctions marked the beginning of SMU's downfall, even before the death penalty case of 1987. The Mustangs scratched out two 6-5 seasons in 1985 and 1986 with many recruited upperclassmen. But far worse days were on the horizon.

In earlier days, the Committee on Infractions *proposed* findings and penalties, which could be appealed to the NCAA Council. SMU appealed the committee's proposals, but the council upheld all the findings and penalties, noting particularly SMU's "history of involvement in previous infractions cases." The council's decision hardly could have been a surprise. The NCAA membership had just made a strong statement about repeat offenders less than two months earlier. At a special convention of NCAA institutions in June 1985, the membership adopted, by a vote of 427–6, "repeat-violator" legislation, authorizing the Committee on Infractions to impose the ultimate sanction—the "death penalty"—on institutions that repeatedly commit major violations. Undoubtedly, the member institutions were thinking of schools like SMU when their representatives voted to adopt the legislation. Not surprisingly, SMU was one of the six schools to vote against the proposal. Fortunately for SMU, the effective date for the new legislation was September 1, instead of a month earlier; otherwise, its death penalty could have come in 1985.

The NCAA legislation has never used the term "death penalty," but it has been part of the popular vernacular since the 1985 special convention. Even NCAA officials use the term, though typically referring to it as "the so-called death penalty." The repeat-violator legislation did two things. First, it defined a repeat violator as an institution that was found by the Committee on Infractions to have committed "at least one major violation . . . within five years after the starting date of the penalties" in a prior major infractions case. Second, the legislation stated that the penalty for a repeat violator "may include . . . the prohibition of some or all outside competition in the sport involved in the latest major violation for one or two sports seasons." So the penalty, if imposed, would deliver at least a temporary death blow—no competition in a sport for at least one season. And if SMU's experience is any indication, the imposition of the penalty can have deleterious effects that last a *long* time.

In 2013 the NCAA adopted major revisions to its penalty legislation, which are discussed in chapter 4. No longer does a specific repeat-violator bylaw exist. The concept instead is subsumed within "aggravating factors . . . that warrant a higher range of penalties." The Committee on Infractions now considers more broadly the history of an institution's major violations—characterized since 2013 as Level I or Level II violations—including "the amount of time between the occurrences of violations." But understand that the basic concept of a repeat violator—and legislation that still allows for the suspension of competition in a sport for both the regular season and the postseason—will remain an important part of the penalty calculus. In part, that is due to a wide body of "case law" from both the infractions committee and the infractions appeals committee that incorporates repeat-violator status into its analysis.

In August 1985, two months after passage of the death penalty legislation, Bill Clements, chairman of the board of governors; Ed Cox, chairman of the board of trustees; President Donald Shields; and the athletics director, Bob Hitch, met on the SMU campus to discuss the future of the payments to football student athletes. Everyone was stinging from the latest NCAA sanctions, and everyone agreed that the payment program had to stop . . . at least for *new* recruits.

A harsh reality was setting in, though. Thirteen players on the 1985 football roster were currently receiving regular monthly payments, and they had been promised those payments as long as they were enrolled at SMU and members of the team. Sherwood Blount had reminded the group back in March, on the eve of his disassociation, that they had "a payroll to meet," hence the title of Whitford's superb book. If payments to *current* players were discontinued, what was the likelihood that one or more of those players, upset by this unexpected turn of events, would turn on the athletics department? Probably pretty high. After all, Sean Stopperich had been a turncoat after a knee injury left him disillusioned and off the field, even while payments to his family continued.

Rocks and hard spots come to mind. If the payments continued and were discovered *anytime in the next five years*, the football program very likely would be shut down, particularly if NCAA investigators also could prove that SMU leaders knew about the payments. But if the payments were discontinued and a disgruntled student athlete spilled the beans, the program would be in jeopardy immediately.

In a high-stakes gamble after the meeting, Clements and Hitch decided to continue the payments, though Cox and Shields had argued against it in the meeting. Remarkably, the payments would continue to come primarily from *Sherwood Blount*, who had been disassociated from SMU athletics just four months earlier. The cash would go to five players who were in their last year of eligibility, five with two years of eligibility left, and three who had three years remaining. So the "payroll" would include thirteen players in 1985, eight in 1986, and three in 1987. By the end of 1987, the program would be completely clean, and no one would be the wiser. After all, the NCAA had been able to tie regular payments only to Sean Stopperich, and he was now gone.

David Stanley, however, was not gone. Recall that he had been recruited, effectively by Sherwood Blount, in the sterling class of 1983. In an all-too-familiar story, Stanley had begun using pain medication in high school to keep at bay the symptoms of a shoulder injury. At SMU he graduated to other drugs, including cocaine. Stanley failed to live up to his potential on the gridiron and eventually wound up in a drug rehab program in early 1985, paid for by SMU (an NCAA violation). As he struggled to regain his footing, an emergency appendectomy early in the fall knocked him out of the entire 1985 football season.

With his frustrations piling up and most of his monthly stipends spent on cocaine, Stanley decided near the end of the season that it was time to leave SMU. The athletics department released him to play elsewhere, but after unsuccessfully seeking to land a scholarship at another school, Stanley came crawling back to Coach Bobby Collins in the summer of 1986. He wanted to be a Mustang again. Collins, still smarting from a postseason ban and mediocre 6-5 record in the 1985 season, wanted nothing of Stanley. As reported in the Whitford book, Collins felt Stanley "had abandoned the program when it was down," so "inviting him back would be unfair to the ones who had stayed."

Stanley's response, in October 1986, was to speak to NCAA investigators, and to a TV producer in Dallas, about the deal he received in 1983 to attend SMU. Stanley said he had been paid $25,000 up front and $750 a month while he was enrolled at smu—$400 to him and $350 to his family. Channel 8 News notified smu officials of the substance of its upcoming broadcast and gave them the opportunity to respond on air. In a public broadcast on November 12, Stanley detailed the payments and identified two football staff members as the individuals who had delivered monthly payments to him. Later, the broadcast showed Stanley and his mother hooked up to lie detectors; they passed.

Prior to the broadcast, athletics director Bob Hitch met with the university's inside counsel and faculty athletics representative. Neither of them had been brought into the loop, so they did not know what to make of the allegations. According to Whitford, Hitch told the others that Stanley was a "drug addict and a lost soul" and, therefore, a liar. After watching the program, in Hitch's presence, they must have had their doubts.

Bill Clements was not present to watch the broadcast; he was on a celebratory trip to Italy. On November 4 he had won back the governorship of Texas from Mark White, the man who had defeated him in 1982.

By today's standards, the ensuing investigation and disposition of the new infractions case were lightning fast, particularly for such a serious case. The infractions report indicates that the investigation began on October 21, 1986, when an enforcement staff member interviewed David Stanley and his mother. The infractions report was released on February 25, 1987, only four months later. Such a speedy resolution would have been unheard of during the ten years I served on the infractions committee.

After the November 12 television broadcast, key smu officials decided to fall on their swords, to a point. They offered ncaa investigators a deal: they would detail and admit to the entire payment program at least from 1985 on, with numbers of athletes and amounts of payments. But the deal included major conditions. Names of participants—boosters, athletics department staff members, and student athletes—would not be disclosed to NCAA officials, including members of the infractions committee. Violations would be stated only in general terms. And effectively, there would be no enforcement staff investigation; the staff would interview only athletics director Bob Hitch and accept his (and thus the university's) version of the facts. Investigators, of course, already had interviewed Stanley and his mother, but accepting the deal meant they would conduct no further interviews, beyond that of Hitch, to confirm what had happened.

Such a deal would be highly irregular. While "joint" investigations often are conducted by enforcement staff and institutional representatives working together, NCAA investigators still work to develop as much relevant information as possible and to ensure the reliability of information upon which violations are based. On the other hand, SMU essentially was offering to hand over on a silver platter a *blockbuster* case, with some of the most serious violations the NCAA had ever confronted, and agreeing to resolve the matter quickly and in full agreement with the enforcement staff.

In the end, the enforcement staff determined that the deal was too good to pass up. An investigator interviewed Hitch, who admitted knowledge of the payment program from the time he arrived at SMU in 1981. But even his name and position would not be disclosed—those implicated in the violations would be identified only as "key athletics department staff members," both in presentations before the Committee on Infractions and in any public reports from the NCAA.

As dirty as the story was, the enforcement staff was getting a sanitized version. The university's key omission, of course, was any mention of the knowledge and involvement of SMU board members. Hitch and head coach Bobby Collins essentially had agreed to take the fall in exchange for favorable buyouts from the university. Universities typically are relieved from any buyout obligations to employees who commit NCAA violations. In this case, however, one certainly can understand

SMU's motivation for accepting all aspects of the deal; even though it was opening itself up to the possibility of the death penalty, the case surely would have been worse had the university disclosed, for example, that the former—and soon-to-be-again—governor of Texas had put his imprimatur on continuation of the player-payment program.

Because the enforcement staff had agreed to SMU's version of the facts, the infractions hearing could be fast-tracked. The Committee on Infractions scheduled the hearing on February 13, 1987, at the legendary Hotel del Coronado, a national historic landmark on Coronado Island, across the bay from San Diego. By the time the enforcement staff and SMU representatives arrived at this grand resort, they had hammered out a stipulated version of the violations, together with proposed penalties. Despite the seriousness of the case—and SMU's repeat-violator status—the enforcement staff had agreed to recommend a set of penalties far less severe than the death penalty. The parties agreed to reductions in coaching staff, scholarships, and recruiting (both on and off campus). But most significant was the staff's agreement to recommend no cancellation of football seasons. The parties differed slightly— the staff recommended canceling all nonconference games for two years, while the university recommended canceling only two nonconference games for two years. But most important was a mutual recommendation that the Southwest Conference schedule remain intact; there should be no death penalty. The legislation permitted the "prohibition of *some or all* outside competition in a sport . . . for one or two sports seasons." The parties' recommendations fit that language, though most observers would define the death penalty as prohibiting *all* competition.

The enforcement staff agreed to these recommendations in recognition of the university's cooperation; after all, it is fairly extraordinary to essentially hand over the facts (or at least one version of the facts) and absolve the staff of its responsibilities to conduct its own investigation and develop its own case. But note that they're only *recommendations*. The Committee on Infractions is the ultimate decision maker, and the enforcement staff gave no assurances to SMU representatives that the committee would *accept* the recommendations. Indeed, if people have doubts about the independence of the Committee on Infractions, the SMU case should go a long way toward dispelling notions that the infractions committee and enforcement staff work in lockstep.

Unlike the infractions hearing in 1985, which lasted three days, the 1987 hearing was conducted in a single afternoon. Why? Because the enforcement staff and SMU representatives had stipulated to the facts and that those facts constituted NCAA rule violations. In many infractions cases, the facts are in dispute, and the conversation among the parties and the committee takes hours, or even days, in order to develop a complete picture of what happened. When the parties are in agreement, the committee typically accepts the mutually agreed-upon version and notes in its public infractions report that "the university and the enforcement staff were in substantial agreement with the facts and that violations of NCAA legislation occurred."

On the other hand, the infractions committee wants to assure itself that the agreed-upon facts are accurate and that the full picture has been presented. Indeed, the committee has been known to adjourn an infractions hearing with an instruction to the enforcement staff to conduct further investigation. That easily could have happened in February 1987. Accounts of the SMU infractions hearing suggest that the committee members aggressively questioned both the enforcement staff and university representatives about the reasons for their unusual confidentiality agreement, with no disclosure of named perpetrators. In the end, though, the committee accepted the parties' stipulated version of the violations, swayed in part by the enforcement staff's insistence that without the university's cooperation, NCAA investigators probably would not have been able to develop a strong case on their own. The enforcement staff's 1985 case against SMU could have been exhibit 1; reliance strictly on voluntary cooperation of witnesses had left a lot of evidence of the payment program undiscovered.

The entire recitation of the violations appears as follows in the infractions committee's public report, released (again, unusually) less than two weeks after the hearing:

> During the period September 1985 through December 1986, monthly payments ranging from $50 to $725 were made to numerous student-athletes in the sport of football from funds provided by an outside representative of the university's athletics interests.
>
> Specifically, subsequent to the conclusion of an NCAA infractions case in August 1985, certain key athletics department staff members agreed that promises made to student-athletes prior to the 1984–85 academic year during the young men's recruitment should continue to be fulfilled. Previous cash payments to the student-athletes had gone undetected by the NCAA, and the involved staff members agreed to continue the payments and to distribute them to the young men. It was understood that such payments would not be made to new student-athletes. An outside athletics representative who had been disassociated from the university's athletics program for involvement in the NCAA infractions case provided the funds for these payments.
>
> As a result of these arrangements, 13 football team members received payments during the 1985–86 academic year that totaled approximately $47,000, and eight student-athletes continued to receive payments from September through December 1986 that totaled approximately $14,000. Payments were not continued subsequent to December 1, 1986, and reportedly, all but three of the student-athletes have exhausted their eligibility.

While the Committee on Infractions accepted this brief, sanitized, stipulated version of the violations, penalties were another matter. This was SMU's seventh major case involving football, including its *fifth* in the last thirteen years—a record the committee characterized as "nothing short of abysmal." Even with this abysmal record, the committee may have accepted the enforcement staff's penalty recommendation . . . had it not been for the NCAA's special convention in 1985, at which the membership addressed the matter of repeat violators. The committee was succinct: "As a committee of the Association, the Committee on Infractions is bound by the judgment of the membership. That judgment was made absolutely clear in the recently adopted legislation and provides that serious repeat violators are to receive heavy penalties."

The committee went on in its report to catalog other aggravating factors. By its cheating, SMU had gained a serious competitive advantage—"a winning record and national prominence for its football program." Those "key athletics department staff members knew full well the cheating . . . was continuing, and those individuals *deliberately failed to disclose* this fact." I can't help but believe that the statement in the stipulated facts that previous cash payments "had gone undetected by the NCAA" was a bit galling to the committee. The payments had gone undetected, of course, because university officials had engaged in a conspiracy of silence. SMU officials had given assurances to the committee just two years earlier, at the 1985 infractions hearing, that (1) "all known violations had been disclosed" and (2) the involved boosters had really been disassociated. Yet here was Sherwood Blount (though not named in the report) being "requested by key athletics department staff members to continue to fund the payments that were distributed through the athletics department."

Against those factors, then, every subsequent, *potential* death penalty case must be measured—an abysmal track record as a repeat violator, egregious violations that stand out among major infractions cases, deliberate concealment of known violations, active participation in violations by "key athletics department" personnel, the use of disassociated boosters, the gain of a substantial competitive advantage through cheating, false assurances (aka flat-out lying) to the Committee on Infractions in prior cases . . . and the list goes on. The committee, for example, also took to task the three football players who remained eligible even after being on the payroll in past years. Those players refused to come forward and identify themselves.

And today, of course, we know many more of the facts behind the smu payment-to-players program. Because of David Whitford's *A Payroll to Meet* book, for example, we know most of the excruciating details of involvement of the governing board in the violations. The media uncovered many of the hidden details shortly after the death penalty was announced. Bill Clements, for example, came clean with writers from the *Dallas Morning News* on March 2, 1987, just five days after the infractions report was released and just weeks after taking office for his second term as governor of Texas. So to the list of factors comparing future cases to smu, one can add active involvement in violations at the highest levels of university governance.

Most people who have heard of the smu death penalty case believe that the infractions committee leveled a two-year suspension of the football program. In fact, the committee imposed a complete ban only for one year; the second year, in 1988, was limited to "no more than seven games or scrimmages against outside competition, none of which shall be a 'home' game." So a Mustangs team could have played a full Southwest Conference slate in 1988, as long as it was willing to play (and the conference office was willing to schedule) every game on the road. smu administrators had been humiliated enough; they canceled the entire 1988 season.

smu football climbed back into the saddle in 1989. After a two-year hiatus and shattered recruiting, perhaps it was a miracle that the Mustangs won even two games during the 1989 season. They dropped back to 1-10 seasons in 1990 and 1991 and then struggled for years to become even a shadow of what they once had been. In the two decades following the death penalty, from the 1989 season through the 2008 season, SMU managed only *one* winning season, a 6-5 campaign in 1997. It averaged only three wins per seasons over that twenty-year stretch, compiling an overall record of 59-164-3.

Observers often question whether NCAA sanctions have any real teeth. Studies have shown that most schools rebound pretty quickly, even after serious sanctions have been imposed. Alabama, for example, had a run of four major infractions cases (three involving its football program) over a fourteen-year period from 1995 to 2009. One of those cases, in 2002, resulted in a two-year postseason ban on the football team. Yet in ten seasons from 2008 to 2017, the Crimson Tide won five national championships, compiling an almost inconceivable 125-14 record. Hell, even Penn State was 8-4 the season after it accepted some of the harshest penalties in history. Four years later, Penn State was a Big 10 champion, ranked fifth in the country and playing in the 2017 Rose Bowl. Its opponent was USC—another team that recovered nicely, thank you, from very harsh sanctions. In the final AP poll in January 2017, USC ranked third and Penn State ranked seventh.

The death penalty against SMU, however, bit hard. The team finally managed a respectable four-year run, with three winning seasons, from 2009 to 2012 under head coach June Jones, but even during that short stretch, the team averaged nearly six losses per year in compiling a 30-23 record. The program hit rock bottom again in 2014, with a 1-11 record. For other institutions that have watched SMU's now decades-long plunge from the very pinnacle of college football, the prospect of another death penalty is scary indeed. And it's understandable that for SMU fans like Nathan Darrell Ford, any major case involving their beloved Mustangs must feel like a hatchet in the spine.

Ford, you will recall, was distressed over sanctions imposed in 2000, the result of SMU's eighth major infractions case involving the football program. Among other violations, an assistant coach encouraged, and then arranged for, an academically challenged recruit to have someone else take his ACT for him so he could qualify for initial eligibility. After the deed was done, the coach paid the real exam taker $100 for his good work in achieving a qualifying score. Later, the coach encouraged the recruit to lie to investigators. Due in part to this outrageous conduct, the Committee on Infractions imposed several penalties on SMU's football program, including two years of probation, a vacation of wins in the games in which the recruit later competed while ineligible, and a reduction in the number of expense-paid recruiting visits for prospects. All in all, a pretty routine, run-of-the-mill set of penalties, despite Ford's characterization. The assistant coach, however, was subject to an unusually harsh penalty—a seven-year show-cause. I can count on one hand the number of individuals, in my nearly ten years on the infractions committee, who were subject to show-cause penalties of seven years or more.

Aside from this one assistant coach's egregious behavior in the 2000 case, SMU had a relatively clean slate for nearly twenty-five years. Perhaps the death penalty provided exactly the jolt SMU and other schools needed. In 2011, however, SMU made a return trip to the Committee on Infractions for a record-setting ninth time. But this time, for a change, a sport besides football was the center of attention. Men's basketball staff members had made impermissible text messages to parents of recruits. In the big scheme of things, it was a pretty minor case, and the head coach self-reported the violations when he learned of them. The committee imposed a two-year probation and accepted some modest recruiting restrictions self-imposed by the university.

The following year, in 2012, SMU hired legendary coach Larry Brown to coach its men's basketball team. Brown is a Naismith Hall of Famer; he remains the only coach ever to win both an NCAA championship (with Kansas in 1988) and an NBA title (with the Detroit Pistons in 2004). Brown also had left two other college programs on the eve of NCAA sanctions. A Brown-coached UCLA team reached the NCAA finals in 1980 (losing to Louisville in the title game), but that Final Four appearance later was vacated by the Committee on Infractions because of recruiting and extra-benefit violations. In 1988 Brown led a Kansas team to the NCAA title and then left to become head coach of the NBA's San Antonio Spurs. Later that year, the infractions committee found that serious recruiting violations had been committed in 1986. The committee also cited the institution for a "disturbing failure to exercise appropriate institutional control" over its men's basketball program. The committee banned Kansas from defending its NCAA title in 1989, the only time a reigning champion has been barred from postseason play.

The violations at both UCLA and Kansas occurred on Brown's watch. Although the infractions committee made no findings against Brown himself, it did note in the Kansas case that "actions known by . . . the head coach to be violations were not reported to appropriate members of the university's administration." At the time, Kansas was a repeat violator under the new repeat-violator legislation that the NCAA membership had passed three years earlier. In backing off harsher sanctions, the committee noted that "the coaches who were involved in this case are no longer at an NCAA member institution." Brown already had left for San Antonio.

It did not take long for Brown to have success at SMU. During the 2014–15 season, his Mustangs team won twenty-seven games, and SMU made its first NCAA tournament appearance since 1993. Three months later, in June 2015, Brown and other SMU officials were before the infractions committee to address allegations of academic fraud involving one of the men's basketball players. The case also involved serious rule violations in the men's golf program. During the summer of 2013, in Brown's second year at SMU, an administrative assistant he had hired committed academic fraud by completing coursework for a prized recruit, a McDonald's All-American.

The committee found that the assistant "obtained the student-athlete's username and password to his online summer course" and "completed all of the student-athlete's assignments and exams" for the course. The player received academic credit and a grade of A- for the course, even though he did no work.

Brown was not implicated in the fraud; later, though, he was "confronted with confessions" from both the student athlete and the administrative assistant that the fraud had occurred, but "he took no action." Ultimately, the infractions committee cited Brown for failing to report violations, failing to "promote an atmosphere of compliance" in his basketball program, and "initially lying to the enforcement staff during the investigation." For his "multiple severe violations," Brown received a two-year show-cause penalty that included a suspension from 30 percent of the 2015–16 season. And after SMU had finally returned to the NCAA tournament in 2015, it was banned from postseason competition in 2016. Brown resigned from his coaching position at SMU in July 2016, leaving a roster deeply depleted by scholarship reductions through 2019.

The 2015 infractions case rendered SMU a record-setting *ten-time* major violator.

The football players were not the only stars at SMU in the eighties. Jon Koncak arrived on campus in 1981. A seven-foot center on the men's basketball team, he was one of the best players ever to wear a Mustangs uniform. Indeed, SMU retired his jersey in 2008 to recognize his accomplishments. Koncak was a member of the U.S. Olympic team in 1984, a consensus second-team All-American as a senior in 1985, and the number-five overall pick in the 1985 NBA Draft. He played ten years for the Atlanta Hawks.

Following the imposition of the death penalty on the football team, SMU hired a private investigation firm to review the entire athletics department. In 1988 Koncak told one of the investigators from the firm that he had received thousands of dollars in cash from boosters during his junior and senior years at SMU. He identified two boosters who were among the nine disassociated from the athletics program in April 1985 for payments to football players. Koncak said he knew of other basketball players who also received payments. While the payments came from boosters, Koncak told the investigator that he believed "very strongly" that his head coach at the time knew about the payment program. That coach was Dave Bliss.

3

Unethical Conduct

Sports do not build character. They reveal it.

HEYWOOD BROUN

Fewer than one hundred miles down I-35 from Dallas and SMU lies Waco, a place that has become synonymous with the 1993 deaths of seventy-five people during a confrontation between David Koresh's Branch Davidians and federal agents. Timothy McVeigh used "Waco" as a rallying cry, two years to the day later, when he bombed the federal building in Oklahoma City, killing 168 people, including nineteen children, mostly from the building's childcare center, and wounding hundreds of others.

Waco seems to have had a disproportionate share of bad news over the last century for a town of its size. In 2016 the town experienced the one hundredth anniversary of the "Waco horror," when Jesse Washington, a black seventeen-year-old, was seized from a courtroom by a mob after he had been found guilty of murdering a white woman. The mob dragged him by a chain to the town square, where he was tortured, mutilated, and burned to death in front of fifteen thousand residents, including the mayor and the chief of police. In 1953 a tornado hit downtown Waco, killing 114 people. It remains the eleventh-deadliest tornado in U.S. history. Very recently was the Twin Peaks shootout. On May 17, 2015, a dispute between rival biker gangs broke out at the Twin Peaks Restaurant. A shootout ensued, resulting in nine deaths, twenty injuries, and nearly two hundred arrests.

Not all the news has been negative. Dr. Pepper was invented in Waco in 1885 at Morrison's Old Corner Drug Store and to this day remains a hit among soda aficionados. During his presidency, George W. Bush established his "Western White House" on his ranch in Crawford, not far from Waco. Joanna and Chip Gaines have been the toast of the town with their *Fixer Upper* TV show and Magnolia empire. But the big thing going in Waco is Baylor University, which has emerged in recent years as a powerhouse in college athletics. The school has long-standing traditions of excellence in tennis and in track and field, but now it has become a force to be reckoned with in the so-called "major" sports. The university's women's and men's basketball programs have excelled; the women won a national title in 2012 with a perfect 40-0 record. Until a sexual assault scandal slowed things down in 2016, the football program had won an average of ten games per season over the five prior seasons.

The recent heights in the athletics department have been a welcome change from the depths of 2003.

On July 25, 2003, in the hot Texas sun, the body of Patrick Dennehy was found decomposing near a gravel pit several miles southeast of Baylor's Waco campus. The cause of death was two gunshot wounds to the head, both above the right ear. Patrick Dennehy was twenty-one years old; at the time of his death, he was a member of the Baylor Bears men's basketball team.

Dennehy had gone missing several weeks earlier. He had attended his last class of the year on June 12 and had spoken to a friend on June 14, but he had not been heard from since. It was the weekend of Father's Day, and his mother and stepfather were surprised that he did not call home. After days of worrying, they called the Waco police on June 19 to report that Dennehy was missing.

On July 21, four days before his body was discovered, Dennehy's girlfriend back in Albuquerque, Jessica De La Rosa, made another call—to the NCAA enforcement staff. The information she provided suggested potential violations within the Bears basketball program. The next day, representatives of Baylor University also notified the enforcement staff that they were investigating allegations of major infractions within the men's basketball program. And so began one of the most disturbing odysseys of corruption and deceit in collegiate athletics history.

The disappearance and murder of one of their own sent some members of the coaching staff of the Bears basketball team scrambling, not for answers to the senseless violence, but to use this tragedy to cover up their own noxious behavior. Much of what followed, and had already occurred, could be loosely and generously described as "unethical conduct." Most people with a moral compass understand unethical conduct as a general term. It also has special meaning in the realm of collegiate athletics and NCAA rules and regulations. Unethical conduct is the most serious rule violation that can be committed by an individual, and it can take a variety of forms. In the Baylor case, it took two principal forms: (1) knowing involvement in major violations, and (2) providing false or misleading information to investigators. Once everyone came clean and admitted to their misconduct, it became clear that the Baylor infractions would epitomize unethical conduct.

At the center of this odyssey and resulting criminal investigation, internal university investigation, and NCAA investigation was the head coach of Baylor's men's basketball program, David Gregory Bliss. Bliss has a superb pedigree. He holds an MBA from Cornell University, where he played basketball as an all–Ivy League guard and was captain of the baseball team. He is a member of the Cornell Athletic Hall of Fame and has been a frequent speaker for the Fellowship of Christian Athletes. He has amassed over five hundred career wins in Division I men's basketball, boasting a .616 winning percentage. Bliss started his coaching career as an assistant to Bobby Knight at West Point and later was on Knight's staff during some of the glory years of Indiana basketball in the 1970s. Prior to the head coaching job at Baylor, Bliss had been head coach at Oklahoma, SMU, and New Mexico. He remains New Mexico's all-time-winningest coach, with seven NCAA tournament appearances. His best season was 1995–96, when the Lobos went 28-5.

Bliss is also a wolf in sheep's clothing, in the eyes of many. As one former player put it, "He's a liar, for one, a used-car salesman. . . . Everything he said or did was just a means to make him richer and more powerful and to feed his ego." The speaker, Rob Robbins, played for Bliss at New Mexico from 1988 to 1991, graduating as the school's second-leading scorer.

Bliss had moved to New Mexico in 1988 from SMU, where he had been the men's basketball head coach during the major football infractions cases, the conduct that predated them, and the resulting death penalty. He, like many others with an out, jumped ship for greener pastures shortly after the death penalty was handed down, but there was probably more to the story.

Bliss was head coach at SMU from 1980 to 1988, right in the heart of the years when the football boosters' cash-to-players program was in full swing. The basketball program apparently was not immune. Star center Jon Koncak, who graduated in 1985 as a second-team All-American, later admitted in an interview with the *Fort Worth Star-Telegram* to receiving booster payments.

The *Star-Telegram* had obtained a copy of an internal NCAA memo written by Robert Stroup, an enforcement staff member who had investigated the SMU men's basketball program. The memo had summarized a report by a Dallas private investigation firm, which SMU officials had hired after imposition of the death penalty to review the entire athletics department. The report had confirmed major violations in the basketball program, including the payments to Koncak. Stroup, however, had been directed by his supervisor to back off the investigation. As he later told the *Star-Telegram*, the investigation "was at a point where there could have been another major case, but, back then, cases would take two, three years to complete. It was just kind of decided, 'We gave them the worst [the death penalty]. What more can we do?'"

The death penalty was indeed extraordinary, but it fell on the football program. One could question the propriety of backing off a basketball investigation, but it's also understandable that the NCAA, had it pursued SMU in yet *another* major infractions case, could have been viewed as piling on. In any event, the investigators' report had not implicated Bliss directly in the violations, so he was free and clear to take his show to Albuquerque.

Despite his track record prior to Baylor, Dave Bliss did not kill Patrick Dennehy. The assailant was Carlton Dotson, Dennehy's fellow teammate and roommate. Dotson was a transfer from Paris Junior College in eastern Texas, recruited to Baylor the same year as Dennehy. In late June 2003, a month before Dennehy's body was discovered, the Waco police secured a warrant to search Dennehy's computer. The affidavit in support of the warrant cited an informant who said Dotson told his cousin that he had shot Dennehy in the head during an argument outside Waco. In July Dotson spoke with law enforcement officials, admitted to killing Dennehy, and provided information that led to the location of Dennehy's body.

An odd set of facts emerged. Dotson and Dennehy had both purchased guns, allegedly for protection, because they had been threatened by teammates and had had $300 stolen from their apartment. On the day of the murder, they had gone out to the gravel pit for some target practice. Dotson told authorities that he killed Dennehy in self-defense, fearing that Dennehy was going to kill him. The autopsy, however, clearly negated self-defense. Perhaps Dotson acted out of paranoia, or perhaps he was simply a tortured soul suffering from mental illness.

Many of his actions were bizarre and irrational, including telling authorities at one point that he heard voices and that he was the Son of God.

Dotson ultimately pled guilty to the murder of Patrick Dennehy and in 2005 began serving a thirty-five-year term at the maximum security prison in Huntsville, Texas. We probably will never know what happened near the gravel pit that day—seemingly a random and unforeseeable event outside the scope of basketball, the result of an unstable man reacting to a tumultuous environment. No mystery, however, surrounds the cold, calculating way that Dave Bliss tried to use this unfortunate tragedy to cover up his own misdeeds and lies as they pertained to Dennehy, other players, and his oversight of the Baylor men's basketball program.

The ship first left dock on this absurd voyage when Bliss recruited and signed five new prospects in 2002. Knowing that some of these prospects were questionable academically, he hedged his bets and recruited and signed two more prospects, promising them scholarships. Those additional signees were Patrick Dennehy and Corey Herring. Bliss then turned it over to the gods, and as fate would have it, the first five recruits all met the required academic standards for eligibility. Bliss was now stuck with seven players and five scholarships. Being a man of integrity, questionable or otherwise, he chose to keep the additional two on "scholarship" . . . even if he had to pay them himself. Like the boosters at SMU years earlier, Bliss had promises to keep and a payroll to meet.

And so, with the help of his staff, when the bills came due, Bliss paid them—a clear NCAA violation, but, to be charitable, perhaps one motivated in part by humanitarian instincts. In April 2003 Bliss gave assistant coach Rodney Belcher $2,000 in cash—twenty $100 bills; Belcher passed it along to Dennehy. The following month, Bliss gave Belcher seven money orders for $1,000 each and $132 in cash. Belcher took all the funds to the university cashier's office and paid them to Dennehy's delinquent student account. On May 28, 2003, on behalf of Herring, Bliss gave Belcher $9,132 in cashier's checks and ten money orders totaling $8,689, for a total of $17,821, which Belcher then delivered to the Baylor cashier's office to pay to Herring's delinquent student account.

All was on track. Dennehy and Herring were taken care of, and their student accounts were fully paid. No one was the wiser regarding the source of the funds. Just takin' care of business. Then, just two and a half weeks later, Dennehy went missing . . .

When Dennehy disappeared, Bliss knew that the authorities would follow the money in an attempt to find out where Dennehy was and what had happened. If that money trail led back to the university and, more specifically, to the basketball program and coaching staff, Bliss would have problems. He knew what it would look like, because of what it was: major NCAA violations—impermissible inducements to prospective student athletes, impermissible benefits to student athletes, unethical conduct, and perhaps others. He could come clean right then, admitting to the tuition payments and pleading for mercy on the ground that he was keeping his promises to two young men who had relied on scholarship aid to attend school and play ball. Or he could try to hide what he had done. Bliss opted for the cover-up.

With respect to Herring, the cover-up actually had begun the previous fall. Herring needed $300 a month during the fall semester to pay for living expenses. At Bliss's direction, assistant coach Brian O'Neill flew to Herring's hometown of Buffalo, New York, to personally provide Herring's mother with a false story and paper trail. O'Neill had been with Bliss at New Mexico, and Herring was one of his first recruits to Baylor. As the infractions report would later say, on this trip O'Neill was serving as Bliss's "bag man." He had $900 in cash from Bliss for Herring's mother. In return, she would write three nonsequential checks of $300 each, payable to her son. Even this early in the scheme, and for such a modest amount,

O'Neill had his instructions from Bliss: Herring's mother was to write the checks "at spaced intervals throughout her checkbook to . . . evade detection should someone question three sequentially numbered checks being given to [her son] over a 90-day period."

And what of those money orders and cashier's checks used in May 2003 to pay in full Herring's student account? Not only did Bliss purchase them, but he also forged the signature of Herring's mother on them. And after Dennehy's disappearance, Bliss solidified the cover-up with his own trip to Buffalo. There he obtained Herring's mother's bank statements, from which he "created duplicate versions that reflected bogus deposits and withdrawals in the amount of the tuition payments" Bliss had paid on Herring's behalf.

Herring's payments, then, were covered. Dennehy's were more problematic, because he couldn't be found. When he turned up dead later in the summer, a new challenge presented itself. On the one hand, dead men tell no tales. On the other hand, dead men can tell no lies.

One individual who did agree to provide cover was Dennehy's former AAU (Amateur Athletic Union) coach. In the summer of 2003 Bliss called to ask if he would please tell investigators that he personally gave Dennehy money to pay his tuition. Remarkably, the AAU coach agreed to do so, even though he never made any payments to anyone. Such was the power of Bliss, who of course was attempting to conceal the fact that the payments were from him.

Why would the AAU coach lie for Bliss? The investigation took an interesting turn, and other violations got caught up in the money trail. Bliss had long ago discovered, as many coaches had, that the various AAU programs were fertile ground for prospects. To ensure that those programs provided a heads-up when they had some talent or helped to steer talent a certain way when coaches had their sights set on a prospect, college coaches embraced the American way—showing the AAU coaches some love. And love meant money. During 2002 and

66

2003, in addition to at least $28,600 Bliss personally donated to AAU programs, he was able to solicit booster donations totaling $87,000, hand delivered by Bliss to the Houston Superstars.

Not all such donations are NCAA violations, even though a quid pro quo seems evident. Bliss had disclosed $5,000 of his personal donations, as required on institutional disclosure forms, stating that the $5,000 was to cover his son's travel. His son played for one of the AAU teams. If this was an accurate disclosure, it was well within the rules. But Bliss conveniently left out another $23,600 in personal donations to various AAU teams; when the full scope of the donations (including those of Baylor boosters) was considered, he clearly was doing far more than covering his son's traveling expenses and was doing so to gain a competitive advantage. At least four AAU players from programs receiving donations during this period eventually enrolled at Baylor. When confronted with the donations, Bliss argued that the NCAA bylaws applied only to high school programs and that AAU programs were thus outside the purview of NCAA bylaws. The Committee on Infractions ultimately rejected that argument and tacked on another violation: impermissible financial assistance to prospective student athletes.

The ship was now well out to sea. Transgressions had been made. The cover-up was on. But things would get worse . . . far worse.

A concocted story of the AAU coach making Dennehy's full tuition payments was unlikely to hold up, particularly when the money trail was followed. Bliss needed a backup plan, and he found it, ironically, in the overall character of the players he had recruited. Not all were model citizens. At the infractions hearing a couple of years later, Robert Sloan Jr., then president of Baylor, would put it this way: not only did members of the team have questionable academic abilities, but overall the group was involved in "rampant drug use and serious criminal activity."

Bliss had his out: paint Dennehy as a drug dealer. People would buy that. He got all that cash and paid his bills from the sale of drugs. Could Dennehy refute it? Obviously not. All Bliss needed now was a few players and the coaching staff to say the same. "It doesn't have to be the same story. It just has to have the same ending," according to Bliss.

Getting people to go along was not as difficult as it might sound. Doug Ash, Bliss's top assistant on the coaching staff, was a soldier. He'd been with Bliss from the beginning, when Bliss hired him years before as his top assistant at Oklahoma. Assistant coach Rodney Belcher was newer to the team, but he too had always been willing to go to the mat for Bliss. Both assistants later testified before the infractions committee that they had gone along with everything and played their role out of a loyalty to Bliss. Brian O'Neill was no longer around when the shit hit the fan. He had left the program at the end of the season in April 2003.

The players? Well, players are players; they do as they're told. Bliss went so far as to write out instructions, detailing what the players should tell investigators. In some instances, he even provided them with tape recorders so they could practice what they would tell investigators—that Dennehy was a drug dealer with large rolls of cash. Like practicing for "a high school play," as the chair of the infractions committee put it after the case was over.

Then there was assistant coach Abar Rouse, who also had a tape recorder. Bliss liked him, and he was a good assistant. But he had only been with the program for three months. His first college coaching gig, at his alma mater no less, and he was all of twenty-seven years old. When Bliss's initial request for help in the cover-up went nowhere, he must have thought, *Strong-arm him; he's just a kid.* This was after Rouse told Bliss that he was uncomfortable impugning the reputation of a dead man to cover up illicit payments made by a head coach to a college recruit at the world's largest Baptist university. Bliss then reportedly left a highlighted contract on Rouse's desk.

The highlighted portion indicated that Bliss had the power to hire and fire assistant coaches.

Rouse claimed in a 2013 interview on ESPN's *Outside the Lines* that Bliss actually told him that he would fire him if Rouse did not go along with the plan, which included assigning players to the different assistant coaches, who were then tasked with helping those players lie to NCAA, university, and law enforcement investigators. Whatever exactly transpired, the message was clear. Three months in and Rouse was in a game of hardball, back against the wall—be fired or go along in an amoral, possibly criminal, conspiracy. Rouse went with plan C, tape-recording Bliss talking about the cover-up.

During conversations from July 30 through August 1, Rouse carried a concealed microcassette recorder. Two weeks later, he turned over the tapes to university and NCAA investigators. Bliss's messages were stunning in their depravity: "What we've got to create here is drugs. . . . I think the thing we want to do—and you think about this—if there's a way we can create the perception that Pat may have been a dealer. Even if we had to kind of make some things look a little better than they are, that can save us. . . . Dennehy is never going to refute what we say." In crafting a script for players to tell investigators, "All they've got to remember is that they can tell the story, 'We went up there and everything. And all of a sudden, he walked out with that tray, and it had everything on it that you can imagine. And I knew something different was up. And then he pulled out his roll of bills. And when he pulled out that roll of bills, it scared us and we never went back.'"

Most people probably think assistant coach Abar Rouse acted out of a desire for self-preservation, to give himself some insurance or a card to play if this thing went south. If so, who could blame him? According to Rouse, however, in a 2008 interview with ESPN reporter Dana O'Neil, he acted out of his obligation to the university he loved and to his Christian faith: "I think you have to weigh your career versus how you protect kids. That was the only thought process going through my head. A career is a small thing in comparison to a life, a small thing in comparison to morals and values." He later added, in the 2013 ESPN *Outside the Lines* interview, that part of the reason for taping Bliss was also to protect himself, as he believed that Bliss would fire him and then lie about the cause or do whatever else he needed to do to protect himself. Rouse already had seen Bliss lie, cheat, and scheme, and he believed that this behavior would not stop.

As Bliss scrambled to clean up the money trail and get people in line, investigators began to turn up other questionable conduct and infractions, including additional recruiting violations and the failure to report the results of players' drug tests. The ship was now foundering; it was taking on water, and there was no land in sight.

Bliss eventually could see the writing on the wall. The day after Dennehy's funeral, on August 8, 2003, Bliss and the athletics director, Tom Stanton, both resigned. Stanton resigned largely because of his office's failure to monitor the men's basketball program and protect against infractions but also because he was directly involved in not reporting the failed drug tests. Bliss actually had reported to Stanton that three men's basketball players had tested positive for marijuana, but Stanton failed to follow institutional procedures for reporting the results to the university's office of judicial affairs for determination of disciplinary sanctions and notation on the students' permanent records. As a result, according to the later infractions report, the student athletes "faced no consequences" for their drug use. Stanton also was cited in the infractions report for failing to follow up with the compliance office after he learned that Bliss was soliciting boosters for donations to AAU programs.

To Baylor's credit, once university officials learned of the allegations, they immediately launched a thorough internal investigation. They put a stop to any and all violations, replaced the entire men's basketball coaching staff, and self-imposed significant punishments on the men's basketball program. They also fully cooperated with NCAA investigators and the Committee on Infractions. Even Coach Bliss was remarkably forthcoming and took ownership of his misconduct. He helped with the internal investigation as well as with the NCAA investigation, and he later appeared before the infractions committee to admit to and elaborate on the role he had played. At the infractions hearing, he described his actions as "despicable."

Baylor's self-imposed penalties included a one-year postseason ban; forfeiture of conference tournament revenue; and reductions in official paid visits, recruiting opportunities, and scholarships. The institution also implemented many new procedures and policies regarding recruitment, drug testing, and academic standards.

These corrective measures undoubtedly helped Baylor to put its best foot forward in trying circumstances, but there was little hope for leniency from the Committee on Infractions. The underlying violations were "serious and widespread," in the committee's language. But let's face it—they were not unheard of. Unfortunately, illicit payments to student athletes or AAU programs were part of the infractions landscape. The Baylor case was outrageous because of the cover-up. What makes Dave Bliss a poster child for unethical conduct is his heavy involvement in, and orchestration of, violations as head coach. This was not some rich booster trying to steer players to his alma mater; this was the head coach in the trenches, hands dirty, actually forging financial documents and telling people how and when to lie, not only to NCAA investigators, but to law enforcement officers investigating the murder of one of his players by another one of his players.

Moreover, this was Baylor's third major infractions case within ten years. In 1995 the men's basketball program was sanctioned for infractions related to academic fraud, also resulting in federal felony convictions for three assistant coaches for mail fraud, wire fraud, and conspiracy. Then in 2000 the infractions committee cited the university for major violations in the men's tennis program. This history meant Baylor was a two-time repeat violator when it came before the infractions committee in 2005. Of all the findings or designations in NCAA parlance, perhaps the two most significant, at least for institutional culpability, are "repeat violator" and "lack of institutional control" over an athletics program. This case had both.

Coming out of the 2000 infractions case, the university was required to develop and implement a comprehensive compliance program. Simply put, it failed to do so. Had such a program been in place, many of the major infractions occurring in this case would have been easily detected, reported, and potentially handled before they became worse. For example, Dennehy was recruited as a transfer from New Mexico, where he was a starter and quite a well-known all-conference player, yet at Baylor he enrolled as a walk-on and failed to make any tuition payments for almost the entire academic year—a situation that went completely unquestioned. As noted previously, in 2002 Bliss told athletics director Stanton about the failed drug tests of three players, yet Stanton did not forward the results to institutional authorities as required by the university's own policy. Other examples exist as well; the point is that had someone been watching, there was plenty to see.

Again, to its credit, Baylor outlined a candid assessment of its own deficiencies in a self-report to the NCAA, following the university's internal investigation:

> The former head men's basketball coach obviously failed to adequately supervise and control members of his staff beginning in April 2002, and then actively participated in numerous major infractions of NCAA legislation. . . . The university is embarrassed that its various administrative systems allowed these violations to go undiscovered. There were red flags that should have been noticed. They should have been noticed by members of the administration and faculty. They should have been noticed by the director of ath-

letics. . . . They should have been noticed by the compliance staff (the resources of which were seriously depleted due to illness, personnel shortages, and overwork). They should have been noticed by the financial aid office (which generally attempts to be helpful and accommodating of students and was trying too hard to be helpful here).

According to the university, one of the main reasons the infractions occurred within the basketball program was the deference others paid to head coach Dave Bliss, based on his long, "clean record and good reputation." Everyone from top administrators to university staff deferred to Bliss on all matters pertaining to the men's basketball program. An anecdote may illustrate the point. In August 2003, shortly after Bliss resigned, a former administrative assistant told the *Dallas Morning News* that she often felt frightened by Bliss's behavior during the three years she worked for him. She described his verbal abuse of players and, on one occasion, Bliss throwing a telephone across his office. When she voiced her concerns to the university's director of personnel services, "He told me, 'I've met Coach Bliss. He doesn't act like that. Go back to work.'"

Perhaps Lord Acton was right: "Power tends to corrupt and absolute power corrupts absolutely."

I remember sitting through the infractions hearing and thinking the committee actually might have a second death penalty case on its hands. The elements were all in place—serious and widespread violations; not only a repeat violator but a *multiple* repeat violator; probably a lack of institutional control; perhaps the most serious unethical conduct the committee had seen, when one takes into account all components of the cover-up, including desperate attempts to deceive investigators, multiple participants, and the deliberate demonization of a deceased student athlete. For good measure, the university's thorough investigation even had turned up some academic fraud, though in its football program, not in basketball. It promised to be an interesting deliberation.

In the end, two factors saved Baylor from the death penalty. Had the 2000 case involved men's basketball rather than tennis, I believe the committee would have been close. An institution as a whole, including its entire athletics program, is on the hook as a repeat violator each time major infractions occur within five years of a previous major infractions case. Nonetheless, it is difficult to imagine leveling the death penalty on a basketball program because of violations that occurred within five years of a tennis case—unless, of course, the entire athletics department's compliance program is in a shambles. Baylor's 1995 case, involving academic fraud in the men's basketball program, was serious—the committee *hates* academic fraud—but that had been ten years ago.

Of critical importance were Baylor University's demonstrated cooperation, genuine acceptance of wrongdoing, and strong desire to correct the mistakes that were made. Had Baylor not stepped up, cooperated fully (including conducting a thorough internal investigation), and taken significant corrective measures (including cleaning house), I feel relatively certain it would have joined the ranks of SMU in the death penalty record books. Gene Marsh, then acting chair of the infractions committee, said as much in the NCAA's press conference announcing the penalties:

> We walked up to the edge [of the death penalty] and then stepped back. Their penalties and approach saved their basketball season. . . . We were there; we considered this to be a death penalty case. Then we stepped back and we looked at the cooperation of the school once they had a handle on what their problems were, the honest and frankly blunt approach they took towards describing what their problems were. We thought with the system that we have and the members that we have that you have to give some credit along the way to a school that cooperates.

"But make no mistake about it," Marsh also said, "it's a very serious penalty." Indeed it was. In what has come closest to a partial death penalty, the committee shut down Baylor basketball's *nonconference* schedule for a year. To allow the university to "keep its obligation to the conference," the Bears would be allowed a Big 12–only season. Although the committee did not impose a further postseason ban beyond the one year that Baylor already had imposed on itself in 2004, the short season would present serious obstacles to receiving a postseason bid. The committee also imposed a series of other penalties, including scholarship and recruiting restrictions and a five-year probation, which was the longest probationary period possible at the time. Penalty legislation adopted in 2013 contemplates probationary periods of up to ten years.

Because the committee did not impose a further postseason ban, Baylor's current players and recruits were not automatically eligible for a waiver of the NCAA's transfer rules, which typically require transfers to sit out one year of competition at their new schools. Baylor, however, stepped up yet again, granting a release to every student athlete in the men's basketball program and then successfully petitioning the NCAA and the Big 12 Conference for waivers of their transfer regulations, thereby allowing any and all of their current players to leave and play elsewhere immediately. That decision did result in most players leaving the program. The impact, coupled with the dismissal of the entire basketball coaching staff, thoroughly gutted the program. But at least the Baylor Bears, in some form, would be on the court the next year.

The penalty phase also resulted in show-cause penalties related to Bliss and three of his assistant coaches. A show-cause penalty is the most significant penalty the NCAA can levy that has a direct impact on a specific individual. It also is probably one of the most misunderstood and misrepresented areas of NCAA legislation. Admittedly, the legislation is obtuse, so confusion is understandable. A show-cause penalty, at least by itself, does *not* constitute a ban on coaching, and it is imposed on an *institution*, not directly on a coach.

Show-cause penalties are issued only for serious misconduct; rarely has the committee imposed such a penalty in the absence of *unethical conduct* by a coach or other institutional employee (for example, an administrative assistant or academic counselor engaged in academic fraud). By the time of the infractions hearing, however, most individuals who have engaged in unethical behavior have been fired or have resigned. Typically, they are no longer employed at an NCAA member institution, which means that the NCAA, an association of member institutions, has no authority or jurisdiction over them. In such an instance, the show-cause penalty is directed toward any member institution that may want to hire a tainted individual *in the future*. That is the typical scenario; in some instances, however, the second institution *already has hired* the tainted individual, either because it was unaware of the individual's violations at the previous school or because it was willing to take a risk on the individual, knowing full well that the individual had committed violations and was, or may become, the subject of a show-cause penalty. In very rare circumstances, the original institution may have retained the wrongdoer.

In any case, the current or prospective employer will have to assure the Committee on Infractions that it is or will be taking necessary steps to keep the coach in line. In the language of the legislation, that requires a showing of "appropriate disciplinary or corrective action," which could include restrictions on the coach's duties, such as a prohibition on recruiting activities, or a suspension from coaching for a designated period of time. The legislation at the time of the Baylor case contemplated that the appropriate disciplinary action in egregious cases might include "termination of the coaching contract of the head coach and any assistants involved" in the violations; today's legislation refers more generally to restrictions on "athletically related duties."

The show-cause penalty itself is set forth in boilerplate language. The language of the penalties in the Baylor case is typical:

Therefore, he will be informed in writing by the NCAA that, due to his involvement in the violations of NCAA legislation found in this case, if he seeks employment or affiliation in an athletically related position at an NCAA member institution during a [insert number of years]-year period [insert dates], he and the involved institution shall be requested to appear before the Committee on Infractions to consider whether the member institution should be subject to the show cause procedures of Bylaw 19.5.2.2-(l) [the appropriate disciplinary or corrective action provisions at the time], which could limit his athletically related duties at the new institution for a designated period.

The language of the show-cause penalty suggests that a personal appearance before the infractions committee will be required whenever a tainted coach is rehired or retained. In reality, the institution notifies the infractions committee in writing of the disciplinary measures it has taken or intends to take, and it is up to the committee to accept or reject them. If the committee rejects the measures, *then* the coach (who is once again—or still—a university employee and thus subject to NCAA jurisdiction) and institution may be compelled to appear before the committee to "show cause" why further disciplinary measures should not be imposed. That seldom happens; appropriate discipline almost invariably can be worked out between the university and the committee without a hearing. I don't recall a single show-cause hearing in the nearly ten years I served on the committee.

So let's cut through the technicalities. For all practical purposes, a show-cause penalty attaches to an individual coach, no matter where he or she may go, for a specific amount of time, as stated in the infractions report. Most schools avoid the baggage; they don't want to be hampered by a tainted coach with restrictions, so they stay away. In those cases, then, the penalty effectively acts as a ban on coaching. In the rare circumstance in which an institution believes a coach is worth the risk, it will put forth a plan for disciplining and monitoring the coach, also accepting the principle that should that coach commit another violation during the show-cause period, the institution will be subject to enhanced penalties. For those practical reasons, I will refer to show-cause penalties being imposed on individuals, even though technically they are imposed on institutions.

Note that the show-cause penalty applies only to "athletically related duties." Jim Tressel, former Ohio State head football coach and 2015 inductee into the College Football Hall of Fame, resigned in 2011 after an NCAA investigation led to a five-year show-cause penalty (mostly for failing to report known violations). In 2014, just three years into the show-cause period, Youngstown State hired him as university president. His penalties or restrictions did not follow him to the presidency because it was outside the scope of collegiate athletics in theory; however, recall that college presidents, under NCAA legislation, are ultimately responsible for their athletics programs.

Because NCAA penalties apply only within the realm of member institutions and their employees, individuals subject to a show-cause penalty likewise are free to do as they please, so long as it is not with an NCAA member institution's athletics program. Another high-profile example involves Chip Kelly, former head football coach at Oregon. He left Oregon during an NCAA investigation that resulted in an eighteen-month show-cause order. But because he left the university to become head coach of the Philadelphia Eagles—outside the NCAA's authority—he was free and clear of any penalties or restrictions. Had another NCAA member institution wanted to hire Kelly within that eighteen-month period, though, it would have been saddled with his baggage. Similarly, a tainted coach can even move to another *college* coaching position, so long as the college is not an NCAA member institution. Dave Bliss, for example, later coached at an NAIA school. He was hired just before his show-cause penalty expired, but his new school was free to hire him without restrictions.

In the Baylor case, the Committee on Infractions imposed a ten-year show-cause penalty on Bliss for his wanton unethical conduct, willfully committing multiple and serious violations of NCAA rules and involving everyone, top to bottom—staff, players, players' families, boosters—in his web of deceit. A ten-year show-cause penalty is the longest the committee has ever imposed, and it is reserved for the most egregious misdeeds. Theoretically, the committee could impose a permanent show-cause penalty, similar to the permanent disassociation of a booster, but to my knowledge, it has never taken that step. In my experience on the infractions committee from 2000 to 2010, I saw only one other individual receive a ten-year show-cause penalty, a coach from New Mexico State involved in egregious unethical conduct, including academic fraud.

Assistant coaches Doug Ash and Brian O'Neill received five-year show-cause penalties for their knowing involvement in violations. Assistant coach Rodney Belcher was tagged with seven years. Not only did he knowingly violate the rules, but he lied to the NCAA enforcement staff in his interviews and in the response he submitted to the infractions committee.

In a tidy, sanitized world, that would be the end of it, but in the real world, warts and all, there is always an aftermath. The ship, at this point, lay in tatters, smashed along the rocks, the captain and crew bobbing at sea. No doubt this saga would have a lasting impact on all those involved and hang a dark cloud over the town of Waco.

The rescue from the shipwreck, while certainly not ideal for anyone, was easier for some than others. Doug Ash became a longtime scout for the Detroit Pistons. Brian O'Neill returned to New Mexico, where he became deputy director of the New Mexico Sports Authority. In February 2008 Governor Bill Richardson appointed O'Neill executive director. Rodney Belcher initially coached for the Texas Celtics, a sixth-grade AAU team in Plano. He then was an assistant coach for eight years with the Lady Wildcats, a high school girls' team in Plano, where he became head coach in 2014.

Dave Bliss left Waco for Colorado, where he initially volunteered as an assistant coach at a Denver area high school. He then moved on to become the head coach of the Dakota Wizards, a CBA (Continental Basketball Association) team in North Dakota. He resigned after one year, citing family reasons. Bliss later returned to Texas and in 2010 became the dean of students, athletics director, and head basketball coach at the Allen Academy, a private high school in Bryan, Texas. It didn't take long for controversy to rear its ugly head.

Within six months of Bliss's appointment, he was crosswise with the Texas Association of Private and Parochial Schools (TAPPS), the state's largest governing body for private high school athletics. The association found that Bliss had used improper inducements to recruit two high-profile basketball players from Houston-area public high schools. The athletes, who were entering their senior years, transferred to Allen Academy after being offered tuition at a substantial discount (i.e., 85 percent off the school's $10,000 annual tuition, according to the TAPPS executive director). In addition, the association found that Bliss had forged the signature of Allen Academy's head of school on a transfer form for another student, who eventually decided not to enroll. Both Allen Academy and Bliss admitted that the forgery had occurred. As a result, TAPPS levied a two-year probation against Allen Academy and a one-year suspension for Bliss from any coaching or administrative duties within TAPPS schools.

Rather than accept the TAPPS report and penalties, Allen Academy, which had been a charter member of TAPPS since 1978, simply left TAPPS and transferred its competitive status to the Texas Christian Athletic League (TCAL), a smaller Texas private school association. That year, Allen Academy won the TCAL Class 2A state title, with the help of the two players whose eligibility was questioned in the first place. Bliss coached that team because the TAPPS sanctions were no longer applicable in the TCAL. His Allen Academy Rams went on to win five straight TCAL state titles, the last in February 2015.

In April 2015, just before his ten-year show-cause period expired in June, David Gregory Bliss returned to college coaching. Bliss became the head men's basketball coach at Southwestern Christian University, an NAIA school in Bethany, Oklahoma. In announcing the hire, Southwestern president Reggies Wenyika stated, "Coach Bliss fits well within our mission and culture and embraces what Christian-based education is all about."

We all believe in second chances, and the values of forgiveness and redemption certainly are appropriate for a religiously affiliated school. But I wonder sometimes if President Wenyika got the full memo on Dave Bliss. Perhaps a better fit would have been someone with the belief that "a career is a small thing in comparison to a life, a small thing in comparison to morals and values." Maybe that is what Christian-based education is all about.

This brings us to Abar Rouse, to whom the basketball gods have not been as kind. Good work at ESPN has kept the situation on many people's radars, starting with an *Outside the Lines* interview in 2003 with Mike Krzyzewski and Jim Boeheim, Dana O'Neil's piece in 2008, and then another *Outside the Lines* interview with Rouse in 2013.

Rouse weathered the initial scandal, not being fired or forced to resign as he had done nothing wrong, but in August 2003 Scott Drew came on as head coach. As one would expect, Drew brought in all his own people, and Rouse was out of a job. Thinking he would be able to find a new coaching job somewhere in the vast network of the NCAA, Rouse made inquiries, sent out resumes, and waited. . . . The phone never rang. To date, since he was released from Baylor, Rouse has had one college coaching job, as a graduate assistant at Midwestern

State University, a Division II school in Wichita Falls, Texas. The position paid $8,000 a year. Unable to survive on that salary and adequately provide for his daughter, he was forced to quit and take a job at a manufacturing plant, examining airplane parts on the night shift. After years at the manufacturing plant, he found his way to a federal women's correctional facility as a recreational specialist. As of 2017 he was still with the Federal Bureau of Prisons.

Rouse has stated, "That's all I ever wanted to do, be a college basketball coach," but it seems that college basketball doesn't want Abar Rouse. Jeff Ray, the former head coach at Midwestern State who hired Rouse, provided some insight in a conversation with Dana O'Neil: "Our profession has a distorted view of right and wrong sometimes. I'm right in the middle of it, don't get me wrong. But sometimes the things you see are pretty disgusting. Why is there this black cloud hanging over him? He did nothing wrong. To me, this is all a testimony to the sad state of affairs of our profession."

Rather than beat around the bush, we might as well ask whether Rouse has been blackballed. Was there a secret gathering or a memo that went around among head coaches that said, "*Do not hire Rouse*"? Of course not, but what has occurred seems to have had the same effect. As others have pointed out, this "blackball" scenario comes in part from an unwritten code among coaches that you don't rat on your own. In Rouse's case, that code found a mouthpiece at the highest level of the coaching profession. On the heels of the Baylor scandal, coaches Mike Krzyzewski of Duke and Jim Boeheim of Syracuse expressed their opinions on the matter in a 2003 ESPN *Outside the Lines* episode. When asked about Rouse taping Bliss during the cover-up, Krzyzewski stated, "If one of my assistants would tape every one of our conversations with me not knowing it, there's no way he would be on my staff." Boeheim added, "He didn't do the right thing. The right thing would have been to stand up in a meeting and tell the head coach, I'm not going for this, this is not going to happen." Many people have stated that when this message came down from on high, it was clear—Rouse is out.

Krzyzewski's comment, of course, is disingenuous. Rouse was not taping *every* conversation. He was taping only those conversations pertaining to covering up major NCAA infractions and interfering with a criminal investigation, *after* his head coach threatened to fire him for stating that he was not comfortable going along with an amoral cover-up and a plan to impugn the reputation of a dead man. As for Boeheim's comment regarding what Rouse *should* have done, Rouse tried that once and was told he'd be fired. When pressed on why he didn't try standing up to Bliss a second time, Rouse reiterated that he believed David Bliss would do anything to protect himself and had demonstrated that by his past behavior. Rouse also reminded his interviewer that he was twenty-seven years old, three months into his first coaching job, and "scared out of his mind" by his superior's threats and by what he was being asked to do.

On a side note, Rouse has claimed that he never intended the tape-recordings to become public; he made the tapes to try to help NCAA and university investigators get to the truth. As Rouse stated in Dana O'Neil's piece, "I didn't expose a head coach; I didn't do that. I went to the proper authorities and told them what was going on, and I let that case be heard by them. It would have been handled discreetly. In other NCAA investigations, countless other investigations, the coaching staff and many go in and tell the truth. It's never figured out where that truth came from. It's handled discreetly. My trust and confidence were breached by others."

Rouse also told O'Neil that "principles mean something if you apply them when it's inconvenient." In Rouse's case, that seems to be a lot more than lip service, and if any of the participants in the Baylor scandal deserved a second chance, Abar Rouse arguably belongs at the top of the list. Fortunately, Rouse seems to be in a good place—married with children and working at a good job. In a March 2017 interview with ESPN's

Jeremy Schapp, he described his work in the prison system as teaching, which, after all, is what coaching is all about. He said he was "absolutely ecstatic" about the work he did, describing himself as "very, very happy" and his work as "very fulfilling."

Perhaps Dave Bliss also has deserved his shots at redemption. In a 2009 interview, he told a reporter that he still felt "horrible" about what he had done at Baylor. He added, "However, I also know if I'm going to be any good for God and to try to follow God's plan for my life in the world, then I've got to forgive myself." He has since written a book about his life journey titled *Fall to Grace: The Climb, Collapse, and Comeback of Coach Dave Bliss.*

Bliss certainly is an enigma . . . or perhaps a chameleon. I distinctly remember coming away from the infractions hearing with the impression that Dave Bliss, at bottom, was a good guy and decent human being who made appalling mistakes but deserved a chance for redemption. The chair of the infractions committee, Gene Marsh, echoed that impression at the press conference announcing the Baylor penalties. Noting Bliss's contrition and sorrow, Marsh said, "He regrets it deeply. I believe that." At the time, the committee did not know of the investigation of Bliss's basketball program at SMU, because it had been called off short of resolution as a major infractions case. And we certainly did not know what was to come—actions at New Mexico that would lead one of his best players to describe Bliss as "a liar [and] a used car salesman"; the fear he instilled in an administrative assistant at Baylor, who called him "an angry man"; or his troubles even at the high school level at Allen Academy.

Certainly, there is one person for whom Dave Bliss's redemption may be difficult to swallow. In 2013, ten years after his ordeal at Baylor, Abar Rouse reflected on the experience in ESPN's *Outside the Lines* interview: "I have a full understanding now for what the face of evil looks like." When prompted to elaborate, he said, "Dave Bliss."

On Friday, March 31, 2017, Showtime aired a documentary called *Disgraced*. The film revisited the events surrounding the death of Patrick Dennehy in 2003 and Dave Bliss's ensuing attempts at a cover-up of wrongdoing in the Baylor basketball program. The filmmakers interviewed numerous individuals, including Bliss, who, remarkably, repeated his assertion that Dennehy had been a drug dealer. The following Monday, just as the NCAA men's basketball championship was getting ready for tipoff in Phoenix, Southwestern Christian University released a public statement announcing the resignation of the head men's basketball coach, Dave Bliss. The statement included no reasons for Bliss's departure, but it did include the following: "University President Reggies Wenyika affirmed his commitment to seeking new leadership in a manner that is consistent with the University's belief, standards and policies, as a duty to our Christian heritage of providing a values-driven education."

Unlike SMU football, the Baylor Bears men's basketball program rebounded relatively quickly. The early years were tough; Coach Scott Drew had a difficult rebuilding task on his hands and struggled to a 21-53 record in his first three seasons after replacing Bliss. But success was not far away. Since the 2007–8 season, the Bears have made seven NCAA tournament appearances, including two Sweet Sixteen and two Elite Eight appearances. In two of the years the team did not get an NCAA bid, it went on to win the NIT championship one year and finish as runner-up a second year. In 2016–17 Baylor started the season with a 15-0 win streak and was ranked number one in the country for the first time in school history. The 2018–19 season marks Drew's sixteenth year as head coach.

In 2011–12 the Bears garnered thirty wins, an all-time Baylor record. That same year, the men's basketball program was back before the Division I Committee on Infractions. In December 2008 the NCAA enforcement staff spoke with an elite recruit who reported that members of the coaching staff at Baylor had made impermissible (excessive under the rules) recruiting contacts to the prospect and his father. The investigation lasted for over two years, in part because the Baylor *women's* program, which also had surged to prominence, was implicated in recruiting violations as well.

Ultimately, the investigation confirmed hundreds of impermissible telephone calls and text messages to recruits, including dozens by Drew himself. The infractions committee also found that Drew had failed to monitor the recruiting activities of two assistant coaches. One of those assistants engaged in unethical conduct by attempting to influence others to withhold information from investigators. One of his text messages said, "If they ask if any coaches have violated rules, please don't bring up texts. I know you . . . won't. Just paranoid."

Drew was suspended for the first two conference games of the 2012–13 season. During the prior season, Baylor had prohibited him from making recruiting-related telephone calls for two months. The assistant coach with the unethical-conduct finding received a one-year show-cause penalty, and the basketball program self-imposed modest scholarship and recruiting reductions. It could have been far worse: little was made in the infractions report of the fact that this case made Baylor a *three-time* repeat violator.

An interesting fact lies buried in the appendix to the infractions report. The "elite recruit" who first talked to the enforcement staff about the violations was not a Baylor player but a "current Southern Methodist University men's basketball student-athlete."

4

The Infractions

He did *what*?! That was my reaction when I was first introduced to the world of infractions in May 2000. I had been
appointed to the Division I Committee on Infractions just the
month before, and I was preparing for my first infractions
hearing in June. The case involved Howard University, and
the audacity of an assistant baseball coach who recruited players for the university still astonishes me. At the time of their
recruitment, the players were attending college in Oklahoma
and competing in varsity baseball at their respective institutions. So of course they would be coming to Howard as *transfer* students, in which case they would be subject to certain
restrictions: (1) their years of remaining eligibility would be
reduced by the years they already had competed elsewhere;
(2) their transcripts would have to meet academic eligibility
requirements; and (3) for at least one student athlete who was
transferring from a four-year institution, he probably would
have to sit out a year due to the NCAA's transfer rules.

After arriving in Washington DC, however, the players
enrolled at Howard as *new freshmen,* with the full awareness of
the assistant coach who recruited them. The infractions committee did not make a specific finding that the assistant coach
instructed them to do so, but one can make logical inferences.

By indicating that they had not attended any other college, the players not only gained *four years* of eligibility but would be eligible to compete immediately. Moreover, they avoided any issues arising from academic deficiencies at their previous institutions. The boys had been in school to play ball, not necessarily to focus on their academics. As Cardale Jones, the quarterback who led Ohio State to the national championship in football in 2015 infamously put it, "Why should we have to go to class if we came here to play FOOTBALL, we ain't come to play SCHOOL, classes are POINTLESS."

As the Howard case unfolded, this was just the tip of the iceberg. Among dozens of violations, perhaps the most troubling were instances of blatant academic fraud. For example, one baseball player "earned" academic credit in four courses one summer, with an A grade in each course, without attending any classes or completing any coursework. Indeed, the player was not even on the Howard campus that summer (and the courses were *not* online courses). He was back home in Oklahoma, and he was not even aware that he had been enrolled in the courses. The assistant baseball coach denied involvement, but forensic document examiners determined that it was "very" or "highly" probable that the coach had completed enrollment forms, a student loan application, and a promissory note in the player's name. Without the summer credit, the player would have been ineligible to compete during the coming academic year, but compete he did.

The June infractions hearing focused primarily on the sports of baseball and men's basketball and was unusual because Howard was the only institution before the infractions committee over the course of two full days. The vast majority of infractions hearings last, at most, one day, and during that era, the committee typically heard two different cases over the course of a weekend, though these days, committee panels typically meet during the week. The Howard case immediately mushroomed; by the end of the two-day hearing, it was clear that a second hearing would be necessary. Because of information revealed during the hearing, the infractions committee asked NCAA investigators to look into other potential violations.

More than a year later, in August 2001, the committee held a second hearing. In my nearly ten years on the infractions committee, Howard was the only case to spill over into two separate hearing weekends because the violations were so extensive. When the committee issued its public infractions report (fifty-seven single-spaced pages) three months later, the scope of the violations was nearly unprecedented: five separate sports with major violations, including academic fraud, recruiting violations, and improper benefits to student athletes; unethical conduct by five different coaches, including not only deliberate violations but also providing false and misleading information to investigators; and lack of institutional control over the athletics program.

On the heels of Howard's initial hearing, I began preparing for my second infractions experience. The committee met every other month, in the even-numbered months, like clockwork. So my second hearing occurred in August 2000, when the committee heard a case involving the University of Minnesota. The allegations in that case centered on extensive academic fraud in the men's basketball program. After a lengthy hearing, the infractions committee found numerous violations, including approximately four hundred pieces of coursework improperly prepared for student athletes by a secretary in the athletics academic-counseling office. An academic counselor assigned to the men's basketball program had coordinated the efforts of the secretary, identifying student athletes with whom she was to work and focusing her attention on particular courses and assignments. The infractions committee also determined that the head coach of the men's basketball team, Clem Haskins, was complicit in the academic fraud and had provided special benefits, including cash, a car lease, and a trip to Hawaii, to the secretary and the academic counselor in exchange for their activities.

The infractions report, released in October 2000, pulled no punches with respect to the gravity of the case: "The numerous violations found by the committee are among the most serious academic fraud violations to come before it in the past 20 years. The violations were significant, widespread and intentional. More than that, their nature—academic fraud— undermined the bedrock foundation of a university and the operation of its intercollegiate athletics program. By purposeful acts of commission, and, through the absence of effective oversight, serious acts of omission, these violations damaged the academic integrity of the institution."

So this was my introduction to the world of NCAA rule violators—two cases, Howard and Minnesota, that remain among the most serious that the infractions committee has seen. Both cases also resulted in appeals, so in my capacity as the committee's new coordinator of appeals, I got my feet wet in a hurry. By preparing committee responses in both appeals, I became immersed in each case and quickly learned valuable lessons about the appellate process and the workings of the NCAA Infractions Appeals Committee, which reviews decisions of the Committee on Infractions.

Fortunately, most of the cases that come before the infractions committee are not as egregious as these two. Most are much narrower in scope, and the violations are not as extensive or flagrant. On the other hand, it is best to put aside one misconception early—that the NCAA rule book is so extensive that the typical violator is simply tripped up, unsuspectingly, by a complicated and detailed set of rules. That can happen, but such a scenario actually is quite rare in major infractions cases, which typically involve either intentional violations or violations of fundamental, well-known rules.

The NCAA *Division I Manual*, which includes bylaws governing topics such as recruiting, eligibility, and benefits for student athletes, is long—over four hundred pages. Within those pages is an immense amount of detail, so the manual certainly can provide challenges for individuals trying in good faith to stay on the sunny side of rules compliance. On the other hand, much of the manual is devoted to governance and procedural matters that have nothing to do with standards of conduct. Moreover, most NCAA institutions (certainly those that take rules compliance seriously) have developed thorough in-house compliance programs, with full-time staffers whose jobs are to keep their athletics programs on the straight and narrow. These individuals, together with other athletics personnel, such as coaches, have ample opportunities for rules education through in-house training sessions, regional compliance seminars, and other avenues.

In one amusing case, relatively early in my tenure on the infractions committee, an attorney for a coach on the hot seat argued that his client's culpability should be tempered by the fact that the NCAA rule book failed the Gunning Fog Index Readability Formula. The Fog Index, created in 1952 by textbook publisher Robert Gunning, is a mathematical readability formula that purports to measure the level of reading difficulty of a document by focusing on the length of sentences and the number of "big words," with three syllables or more. The committee was not sure whether the attorney implicitly was arguing that his client, a university employee, could read at only a middle school level. In any event, the attorney was unable to convince the committee that the rule book is incomprehensible.

One indication that the world of NCAA infractions is populated by scoundrels rather than unintentional wrongdoers is the prevalence of academic fraud cases. Typically, people know when they're cheating academically, as in the Howard and Minnesota cases. They know what fraudulent academic credit or a false transcript is, and nothing about the rule book will confuse them regarding what is right and wrong.

During my time on the infractions committee, from 2000 to 2010, nearly a quarter of the major infractions cases involved some form of academic fraud. One sobering moment came in a 2002 case involving the University of California at Berkeley. Cal-Berkeley has a well-deserved reputation as one of the country's most respected academic institutions, but at the heart of the case was blatant academic fraud. A professor allowed two football student athletes to enroll *retroactively* in courses that had already been completed. The courses ended in May, and the student athletes enrolled in August. The athletes received C grades in the courses, even though they could not have attended any classes and, based on the evidence, did no work to earn academic credit. Both athletes needed the academic credit to be eligible to compete, and both were allowed to compete during the entire football season in the fall.

Later in my tenure was a high-profile case involving Florida State University, where dozens of student athletes across ten different sports received improper assistance in their coursework. In some instances, university staff members sat beside student athletes as they took online exams and directly provided answers. Remarkably, one of the staff members insisted that providing answers during an exam was no different than any other assistance provided by a tutor. This was the individual Taylor Branch referred to in his *Atlantic* article, mentioned in the introduction, as a "powerless scapegoat." To its credit, the university acknowledged that such conduct was unethical and unacceptable, and once again the infractions committee reminded the NCAA membership that "academic fraud is considered by the committee to be among the most egregious of NCAA infractions."

Everyone involved in intercollegiate athletics will agree with the committee's statement in the Minnesota case that academic fraud "undermine[s] the bedrock foundation of a university." Yet the percentage of major infractions cases involving academic fraud seems likely to *increase*. It is no secret that universities continue to admit many student athletes with marginal academic credentials. And pressures to keep these individuals academically eligible inevitably lead some coaches, academic counselors, professors, and student athletes themselves to cheat.

Jon Duncan, the NCAA's vice president of enforcement, said in January 2015 that academic fraud cases were on the rise, noting that the enforcement staff at the time had twenty such cases open and under investigation, including eighteen at the Division I level. He attributed the increase to several factors, two of which extend beyond athletics: (1) an increase in cheating generally on college campuses and (2) an increase in online courses, which "creates opportunities for mischievous behavior" that do not exist in traditional classroom-based courses.

When students are submitting academic work electronically or are otherwise engaged in distance education (i.e., outside the traditional classroom), ample opportunity exists for someone other than the enrolled student to complete the coursework. For example, in a series of cases in the early 2000s, the Committee on Infractions confronted an ongoing problem with correspondence courses. At the time, such courses offered by Brigham Young University (BYU) were particularly popular. BYU offered an extensive correspondence program, in part as an effort to serve the educational needs of Latter-Day Saints students on missions to far-flung parts of the globe. BYU could do everything right—for example, accepting only proctored quizzes and exams—but no one could know for sure what was happening on the student's end.

After hearing several cases involving academic fraud in BYU correspondence courses, the infractions committee finally had had it. In a February 2007 report on McNeese State University, the committee outlined unethical conduct by an assistant men's basketball coach: "He facilitated academic fraud for . . . two prospects when he arranged for someone other than the prospects to complete quizzes and a test in a math correspondence course." As for proctoring, the correspondence exams were "proctored" by the coach's wife in their family home. After citing several previous cases involving similar types of academic fraud, the committee expressed its exasperation, along with a warning: "Also very troubling to the committee is that academic fraud occurred in the administration of correspondence courses from Brigham Young University. . . . Academic fraud and other problems with correspondence courses (calculation of progress toward degree, for example) have recurred with alarming regularity in infractions cases. The committee once again warns member institutions that they must be especially careful to monitor and review the use of such courses."

Enforcement chief Duncan also noted two athletics-related factors that may have contributed to the rise in academic fraud cases: (1) increased academic standards for student athletes and (2) tying a team's eligibility for postseason competition to its overall academic performance. In recent years, the NCAA's implementation of Academic Progress Rates (APRs) has been heralded as a measure to strengthen the notion of the *student* in a "student athlete." The APR initiative, championed initially by former NCAA president Myles Brand, aims to ensure "the primacy of the academic mission" of NCAA institutions. The APR formulas are somewhat complicated, but the bottom line is that schools now risk significant penalties—loss of scholarships, practice and recruiting restrictions, and postseason ineligibility, among others—if their student athletes do not make adequate academic progress and do not graduate in sufficient numbers.

The goals of the APR program are laudable indeed, but from an infractions perspective, a cautionary note is in order. By placing even greater pressures on student athletes, coaches, and other athletics personnel in regard to academic eligibility, the program has the potential to result in even more instances of academic fraud. That scenario seems to be playing out now, as Duncan suggested.

Duncan was speaking partly in response to what many view as the worst academic fraud case in NCAA history. The fraud occurred over nearly two decades at the University of North Carolina (UNC), where academic counselors steered hundreds of Tar Heels student athletes to sham courses in which the student athletes did little or no work yet received academic credit and high grades. (The UNC case is discussed at length in chapter 10.)

While none of the UNC coaches were directly implicated in the fraud, one particularly disturbing portion of the university's investigative report stated that "it was clear" to the athletics academic counselors "that the coaches had the power over the counselors' employment. . . . It was quite clear to the counselors—at least those in the revenue sports—that they were being evaluated by the coaches and judged by their success in keeping players eligible to play ball."

A similar scenario played out in numerous academic fraud cases that I observed as a committee member. A head coach makes clear to his assistant coaches—and perhaps to others, such as academic advisors—the importance of keeping a particular student athlete eligible. The coach does not direct his subordinates to do anything unethical, simply saying, instead, "Make sure player X is eligible to compete." Later, if things go south, in the form of academic fraud allegations, the coach has a defense of "plausible deniability," and the subordinates take the fall for "choosing" to break the rules.

The NCAA leadership has taken steps to address some of these concerns. In 2013 Jon Duncan created a new academic integrity unit within the NCAA enforcement staff. Kathy Sulentic, an associate director of enforcement, heads the unit. She has indicated that the unit is investigating cases that fall within the scenario above, where "the coach will say, 'We need to get this student-athlete eligible.' Not telling [assistant coaches and support staff members] exactly what to do, but saying 'we need this young man or young woman' and some sort of academic misconduct occurs."

The NCAA membership also approved new legislation in 2013 that makes it easier to hold head coaches accountable for the misconduct of their subordinates. That legislation creates a presumption that a head coach is responsible for violations occurring within the coach's program. The head coach can rebut the presumption by showing adequate monitoring of the program for rules compliance and promotion of an overall atmosphere of compliance. On its face, this new enforcement scheme has teeth. In the past, the enforcement staff effectively had to prove that the head coach knew about the violations, typically with scant direct evidence of such knowledge. The burden now has shifted to the head coach to show that reasonable measures have been taken to *prevent* violations, typically by way of proactive, hands-on monitoring and documentation of rules education.

The legislation also includes significant penalties, including the possible suspension of a head coach for up to a year for very serious violations . . . again, even if the head coach did not participate directly in or have direct knowledge of those violations. That prospect has drawn the attention of some prominent coaches, such as Ohio State head football coach Urban Meyer. In a panel presentation at the 2013 National Association for Athletic Compliance convention, he reportedly stated that it was the first time that head coaches actually feared NCAA bylaws and penalties. He also noted, however, that some coaches, in the reporter's words, may not "feel the urgency until a big-name head coach at a premier program suffers a significant penalty."

Well, that has now occurred. In another high-profile academic fraud case, involving Syracuse men's basketball, the infractions committee in 2015 found, among other violations, that basketball staff members participated in a scheme to keep a star player eligible. The scheme resulted in the commission of serious academic fraud. The committee did not cite head coach Jim Boeheim individually for the fraud, but it did find that he failed to monitor his program adequately and imposed a nine-game suspension on him. As indicated in chapter 2, the committee followed suit later that same year with a suspension of Larry Brown for 30 percent of the 2015–16 season. While SMU typically has not been viewed as a premier basketball program, Larry Brown certainly was a big-name coach.

Finally, as noted previously, the APRs now have sharper teeth as well. In 2012 the NCAA leadership approved a requirement that teams achieve a minimum APR score for postseason eligibility. The University of Connecticut (UConn) men's basketball team was the first premier program to feel the bite.

In 2013, sandwiched between national championships in 2011 and 2014, UConn was prohibited from competing in March Madness because of its low APR scores.

On the one hand, such measures should serve as a strong incentive for schools to focus on academics. On the other hand, the added pressure that comes from facing scholarship or post-season sanctions may encourage even more academic fraud.

Academic fraud, of course, is only one of many violations considered by the infractions committee. The range of possible infractions is quite broad, but most individual violations, in addition to academic fraud, revolve around recruiting, improper benefits to current student athletes, and various forms of unethical conduct. Institutional violations typically involve failure to monitor or control aspects of the athletics program, student-athlete eligibility issues, or financial aid violations (for example, overawarding of scholarships).

I reviewed all major infractions cases involving Division I schools during the ten-year period from January 2000 through December 2009. During that period, there were 109 cases in which major infractions were found, including 90 cases in which a hearing was held before the Division I Committee on Infractions and 19 cases decided by summary disposition, without a hearing. As the following summary shows, several types of violations (what I call the "Big 8," in honor of a time when conference alignments were simpler) and two sports— men's basketball and football—predominate:

The "Big 8"

Recruiting* (67 cases)

Extra benefits** (62)

Unethical conduct (58)

　　Knowing involvement in violations (52)

　　Provision of false or misleading information (29)

　　Failure to cooperate in an investigation (9)

Failure to monitor (50)

Lack of institutional control (37)

Eligibility (ineligible competition, improper certification, etc.) (30)

Financial aid (overawarding grants-in-aid, etc.) (27)

Academic fraud (25)

* Recruiting violations run the gamut: impermissible contacts (e.g., during quiet period, too many contacts per week, contacts of student athletes from other schools); inducements; improper tryouts; booster contacts; presence during National Letter of Intent signing; benefits to high school coaches; excessive entertainment; improper recruiter; improper publicity; use of student athletes in recruiting; etc.

** While recruiting violations involve *prospective* student athletes being recruited to attend an NCAA institution, extra-benefit violations involve an institution's enrolled student athletes. The general idea is that a university employee or a booster cannot provide to a current student athlete a benefit (money, meals, transportation, etc.) that is not available to other students at the university.

Miscellaneous and Less Frequent Violations

Impermissible out-of-season activities (e.g., coach observation; mandatory practice; improper skill instruction) (15 cases)

Exceeding practice limitations (10)

Exceeding coach limit (7)

Failure to report violations (5)

Violation of supplemental pay restrictions (5)

Failure to promote atmosphere of compliance

Failure to report outside income

Impermissible employment of nonqualifiers

Contract for future employment of high school or junior college coach (for delivering a recruit)

Impermissible compensation to volunteer coach

Violations of amateurism rules

Excess number of coaches recruiting off campus

Violation of scouting legislation

Gambling

Sports Involved in Major Infractions Cases (2000–2009)*

Men's basketball (40 cases, 37 percent of all cases)

Football (37, 34 percent of cases)

Multiple (18)

Women's basketball (10)

Men's tennis (6)

Baseball (4)

Men's soccer (3)

Men's track and field (3)

Women's tennis (3)

Women's volleyball (3)

Men's swimming and diving (2)

Women's golf (2)

Softball (2)

Women's track and field (2)

Men's ice hockey (1)

Men's volleyball (1)

Wrestling (1)

Women's gymnastics (1)

Women's rowing (1)

Women's swimming and diving (1)

* Note: If multiple sports were involved, "multiple" is indicated, plus the most significant sport if there was one. If major violations occurred in two or three sports, each sport is listed.

The summary indicates that unethical conduct by university employees (typically coaches) occurred in over half the major infractions cases during the decade. Once again, the breadth of that unethical conduct, which is the most serious violation that can be found against an individual, shows that most violations are not inadvertent violations resulting from an outrageously complex set of rules. Instead, they are deliberate, knowing violations and, accordingly, can and do result in severe sanctions by the infractions committee.

The NCAA enforcement staff and the Committee on Infractions have a steady stream of work. Cases are always in the pipeline, and NCAA investigators always have active cases on which to work. David Price, a former NCAA vice president of enforcement, was quoted in 2007 as saying that his enforcement staff typically received seven or eight tips a day about potential rules violations. Of those, Price estimated that about one in fifteen warranted further investigation. If his numbers still hold up, that means, on average, every other day a lead requires some follow-up.

Price stated that many of the enforcement staff's tips came from fans "trolling online message boards." The use of social media in the discovery, reporting, and even commission of violations is a development of growing importance. In a 2011 tongue-in-cheek "guide to smarter NCAA rule-breaking," a *Sports Illustrated* writer offered the following examples: "North Carolina's football program has a date with the NCAA's Committee on Infractions because former defensive tackle Marvin Austin got too descriptive on Twitter. Jim Tressel is currently unemployed because of a series of e-mails. Bruce Pearl isn't coaching basketball at Tennessee because someone snapped a photo of a recruit at Pearl's house, which was inconvenient because Pearl told the NCAA the recruit hadn't been at his house."

Information today is shared at breathtaking speed, with vast audiences—and even something as primitive as an email message or a photograph can be the downfall of an athletics program, particularly if it goes viral on the internet. Marvin Austin tweeted about the great time he had in Miami. Unfortunately, the persons with whom he had associated in Miami and from whom he had received benefits were agents and their runners, so his actions violated NCAA amateurism rules. Head football coach Tressel's emails at Ohio State revealed that he knew of potential rule violations months before they came to light, but he deep-sixed them. It was impermissible for the recruit at Coach Pearl's house to attend the gathering because he was on an unofficial, rather than official, visit to Knoxville—a minor violation, particularly since Coach Pearl did not invite him to the party. But a quick snapshot from an iPhone and an anonymous letter to the NCAA enforcement staff (with a photo of the coach and prospect standing together and a handwritten question: "Is having ... a 2010 high school recruit in your home an NCAA violation?") led to Pearl's termination, because he did not know about the photo and lied to investigators about the prospect's presence in his home.

One of the lessons of these cases is the ease by which a social media post, email message, or photo can provide evidence of an NCAA rules infraction. Email messages in particular can come back to bite hard, even in matters that go beyond *rule* violations. The criminal case against former president Graham Spanier at Penn State, for example, was based primarily on brief email exchanges in 1998 and 2001 that suggest Spanier knew of possible child sexual abuse by Jerry Sandusky but failed to report the abuse or take measures to prevent its recurrence.

Another lesson is that an initial investigation into an isolated infraction can morph into something entirely different, depending on where the evidence leads. The North Carolina case began as an investigation into student athletes' contacts with an agent but expanded rapidly to include allegations of academic fraud, extra benefits to other student athletes, improper marketing of student athletes to an agent by an assistant coach, impermissible outside income to coaches, unethical conduct by two former staff members, and the university's failure to adequately monitor its football program. The breadth and depth of the allegations led to the firing of the head football coach and the resignation of the athletics director.

The Tennessee case first came to light as a football case rather than a basketball case, after the *New York Times* published an article reporting that NCAA investigators were "focused on the use of recruiting hostesses who have become folk heroes on Tennessee Internet message boards for their ability to lure top recruits." Two days after the *Times* article, a writer for *Sports Illustrated* posted his own article with a photo showing two attractive Orange Pride members posing with two standout football prospects after a high school game. The coeds, decked out in Tennessee orange, were holding a large poster identifying the recruits by name: "Miller & Willis have our Hearts." Typically, student hostesses are considered representatives of a university's athletics interests and are forbidden from engaging in off-campus recruiting activities, so their appearance in Duncan, South Carolina (about a three-hour drive from Knoxville, Tennessee), naturally raised eyebrows about possible NCAA recruiting violations.

The Tennessee case progressed in the media as a football case, with violations that could affect the coaching career of Lane Kiffin, who by that time had moved on from Tennessee to USC. In the end, though, the Committee on Infractions determined that the Orange Pride violation was nothing more than a secondary violation, while violations in men's basketball, including Bruce Pearl's misadventures, were at the heart of a major infractions case.

Social media posts not only can lead to the discovery of NCAA infractions, but they also can constitute violations themselves. Rules governing the use of social media and other modern means of communication are regularly in flux, so coaches and student athletes need to be aware of changes as they occur. Until relatively recently, for example, recruiters were limited to contacting recruits via phone, email, or fax. NCAA bylaws prohibited "all other forms of electronically transmitted correspondence (e.g., Instant Messenger, text messaging)."

Such unrealistic rules often were breached intentionally, but they also resulted in truly innocent violations. Coaches, for example, could email prospects from social media platforms such as Facebook, but numerous coaches were tripped up by their failure to understand the workings of social media— for example, inadvertently sending their messages to the recruits' public Facebook walls rather than to their private, direct-message boxes. Other coaches have violated rules disallowing comments about recruits on the coach's own social media accounts—for example, "I was so excited to hear that J.C. Copeland committed to play for the Vols today!" That message posted to Lane Kiffin's Twitter and Facebook accounts in 2009. Unfortunately for Tennessee, the prospect's "commitment" was only verbal and came before he signed a National Letter of Intent, so he was still a recruit, making the post a violation.

Social media activity by *fans* also can be problematic— for example, when fans use social media in their own efforts to "recruit" prospects to their alma maters or other favorite schools. Depending on the circumstances, such fans can be considered boosters, who are prohibited from recruitment contacts. One can imagine the difficulty of monitoring fans' social media activity for potential recruiting violations. When Duke compliance officials, for example, asked the creator of the "John Wall Come to Duke!" Facebook group to stop its activities, he changed the group's name to "Wohn Jall Come to a School in Durham!" and the group kept posting.

Of course, documentary evidence in the form of a social media post, email message, or photo is not necessary to form the basis of a major infractions case. The ease with which other violations can be detected demonstrates the sheer idiocy of some infractions. A simple hypothetical will illustrate the point: Assume that a coach provides an improper recruiting inducement (cash, clothing, etc.) to a hot prospect and is successful in enticing the prospect to the coach's campus. The student athlete, however, fails to live up to expectations and ends up riding the pine. When he finally becomes disillusioned enough with his lack of playing time that he decides to quit, or transfer to another school, might he be inclined to report the recruiting inducement simply because he is disgruntled about how he was treated at the school?

In the St. Bonaventure case discussed in chapter 1, other schools had looked at the ballplayer from Coastal Georgia because of his basketball talent, but they had concluded that his welding certificate was insufficient to make him eligible. What would they have thought when they saw the athlete on the court, competing for St. Bonaventure? Did the Bonnies' coaching staff simply take their chances and assume that all their competitors would never have had contact with (or not remember their contacts with) the prospect?

In 2007 the Committee on Infractions considered a case involving the men's tennis team at Temple University. In that case, the head coach allowed an ineligible student athlete to compete in eleven matches under an *assumed name*—that of a former student athlete who had left the team. The fraudulent participation was uncovered by another team during the conference championship. As noted in the public infractions report, "coaches from another Atlantic 10 member institution recognized that one of Temple's student-athletes ('student-athlete 1'), a young man they had at one time attempted to recruit, was competing for Temple but was not listed on the team's lineup for that particular match. They also noticed the name of a student-athlete ('student-athlete 2') in Temple's lineup who was not competing in the event. The other institution's coaches were familiar with student-athlete 2 because he had previously competed against their team."

Many infractions are self-reported by schools that have discovered their own violations. Indeed, the NCAA *expects* schools with serious compliance programs to self-report violations on a fairly regular basis. Some rule violations are inevitable, and if an institution never reports any violations, it is suspect. NCAA bylaws require reporting whenever a violation is discovered, and failure to report is a serious offense in itself.

Until recently, many infractions battles were fought over whether a case or a particular violation was "major" or "secondary." Secondary cases were reviewed solely by members of the enforcement staff, who then imposed penalties if violations were found. The Committee on Infractions did not see those cases, although an institution could appeal penalties to the committee. That rarely happened. The bulk of the committee's work, then, was devoted to major cases, which involved at least one major violation. Secondary violations could be resolved by the committee if they were part of a major case.

It was easy to distinguish a major case from a secondary case—the former included an allegation by the NCAA enforcement staff of at least one major violation. A major violation was defined in NCAA legislation in terms of what it was *not*; a major violation was any violation that was not secondary. A secondary violation was defined as having three elements: (1) it was *"isolated or inadvertent* in nature"; (2) it provided or was intended to provide "only a minimal recruiting, competitive or other advantage"; and (3) it did not involve a "significant impermissible benefit (including, but not limited to, an extra benefit, recruiting inducement, preferential treatment or financial aid)."

As a member of the infractions committee, I was always troubled by the first part of the definition. Because a violation was defined as secondary if it was *either* isolated *or* inadvertent, many intentional rule breakers were let off the hook with little, if any, penalty. Coaches who made improper phone calls to recruits (for example, calling during a dead period or exceeding weekly call maximums) typically fell into this category. Coaches knowingly violated the rules but knew that such violations were considered minor and typically were processed as secondary infractions, with light penalties. In my mind, coaches who intentionally violate the rules have no business serving as leaders of young men and women. Thus, I always felt that the word "or" should be changed to "and" in the first prong of the secondary definition; if there was evidence that an individual committed a violation *intentionally*, it should have constituted a major violation and subjected the perpetrator to significant sanctions.

The "major" and "secondary" definitions provided a workable dichotomy for decades, but shortly after his appointment as NCAA president in 2010, Mark Emmert declared a preference for a multitiered violation structure. He initially suggested as many as five different categories of violations, but an appointed enforcement working group and the NCAA Board of Directors ultimately decided on four: (1) "severe" breaches of conduct (Level I); (2) "significant" breaches of conduct (Level II); (3) breaches of conduct (Level III); and (4) "incidental" infractions (Level IV). Cases involving Level I and Level II violations are further categorized into sublevels based on aggravating and mitigating factors.

This new violation structure took effect on August 1, 2013. Whether it represents an improvement over the former major-secondary model remains to be seen. Clearly the new structure is designed to cabin the Committee on Infractions' discretion, in part to provide rule violators better notice of the infractions and the level of seriousness of those infractions. The committee's discretion on imposition of penalties also is constrained with new penalty guidelines. Of course, judgments still must be made about what is "severe," "significant," or just a run-of-the-mill "breach of conduct" and about the weight to be accorded to aggravating and mitigating factors. Thus, it would appear that both the enforcement staff (in bringing the allegations) and the Committee on Infractions (in making findings) retain ample discretion in categorizing violations as they see fit.

Another goal of the violations restructuring, according to the NCAA, was to "focus [the NCAA's] primary [enforcement] resources on the most serious infractions cases," hopefully resulting in "greater accountability for the most serious offenders." That goal is furthered in part by assigning only Level I and Level II cases to a hearing before the Committee on Infractions. Level III and Level IV cases are resolved internally, by the NCAA enforcement staff. Again though, whether this represents an improvement over prior practice is debatable, because the vast majority of Level III and Level IV cases would have been classified as secondary under the old model. As such, they would have been handled by the enforcement staff, without committee involvement.

Level IV cases are truly minor. Indeed, the examples the enforcement working group put forth initially to illustrate a Level IV violation simply provide fodder to those who contend that the NCAA rule book is a model of overregulation: "Institution used too big of an envelope to send recruiting correspondence to PSA [prospective student athlete]; SA's picture was not in camp counselor section of camp brochure; Institution provided cream cheese with the bagels available to SAS."

Really? The bylaws actually govern things like what can be put on the bagels? Surely it is gratifying to learn that the NCAA's "primary resources" will not be focused on such violations in the future . . . though I can assure the reader that they were not in the past, either.

The definition of a Level III violation is very similar to the old definition of a secondary violation. A Level III "breach of conduct" in the new violation structure is a violation that is "*isolated or limited* in nature; provide[s] no more than a minimal recruiting, competitive or other advantage; and provide[s] no more than a minimal impermissible benefit." Some subtle differences exist between the two definitions, but clearly the Level III definition was patterned after the three-part secondary definition. That was confirmed in the enforcement working group's final report, which categorized Level III violations as "currently secondary violations."

Interestingly, "isolated or inadvertent" in prong one of the former secondary definition has become "isolated or limited," which still leaves open the possibility that many *intentional* rule breakers will be dealt with leniently. For example, presumably deliberate and knowing, but "isolated or limited," impermissible phone calls to recruits would escape the scrutiny of the Committee on Infractions because they also would not provide "more than a minimal" recruiting advantage or include more than a minimal benefit. That conclusion is reinforced by the examples included by the enforcement working group: "Assistant women's basketball coach telephoned a PSA prior to April of the PSA's junior year in high school." That violation, even if the assistant coach knew of the recruiting restriction (and a basic one it is) and deliberately flouted it, would be classified as Level III. As for Level II, the working group submitted the following example: "Men's basketball coaches made 68 impermissible telephone calls and sent 42 impermissible text messages to 6 different PSAs over a 9-month period."

Obviously, there is a chasm between those two examples, and one can hope that it does not take 110 potentially deliberate violations to rise to Level II. The limitless scenarios between 1 violation and 110 demonstrate the latitude the restructuring gives to the enforcement staff, whose charging decisions dictate whether cases reach the Committee on Infractions. While the enforcement staff had similar discretion in alleging either major or secondary violations, the multilevel violations structure and the NCAA leadership's complementary goal to process infractions cases more quickly and efficiently seem guided to encourage the enforcement staff to classify cases as Level III or Level IV if at all possible—thereby focusing the NCAA's enforcement efforts on the most serious violations.

The real impact of the new violations structure seems to be a subdivision of major violations into Levels I and II. Cases involving either level of violations are processed similarly, with a hearing before the Committee on Infractions, but new penalty guidelines dictate harsher sanctions for Level I violations, so classification is important. The bylaws do not make that classification easy; the new definitions necessarily will be in the eye of the beholder. Level I violations—"severe" breaches of conduct—are those that *seriously undermine or threaten* the integrity of the NCAA Collegiate Model." Level II violations—"significant" breaches of conduct—only "compromise" the integrity of the collegiate model. Okay, if that's not particularly helpful, try this: Level I violations include "any violation that provides or is intended to provide a *substantial or extensive* recruiting, competitive or other advantage, or a substantial or extensive impermissible benefit." Level II violations provide "less than a substantial or extensive," but "more than a minimal," advantage or benefit. Level III violations, as noted previously, provide "no more than a minimal" advantage or benefit.

The new bylaws do include examples of potential infractions in each category, but with serious qualifying language: "the following, *in appropriate circumstances, may* constitute a severe breach of conduct." Included as an example of a potential Level I violation is academic misconduct. Yes, both the NCAA membership and the Committee on Infractions are particularly troubled by academic fraud, but like any other type of violation, academic misconduct can run the gamut, from an isolated incident in which a tutor provides a bit too much help on a student athlete's paper to widespread fraud like the four hundred papers in the Minnesota case or blatant credit-for-no-work scams, as occurred in the Howard and Cal-Berkeley cases.

In every case, then, the Committee on Infractions still must consider all the circumstances, including aggravating and mitigating factors, in assessing the seriousness of violations and imposing penalties. This the committee has always done, but perhaps the new guidelines will be beneficial by encouraging the committee to be more explicit in its public infractions reports about the factors on which its decisions are based. As a former advocate for the committee in appeals, I fiercely resisted formulaic approaches to these decisions. On the other hand, if the new bylaws help with the *perception* that the committee is operating within consistent guidelines, and that perception lends legitimacy to the process, the entire NCAA membership will be better served.

5

Parasites

What is required is a full frontal attack to turn these
parasites into pariahs and to visibly, forcefully and
emphatically exclude them from any participation
or entrée into athletics programs.

NCAA DIVISION I COMMITTEE ON INFRACTIONS

The blood was "everywhere," according to Jim Neal, describing reports he had received about the death of Logan Young that morning in Memphis. Neal, a high-powered attorney in Nashville, probably figured he'd seen it all. During an illustrious career, he had secured the only criminal conviction of Jimmy Hoffa; prosecuted John Mitchell, John Erlichman, and H. R. Haldeman for their participation in Watergate; and defended a variety of clients in high-profile cases, including Ford Motor Company following Pinto gas tank explosions, Elvis Presley's doctor for allegedly overprescribing addictive medications to the King, Exxon after the Valdez oil spill in Alaska, Louisiana governor Edwin Edwards on racketeering charges, and movie director John Landis after a helicopter crash on the set of *Twilight Zone: The Movie* killed actor Vic Morrow and two others.

In the early 2000s Logan Young was almost as notorious, both in Tennessee and in Alabama, where his actions helped to bring down one of the most powerful football programs in American sports history, the Crimson Tide of the University of Alabama. After a scheme to steer a highly prized recruit to

'Bama—by buying the recruit's high school coaches—drew the attention of federal prosecutors, Jim Neal was the man to defend Logan Young. In 2005 Neal defended Young on federal criminal charges of money laundering and conspiracy to commit racketeering. The defense did not go well; Young remains one of the few individuals ever convicted of a *crime* for activities relating to violations of NCAA rules.

When Neal first began receiving phone calls on the morning of Tuesday, April 11, 2006, there was reason enough to suspect foul play in Young's death. Young reportedly had told friends in the weeks prior to his death that he had received anonymous threats for his role in the Alabama infractions case. Two years earlier, in May 2004, an attorney working on a defamation suit arising from the Alabama case reported that he had been attacked in his law office and knocked unconscious, with the perpetrator escaping with key documents in the case.

A housekeeper employed by Young had entered his home to report for work shortly before 9:00 a.m. on April 11. In a 9-1-1 call, she reported that there was blood throughout the house, and Young, who was lying on the floor in his second-story bedroom, appeared to have been beaten to death. Later that day, a Memphis police spokesperson confirmed Neal's initial fears. Sgt. Vince Higgins issued a statement that the police were "treating it as a mystery homicide," noting that officials likely would need fingerprints and dental records to confirm the identity of the victim. "Suffice it to say," said Higgins, "there was quite a physical struggle in this and this individual was injured severely. . . . The nature of the attack was brutal. The entire house is a crime scene."

In what must have been colossally embarrassing circumstances, however, the police department reversed course two days later. On Thursday the thirteenth, a police spokesperson announced at a press conference that Young's death was an accident, not a murder. An Associated Press report that afternoon stated,

Homicide Lt. Joe Scott said police believe Young tripped while carrying a salad and soft drink up a set of stairs and hit his head on an iron railing. The fall onto the railing opened a large gash across the top of Young's head and he dropped to the floor bleeding profusely, Scott said at a news conference.

After lying on the floor for some time, Young got up and walked bleeding through several rooms of his spacious, two-story house before ending up in his second-floor bedroom, Scott added. His housekeeper found the body beside his bed Tuesday morning.

"There was a lot of blood," Scott said.

Young, who was divorced and lived alone, apparently tried to slow the bleeding with towels from the kitchen downstairs and a bathroom upstairs, and two towels soaked with blood were found on the bed. He walked past several telephones but didn't place an emergency call, Scott said.

Conspiracy theorists, of course, have had a field day with Young's mysterious death, particularly in light of the gruesomely described scene and the initial assessments of both the police and the housekeeper.

Certainly Young's death is the most grisly chapter of the Alabama infractions case, which arguably began in the 1960s, when Young's father, Logan Young Sr., established a friendly relationship with Paul "Bear" Bryant, the legendary Alabama head football coach. The two apparently hit it off during Bryant's recruiting trips to Memphis, and during a time when booster involvement in recruiting was less restrictive, Young Sr. would help to steer Memphis-area talent to his friend in Tuscaloosa. Young Sr., who accumulated significant wealth from a food and beverage business, left the business to his son when he died in 1971. Young Jr. embraced not only the business but also his father's relationship with Bear Bryant, along with a new-found fanaticism for Alabama football, despite the fact that he never attended school there and his hometown had a Division I football program of its own.

Over the years, Young's support of Alabama football—financial and otherwise—garnered him what the NCAA Committee on Infractions later described as "favored access and 'insider' status" within the program. He had his own skybox in the football stadium, befriended the athletics director, attended prominent social events with university trustees, was granted access to nonpublic football practices, and visited summer football camps. More importantly, as reported in the committee's infractions report, Young was "a self-proclaimed recruiting junkie" who was well-known "among college football coaches who recruited the Memphis area."

In 1999 Young came to the attention of Lynn Lang, a local high school football coach. Lang was the head coach at Trezevant High School in Memphis, and he was blessed to have on his 1999–2000 team a hot commodity—Albert Means, a huge defensive lineman who was expected to be heavily recruited by the top Division I schools. Means had grown up poor, with a single mother, but Lang had earned the mother's trust by buying clothes for Albert and occasionally paying grocery or other bills for the family. Consequently, Lang and his assistant coach, Milton Kirk, felt that when the time came for Albert to decide where he should play college ball, Lang could control Albert's decision.

Both Lang and Kirk knew that in Memphis, blue-chip prospects could be marketed, to the financial benefit of the prospects' high school coaches. So in the spring of 1999, as Albert was completing his junior year of high school and anticipating heavy recruitment by top Division I football programs, Lang and Kirk devised a marketing plan. Quite simply, they would control access to Albert by college recruiters and put a price on him, so recruiters had to pay to play. The price was based on a similar scheme that Lang and Kirk believed another Memphis high school coach was using to market his top players—enough to get both Lang and Kirk new vehicles (SUVs would be nice) in addition to $100,000 in cash to Lang. After all, he was the head coach, and that comes with its own perks.

After spring ball ended on college campuses around the country, recruiters did indeed come calling, seeking to talk to Albert Means. Lang, the gatekeeper, got the word out about the price of poker: a hundred grand and a couple of suvs. According to later testimony of both Lang and Kirk, an assistant coach at Alabama who recruited the Memphis area was not deterred. The coach needed a little time to make some arrangements, but someone representing the Crimson Tide would be back in touch. Soon thereafter, Logan Young called Lang: 'Bama was interested.

By this time, of course, Young was well-known in both Memphis and Tuscaloosa as an Alabama booster—what the NCAA euphemistically refers to as "a representative of the university's athletics interests." Not only did he assist in the recruitment of Memphis prospects, but he also could be counted on for other types of assistance. For example, within months of his arrival in Tuscaloosa from Tallahassee, another Alabama assistant football coach received two loans from Young—a $1,600 loan in June 1998 and a $55,000 loan several weeks later. According to the promissory note, the latter loan was to be paid back within a year—by July 1999—but Young was forgiving. Payment eventually came in May 2001. Both loans were found to be NCAA violations in the upcoming infractions case.

Lynn Lang's gross salary at Trezevant High for the 1999–2000 academic year was $37,208, but by November 1999 he was driving a brand spanking new, 2000-model, full-size suv with a list price just under $37,000. Young had delivered for the Tide. In October, Lang and Young had met through an intermediary, a former high school football coach at another Memphis school who knew Kirk and was now assisting Young in his recruiting efforts. After the meeting, Lang picked up Kirk after football practice. Lang had left practice early to meet with Young; Kirk was in charge. According to Kirk's later statement, the two men went to the branch office of a local bank, "deposited a substantial amount of cash in the bank's drop box," and then headed to a strip club to celebrate.

Thus began a period of extravagant spending by Lang. As the infractions report puts it, his "standard of living noticeably improved." Another high school coach described Lang's apartment as "full of new furniture and expensive entertainment equipment." Not all his spending was in keeping with what one would expect of a coach of young high schoolers; Kirk later reported that Lang began dropping "between $100 and $300 three to four times a week" at the strip club.

Kirk arranged for Lang's SUV purchase in November, through an acquaintance at a local auto dealership. Lang paid only $5,000 down, but the balance—or even his new $744 per month car payments—would be no problem. Young's initial bag of cash was only a down payment in itself; he had promised to make good on Lang's original proposal, and Lang was to contact Young when he needed additional installment payments. Those payments—and the high school coaches' expenditures, including their auto purchases—were to be in cash to avoid a "paper trail." Young made two further payments by January 2000, bringing his total thus far to about $30,000.

One big caveat, of course, was attached to the payments: if Albert Means did not commit to Alabama, the deal would be off and Lang would have to pay back the full amount of the payments advanced by Young. Of course, Lang had already blown through most of the money, so the pressure was on. But Lang was confident—he had treated Albert and his mother well, so they surely would be amenable to his guidance on where Albert should go to school.

National Letter of Intent Day, when high school athletes formally commit to competing for particular colleges, did not come until the following month, February 2000. That gave Lang time, remarkably, to continue marketing Albert to other universities. Unlike Young, Lang had no allegiance to Alabama; if someone else was willing to come up with a better deal, Lang was all ears. By now, of course, he was in hock to Young to the tune of $30,000, so the new price for Albert was roughly

$200,000, enough for his $100,000 "fee," two new SUVs, and repayment of Young's $30,000.

No one bit on the full deal, but at Logan Young's criminal trial in 2005, Lang testified under oath that he received some money from representatives of both Georgia and Kentucky. He also said five other schools—Arkansas, Memphis, Michigan, Mississippi, and Tennessee—offered financial inducements of their own. Arkansas, Lang said, offered him an assistant coaching job paying over $80,000 per year or $150,000 in cash for delivering Albert and one of his teammates. Lang also testified that Michigan, Mississippi, and Tennessee offered cash and that Memphis came up with a more creative proposal—free law school for Lang's wife.

Who knows whether Lang was telling the truth. Coaches from Georgia and Memphis offered their own sworn testimony during the criminal trial that Lang was lying about allegations related to their programs. Lang did not cooperate with the NCAA investigation, declining to talk with the enforcement staff. And because his assertions did not come until February 2005, five years after the marketing of Albert Means, NCAA investigators would have been severely handicapped in developing leads, let alone dealing with the statute of limitations, which limits the time period in which allegations of NCAA violations may be brought. The general statute of limitations for NCAA violations is four years, although there are exceptions to the general rule.

In any event, Albert Means signed his National Letter of Intent, committing to the University of Alabama, in February 2000. Lang and Kirk celebrated the following night—at Lang's usual haunt, the strip club—and made plans to finalize the scheme. Albert was going to Alabama; it was now time for Young to fulfill his end of the bargain. To avoid suspicion, though, they agreed to have Kirk wait until the school year was over in May to purchase his SUV.

When May rolled around and Lang told Kirk he would have to wait a while longer for his vehicle, Kirk was more than upset. He did not know how much money Lang had received from Young, but he could see that Lang was living the high life, while he had not received a dime. That summer, Kirk decided to let people know that Lang was a scoundrel. He started with Albert Means's mother, who presumably did not know about the plan to market her son. As the investigation unfolded later, no evidence surfaced that either Albert or his mother knew about the scheme until the summer of 2000. Kirk told Albert's mother that he understood the scheme to include a significant payment to her. He later stated that he had "insisted" to Lang at the outset that there be something in the deal for Albert and his mother. Albert's mother had not received anything beyond Lang's usual, occasional financial assistance.

Kirk also complained about Lang to others, including the Alabama assistant coach who had facilitated the initial contacts between Lang and Young, as well as to a head football coach at another Memphis high school. As the word got around, eventually it found its way to the NCAA enforcement staff, who contacted Kirk in July to see if he would be willing to talk. Kirk was willing; as the infractions report states, "a series of interviews ensued."

At the time, the NCAA enforcement staff already was investigating allegations of other rule violations at the University of Alabama. As is often the case, information that comes to light during the course of an investigation can turn the investigation in a completely different direction. The new information also can open up the university to thorough scrutiny in areas that were not even contemplated at the beginning of the investigation. Such was the case with Milton Kirk's statements to the enforcement staff in the summer of 2000 about what happened in the recruitment of Albert Means.

Eventually, Kirk also spoke with representatives of the Memphis School Board and the U.S. Attorney's Office. Federal prosecutors initiated a criminal investigation under the RICO (Racketeer Influenced and Corrupt Organizations) statutes. One ordinarily thinks of the Mob (organized crime) as involved in racketeering, and federal prosecutors' use of RICO statutes in a broad range of cases has been criticized in some circles. But the actions of Young, Lang, and Kirk fit within the statutes, so the feds were off and running.

Running parallel to the feds were NCAA enforcement staff members. As is also often the case, NCAA investigators worked cooperatively with representatives of both the University of Alabama and the Southeastern Conference (SEC). At least in its latter stages, the investigation truly was a joint investigation conducted by personnel from both the NCAA and the university, with the assistance of an SEC investigator. As discussed in other parts of this book, this cooperative principle at the heart of NCAA governance often leads to debates about how much credit a university should be given in the assessment of penalties for its earlier cooperation in the investigation.

What made the Alabama case even more interesting was the involvement of Gene Marsh, the university's faculty athletics representative. At the time, Marsh was a relatively new member of the NCAA Division I Committee on Infractions. A law professor at the university, Marsh had represented the university in an earlier infractions case before the committee, and his sterling performance led the committee to extend an invitation to him to join as a member when the committee had a vacancy.

My time on the committee overlapped with Gene's by eight years—he does indeed have a brilliant mind, immense integrity, and an in-depth knowledge of intercollegiate athletics. So when Alabama found itself in infractions trouble again, it was only natural that the university would ask him to lead its investigation. Questions would surface later about whether the infractions committee could be impartial when one of their own was in the dock. One thing was clear at the outset, though—with Gene Marsh at the helm, there would be no secrets. The university and the NCAA investigators would work in tandem to get to the truth, as the cooperative principle is designed to work.

The investigators' principal witness, of course, was Milton Kirk. Not only was he willing to talk about the details of the Albert Means marketing scheme, he also cooperated with the federal criminal investigation and ultimately pled guilty to one count of racketeering conspiracy. In exchange for his cooperation, prosecutors recommended a relatively light sentence, and Kirk was sentenced to six months in a halfway house, three years of probation, two hundred hours of community service, and a $1,000 fine.

The NCAA enforcement staff has a difficult task in determining whether to rely on particular witnesses. Ulterior motives are common, so assessing credibility can be a challenge. Typically, the enforcement staff will not rely on the statements of an individual unless that person's statements can be corroborated by other witnesses or other evidence, or other factors exist that point toward the person's reliability. In Kirk's case, his statements led to other sources, in addition to documentary evidence such as phone records. That evidence ultimately was presented to the Committee on Infractions, which found Kirk to be credible because "(1) much of the information he provided was against his own interest, subjecting him to criminal prosecution as well as loss of employment; (2) the information he provided was internally consistent; (3) his information was corroborated by at least 10 other individuals as well as by documentary evidence; and (4) his information was found credible by both the Memphis School Board and by the federal district judge who accepted his guilty plea."

The investigators, then, began to build a solid case that Logan Young had provided improper payments to Lang to induce him to steer Albert Means to Alabama. Not surprisingly, federal prosecutors would characterize the payments as bribery and bring federal bribery charges against all three participants—Young, Lang, and Kirk. What troubled NCAA investigators even more was that Young was no run-of-the-mill booster. His insider status within the Alabama athletics department—as a skybox holder with special access to the football program and a personal relationship with prominent university officials, including the athletics director—made him highly visible.

It's exceedingly difficult for athletics departments to control, or even monitor, the activities of all its boosters. Departments can provide educational materials to their financial supporters, typically in the form of flyers or pamphlets explaining relevant NCAA rules and often accompanying season ticket renewals. But if a booster goes rogue and decides to disregard pleas by the athletics department, there is little to prevent the booster from breaking the rules—for example, by directly providing money, vehicles, housing, loans, or other inducements to prospects, their family members, or even their high school coaches.

The difficulty for NCAA officials in such situations is in assessing *institutional* responsibility for booster violations. The NCAA, as a membership organization, has authority over its member institutions and their employees and student athletes, but it does not have authority over third parties such as boosters. In other words, the infractions committee can impose sanctions against a university for the rule violations of its boosters, but it cannot penalize boosters directly. Not surprisingly, then, institutions attempt to minimize their own responsibility, and culpability, for the actions of rogue boosters.

Unfortunately for the Crimson Tide, Logan Young's special access and insider connections to the athletics department at Alabama would make any arguments of rogue status difficult. After all, Kirk had identified an Alabama assistant coach as the person who first brought together Lynn Lang and Logan Young to make the deal on Albert Means.

Investigators later learned of other rule violations: Young's personal loans to another Crimson Tide assistant coach and Young's impermissible recruiting contacts with prospects or their family members—one at a summer football camp and another in Young's hotel suite in Nashville before an Alabama-Vanderbilt game. The latter incident involved a meeting with a prospect's father. An Alabama associate athletics director witnessed the incident but did not report it as a violation. This individual later was elevated to athletics director. Most troubling of all, however, was the revelation that Young's "buying" of Albert Means was not an isolated incident.

One of the more interesting aspects of the Alabama infractions case was the use of statements by an unidentified witness—unidentified, that is, to both the public and the Committee on Infractions. The use of such witnesses in infractions cases is exceedingly rare; NCAA bylaws prohibit the enforcement staff's use and the infractions committee's consideration of confidential sources. One can understand the reasoning behind this legislation; it would be unfair for the NCAA to use the testimony of a secret witness whom another party has no opportunity to interview or otherwise confront. In the Alabama case, however, the witness was not confidential in this classic sense; the identity of the witness was secret neither to the enforcement staff nor to the University of Alabama. The two parties conducted their investigation jointly, and they jointly developed the testimony of this witness. At the later infractions hearing, university representatives consented to the use of the witness's statements.

Among those statements was the witness's account of a conversation with Logan Young. During that conversation, according to the witness, Young stated that since 1994 he "had 'bought' every prospect out of Memphis" that had signed with the University of Alabama. (For those wondering about hearsay, traditional rules of evidence that govern the use of hearsay in court proceedings do not apply in infractions hearings.) And it was not just prospects out of Memphis—the investigation revealed that Young had paid $20,000 in 1995–96 to try to secure a blue-chip prospect from northeastern Alabama.

Payment to the Alabama prospect was old school: bags of cash. According to statements of fact agreed to by both the

University of Alabama and the NCAA enforcement staff, Young collaborated with another booster who served literally as bagman, delivering $10,000 in $100 bills on two separate occasions to the prospect and his father. This is the same father later discovered in Logan Young's hotel suite by the university's associate athletics director. The first payment, in the fall of 1995, was delivered to the prospect's home in a white plastic grocery bag; the second stash of $100 bills came in Memphis in January 1996, in a large brown envelope.

The payments worked their magic; in February 1996 the prospect signed a National Letter of Intent to attend the University of Alabama. In a perverse twist of fate, however, the prospect slipped on the *student* responsibilities of being a student athlete—he failed to meet the NCAA's academic eligibility requirements and was unable to enroll at 'Bama. And to rub salt in the wound, he later chose to attend one of the Tide's fiercest SEC rivals, the University of Tennessee. That was after he attended another high school to correct his academic deficiencies and was offered a sweet deal by the middleman booster to consider signing again with Alabama the following February: "(1) $5,000 cash, (2) $500 a month, (3) $500 for each football game he started, and (4) $5,000 each Christmas to his mother while he was enrolled."

The Alabama investigation yielded a blockbuster case. The allegations relating to the recruitment of Albert Means and the Alabama blue-chipper involved, in the words of the Committee on Infractions, "some of the largest money amounts alleged in any infractions case in the NCAA's history"—perhaps comparable to the payments in the infamous SMU death penalty case, though not as widespread. The enforcement staff also alleged other violations, but none as serious as the buying of recruits. The violations, for example, included the two personal loans Logan Young made to the Alabama assistant coach and the coach's subsequent failure to be forthcoming with investigators when asked about the loans, violating NCAA "principles of honesty and cooperation."

As noted earlier, the enforcement staff and the university conducted the investigation jointly, and Gene Marsh's leadership on the university side ensured that there would be no surprises at the time of the hearing before the Committee on Infractions. Indeed, in any truly cooperative investigation, the heavy lifting is done prior to the hearing. The enforcement staff and university representatives meet at a prehearing conference to determine how the case will be presented to the committee, and typically the parties are in agreement heading into the hearing. That agreement is manifested in boilerplate language in the public infractions report: "The enforcement staff and the university were in substantial agreement regarding the facts of the findings and that violations of NCAA legislation occurred."

That is precisely the language used in the Alabama report in relation to the $20,000 payment to the recruit from northeastern Alabama. When the parties agree to the facts, there is little incentive or need to rehash the details at the infractions hearing. As for the Albert Means recruitment, university officials agreed that Lynn Lang "manipulated the recruitment of [Means] for his own personal profit" but also "believed the evidence was inconclusive" regarding whether Logan Young provided funds to Lang. In that instance, the infractions committee thoroughly examined the evidence, including the corroborated statements of Milton Kirk and Logan Young's own statements to others, including the unidentified witness, about his payments to Lang.

Doubt about Young's involvement, of course, would make *institutional* responsibility more tenuous. It is difficult enough to hold universities accountable for the actions of third-party boosters; it would be even more difficult to assign blame to a university if it is unclear whether a university booster was even involved in the violations. In the end, though, the evidence was overwhelming, even to find Young guilty beyond a reasonable doubt in his subsequent criminal trial. The bar for finding an NCAA violation is much lower and, frankly, based on a pretty mushy standard: the Committee on Infractions "shall base its decision on information presented to it that it determines to be credible, persuasive and of a kind on which reasonably prudent persons rely in the conduct of serious affairs."

It is unlikely that University of Alabama representatives were surprised by the findings in the Committee on Infractions report. The parties agreed to most of the violations, and any fact disputes were relatively minor. What probably did surprise university officials, however, was the tone of the report. Infractions reports (now called public decisions) typically are straightforward—just the facts, ma'am—without a lot of commentary or editorializing. In this case, though, the committee's frustration with booster cases reared its head:

> While rogue athletics representatives are new neither to infractions cases generally nor to the infractions history of this university, their level of involvement and spending is an increasingly visible and major problem in intercollegiate athletics. Such rogue athletics representatives demonstrate a profound and worrisome immaturity in the satisfaction they derive from close and continued intermingling with college and even high-school age student-athletes. Even if sincere, their claimed motivation for cheating—helping a university to recruit blue-chip athletes—betrays a lack of integrity and "win-at-all-costs" attitude that undermines and cheapens athletics competition and corrupts the ethics and maturation process of the young people they claim to be "helping." The failure of these athletics representatives to heed past lessons about the serious consequences caused to a university and athletics program by their reckless irresponsibility makes clear, moreover, that their prime motivation is self-aggrandizement and the gratification they derive from close contact with athletics programs and coaches.

All true, to be sure, but still extraordinary in a public infractions report. Recognizing that the majority of boosters are ethical and well meaning, the committee's lecture continued:

The actions and attitudes of these [rogue] athletics representatives damage the reputations of the vast majority of athletics representatives and fans who value fair competition and
ethical conduct. Their actions and attitudes force universities
to hold at arms length and to develop an investigative, even
an adversarial, stance with the vast majority of responsible
and reputable representatives and supporters of their universities and athletics programs whose interest and support
are critical to the continued health of an athletics program
and university. Their actions and attitudes corrupt the young
people with whom they come in contact and can even blight
careers of initial great promise. Their actions and attitudes
may provide short-term competitive success but only at the
cost of an athletics program sorely weakened once violations
are uncovered and penalties assessed.

Surely that last sentence signaled what was to come—the committee's attempt to *sorely weaken* the Alabama football program and to warn other universities that they, too, will suffer
serious consequences *once* (not *if*) violations are uncovered.

In its coup de grace, the committee quoted Roy Kramer,
the commissioner of the Southeastern Conference, who had
characterized rogue boosters as "parasites" at the infractions hearing: "These rogue representatives are the 'parasites' of intercollegiate athletics. What is required is a full
frontal attack to turn these parasites into pariahs and to
visibly, forcefully and emphatically exclude them from any
participation or entrée into athletics programs."

The committee also seized the opportunity to address institutional responsibility for booster conduct, particularly the
actions of high-profile boosters:

> There is no doubt that institutional control obliges a univer-
> sity to monitor the conduct of athletics representatives. The
> committee recognizes, however, that in the concentric cir-
> cles of institutional responsibility, the conduct of representa-
> tives typically sits on the outermost circle. But those athletics

representatives provided favored access and "insider" status, frequently in exchange for financial support, are not the typical representative. Their favored access and insider status creates both a greater university obligation to monitor and direct their conduct and a greater university responsibility for any misconduct in which they engage.

This case is an apt illustration of the unequivocal obligation to monitor closely those athletics representatives whose financial contributions provide a level of visibility, insider status, and favored access within athletics programs. Their insider status not only gives credence to their claims of authority within a program but also, and however unintended, serves to reward them for the illicit activities in which they engage. Moreover, special access and insider status likely ease the way for illicit conduct by rogue representatives both by identifying prospects for them and by fostering (or contributing to) the belief of prospects and their parents that the representative's conduct is sanctioned by the university and in its best interest as well as that of the prospect.

The committee's language—and tone—did not bode well for the University of Alabama. Logan Young, involved in both of the major sets of violations, was considered an insider, and that status meant enhanced institutional culpability. And of course, the nature of the violations—large cash payments to influence recruits or their coaches—was viscerally abhorrent.

Ultimately, what's important to an institution in an infractions case are the penalties imposed by the Committee on Infractions. University officials can live with harsh language; few people ever read the language of infractions reports anyway. But penalties are always reported in the media, and penalties have a direct impact on an athletics program. In addition to weakening a team's competitiveness, harsh penalties may influence recruits not to come to the university, current student athletes to leave for greener pastures, fans to stay away from games, financial supporters to withhold contributions, administrators to fire coaches, and a host of other adverse reactions.

Alabama's penalties were severe, at least in comparison to the general run of infractions cases. Most notably, the committee imposed five years' probation, a two-year ban on bowl game participation, substantial scholarship reductions in the football program (twenty-one scholarships lost over three years), and permanent disassociation of three boosters involved in the violations. As noted previously in the discussion of the SMU cases, the probationary period is mostly symbolic. Five years has been the maximum ever imposed (although new penalty legislation contemplates the possibility of longer probationary periods in egregious cases), so the Alabama probation penalty sounds tough. As a practical matter, however, the probation adds little to penalties beyond a requirement that the university file annual compliance reports. The disassociation has little practical effect either, except on those disassociated, and in this case, the university did not even appeal that sanction. The bowl ban and scholarship reductions, though, could have the kinds of significant impacts noted above.

The penalties could have been worse, up to and including the death penalty. The death penalty historically has been reserved for repeat violators whose infractions history exhibits a blatant disregard for the rules. In February 2002, when the infractions report in the Alabama case was released, the University of Alabama was a rare *two-time* repeat violator. The case involving Logan Young was the university's third major infractions case in a period of about six years, and remarkably, all three involved boosters.

In August 1995 the Committee on Infractions issued an infractions report finding major violations in the football program. Among the violations was a student athlete's receipt of six impermissible deferred-payment loans totaling $24,400—serious money. Boosters facilitated some of the loans. Among the penalties imposed and later upheld on appeal was a one-year ban on postseason (bowl game) competition.

More importantly, though, beginning in the summer of 1995, Alabama entered a five-year repeat-violator period. The message to the university in 1995 was intended to be clear: You have just been found to have committed major violations, so keep your nose clean. If we find you committing any more violations in the next five years, it suggests that you have not taken us seriously, and you will be penalized even more harshly under repeat-violator principles.

Logan Young must not have gotten the memo. In September 1995, *one month* after the report was issued, he was meeting in his hotel suite with a recruit's father and arranging for the first $10,000 payment to the recruit later that fall. In the summer of 1998 he made two impermissible loans to an assistant football coach, and the following summer he began discussions with, and payments to, Lynn Lang in connection with Albert Means's recruitment. Of course, none of Young's actions were discovered until the summer of 2000, when Milton Kirk first came forward and the NCAA enforcement staff began its investigation into recruiting violations in the football program. Nonetheless, any major violation between June 1995 and June 2000, if discovered, would subject Alabama to repeat-violator penalties.

In the meantime, the university was facing another serious problem. In January 1998 an assistant *basketball* coach attempted to solicit $5,000 from boosters to pay a prospect's high school coach. The goal, of course, was similar to that in the recruitment of Albert Means— induce the coach to steer his player to Alabama. Things went south, unfortunately, for the Crimson Tide assistant coach—the boosters turned him in. Thus began another major infractions case, with a university employee, rather than a booster, as the culprit. The Committee on Infractions issued its next report, finding a major violation in the basketball program, in February 1999.

Alabama was a repeat violator in the 1998–99 basketball case. It did not matter that a different sport was involved; once the major infractions decision was handed down in 1995, the entire *athletics program* had to prevent major infractions, in all sports, for a five-year period in order to avoid repeat-violator status. The university avoided significant penalties in the basketball case because it acted promptly and appropriately after the boosters blew the whistle, including self-reporting the violation to the NCAA enforcement staff. Nonetheless, a major violation involving unethical conduct by the assistant coach had occurred, and the infractions committee extended the university's repeat-violator period, which originally was to expire in June 2000, to November 2003 (five years from the date of the infractions hearing in November 1998).

So the university's second major infractions case in less than four years was resolved in February 1999. Later that spring, according to Lynn Lang and Milton Kirk, they hatched their marketing plan for Albert Means and pitched it to an Alabama assistant coach, who connected them to Logan Young. Young's first payment to Lang—to buy Means's enrollment at Alabama—occurred in the fall of 1999.

One can begin to understand, then, why the Committee on Infractions, in November 2001, when the University of Alabama appeared before it for the *third* time in six years, wondered if the university had taken to heart the committee's earlier messages . . . and why it may have felt compelled to use harsh language about boosters in its soon-to-be-issued public report.

The report pulled no punches. Because of (1) the university's two-time repeat-violator status, (2) its responsibility for the actions of insider boosters like Logan Young, and (3) "some of the most serious [recruiting violations] in recent memory," the Committee on Infractions "very seriously considered" the death penalty for Alabama football. The imposition of the death penalty was "a very close question" for the committee. The chair of the committee, Tom Yeager (then commissioner of the Colonial Athletic Association), reiterated the point in the NCAA press conference announcing the findings and penalties in the Alabama case: the university was "absolutely staring down the barrel of a gun."

What saved Alabama in this case? The infractions report suggested that the committee's decision came down to a comparison to SMU, where there was "a demonstrated blatant disregard for NCAA rules that permeated throughout the entire university and its governance structure." In contrast, Gene Marsh and others at the University of Alabama had demonstrated a cooperative spirit and a commitment to get to the bottom of the matter: "University officials cooperated fully with the enforcement staff, often at great personal criticism, in a diligent effort to develop complete information regarding the violations. Had this candor and cooperation been lacking, the death penalty (as well as substantial penalties in addition to those imposed in this case) would have been imposed."

Despite its abysmal recent infractions history and its escape from the death penalty, immediately after release of the committee report, the University of Alabama announced its appeal of both findings and penalties, thus sending the case into the wonderland of infractions appeals.

6

The Rats You Are

I'm not saying I haven't had sex with girls at the Mirage . . .

BILL BAYNO

Gotta love Vegas. One can almost be assured that a colorful cast of characters will be involved in any NCAA infractions case associated with Sin City. And for a program out of the modest Mountain West Conference, the athletics department at the University of Nevada at Las Vegas (UNLV) has generated more than its fair share of attention from NCAA investigators.

Just before Christmas 2000, the *Los Angeles Times* ran an article aptly titled "Another Desert Storm." *Times* sportswriter Steve Henson captured the essence of UNLV's latest run-in with the NCAA:

LAS VEGAS—This place invites mischief. Read the travel brochures. The NCAA investigates any type of mischief. Read the rule book. Inevitably, the watchdog turns its attention to the team in the town of temptation. Read the help-wanted ads.

Bill Bayno was fired last week as basketball coach at Nevada Las Vegas amid mischief aplenty, joining Jerry Tarkanian and Rollie Massimino as Sin City casualties. In five-plus years, Bayno apparently deteriorated from a button-down prodigy as a Massachusetts assistant to a Vegas-type with a wandering eye for strippers and a blind eye toward a booster who Lamar Odom says provided "hundred-dollar handshakes."

On December 12, 2000, the NCAA Committee on Infractions

handed down penalties against the UNLV men's basketball program that included a four-year probation and a one-year ban on postseason competition. The university "reassigned" Bill Bayno, the head coach, within hours of the committee's public release of its report.

Most, if not all, coaching contracts permit a university employer to fire a coach if the coach knowingly commits NCAA rule violations. In this case, however, the infractions committee made no finding that Bayno was directly involved in any recruiting or extra-benefit violations. Recruiting inducements are made to *prospects*; extra benefits are provided to student athletes who have already enrolled at the institution. Both types of violations occurred in the UNLV case.

Bayno had a few strikes against him, though, not the least of which was a poor start to the 2000–2001 season—3-4, including a loss to UNLV's upstate rival, Nevada–Reno, which had *nothing* comparable to UNLV's rich history of success in men's basketball. Most damaging, certainly, was the infractions committee's finding that the booster with the "hundred-dollar handshakes" was "a close friend" of Coach Bayno. That booster, identified in the infractions report as "a Las Vegas dentist" and in numerous media reports as David Chapman, had provided Lamar Odom, a blue-chip recruit, with cold, hard cash during his recruitment in the summer of 1997. The payments, which occurred on frequent occasions, totaled roughly $5,600.

The infractions committee also concluded that the university had "failed to adequately monitor" the men's basketball program to ensure compliance with the rules—in particular, failing to monitor the activities of boosters and the athletes with whom they came into contact. Bayno's attorneys, who were threatening legal action for wrongful termination, highlighted the fact that the committee found *the university*, not Bayno individually, to be delinquent in its monitoring responsibilities. But individuals ultimately act on behalf of the institution, and the infractions report at least implied that Bayno was as responsible for the failure to monitor as anyone:

"Finally, given the added fact that the athletics representative in question was a personal friend of the head men's basketball coach, the committee concluded that the institution's athletics staff either knew or should have been in a position to know of potential improprieties involving the athletics representative and the prospect, yet nothing was done to monitor or discourage this relationship."

The case could be seen as a precursor to the Alabama case, where the infractions committee leveled harsh sanctions in part because Logan Young had close personal connections to individuals within the athletics department. Dr. Chapman, as a close friend of Bayno, probably would be viewed as having insider status as well.

Two other factors may have been the death knell for Bayno. One was the unsavory reputation of UNLV's men's basketball program. Longtime head coach Jerry Tarkanian had been remarkably successful (one of the winningest coaches in NCAA history), but he also had become something of a poster boy for troubles with the NCAA. He was involved in a major infractions case early in his UNLV career in the 1970s and then, in the late 1980s, was implicated again in violations centered on the improper recruitment of a top prospect named Lloyd Daniels. And it probably didn't help when a photo appeared in the *Las Vegas Review-Journal* of three of Tarkanian's players drinking beer in a hot tub with Richard Perry, who had a longtime history of sports fixing, including involvement in a college basketball point-shaving scandal at Boston College.

Tarkanian resigned from his position at UNLV in 1992. His successor, Rollie Massimino, lasted only two years before the university bought out his contract amid a scandal relating to a secret salary supplement that paid Massimino nearly 75 percent more than the publicly reported salary the university's board of regents *thought* it had approved. Massimino's departure came just before the start of fall practice in October 1994, and the university hurriedly brought back Tim Grgurich, a respected NBA assistant coach who earlier had served as Tarkanian's longtime top assistant. A return to the glory years did not pan out, though—Grgurich lasted all of five months before resigning in March 1995, citing exhaustion and lingering bitterness about how UNLV administrators had treated Tarkanian and his staff.

So when Bayno came aboard in 1995, he knew full well that the basketball program would be under extra scrutiny because of UNLV's past infractions history . . . and that any missteps with NCAA rules could mean his downfall. The timing could not have been worse for Bayno. Tarkanian had taken his fight with the NCAA enforcement staff to court in the 1980s—indeed, all the way to the U.S. Supreme Court. Because of the lengthy litigation, the infractions case involving Lloyd Daniels's recruitment was not resolved until 1993, which meant that the violations on Bayno's watch in 1997 involving Dr. Chapman and Lamar Odom put UNLV squarely within the five-year repeat-violator window. Worse yet, also similar to the Alabama case, the infractions in 1997 were similar to those in the 1993 case—improper booster involvement in the recruitment of highly touted prospects.

The crowning blow for Bayno may have come from his association with a criminal defendant named Steve Kaplan. Federal court documents released months earlier suggested Kaplan had recruited strippers to travel to Vegas to have sex with Bayno at the Mirage Hotel. Bayno's response to the accusations? As quoted in a *Sports Illustrated* article, "I'm not saying I haven't had sex with girls at the Mirage, but if it was arranged by Steve Kaplan, it was unbeknownst to me."

A few years before Logan Young went on trial in Memphis on charges related to racketeering, another racketeering trial caught the nation's attention in Atlanta. The trial in federal court of Steve Kaplan and several others began in May 2001. At the time, Kaplan was owner of a strip club in Atlanta called the Gold Club. But this was no ordinary strip club—its clientele included many high rollers from the sports and entertainment world. Celebrities such as George Clooney, Mick Jagger, Michael Jordan, Madonna, Donald Trump, and Bruce Willis, not to mention the king of Sweden, were reputed to have patronized the club.

Kaplan, the club's multimillionaire owner, had a lot of friends, including one Bill Bayno. Among Kaplan's other associates were some rapscallions. In the trial's early stages, the prosecution focused on Kaplan's alleged ties to organized crime, particularly the Gambino organization once led by John Gotti. Gotti's nephew John DiGiorgio testified early in the trial about loan sharking back in the day with Kaplan's father. Describing DiGiorgio, an article in the *Augusta Chronicle* stated that "the former owner of Bobby and Johnny's Chicken and Ribs made it clear that he's no snitch and was only testifying because the government had him on tape." The article continued, "That same day, David Campo—real name David Mauricio Cajiao—a Colombian-born former drug dealer and car thief in the government's witness protection program, testified wearing a fake beard, glasses and a ball cap pulled over his eyes. He described doing drugs and sipping champagne with John Gotti Jr. at Mr. Kaplan's Florida nightclub, Club Boca."

In December 2000, when the UNLV infractions report was released, federal prosecutors were preparing for Kaplan's trial. They were attempting to prove not only the Gold Club's ties to organized crime but also that the club committed credit card fraud (some customers found surprisingly large charges to their cards after visits to the club's VIP rooms) and essentially pimped strippers to prominent customers. Presumably, Coach Bayno's reputation took one squarely on the chin, at least for those in Vegas who were aware of his Kaplan connections. His public image took a further hit a couple of weeks later when *Sports Illustrated* told the Kaplan story on Christmas Day 2000. Nonetheless, Bayno challenged the university's actions against him and ultimately reached a settlement with UNLV under which the university bought out the remaining two years of his contract for $400,000.

Like officials at the University of Alabama, UNLV's president announced that the school would appeal part of the sanctions imposed by the Committee on Infractions. In particular, the one-year postseason ban, according to President Carol Harter, was unfair to innocent student athletes still at the school who had nothing to do with the violations. The appeal would be to a five-member NCAA Infractions Appeals Committee, a body created in 1992, ironically, as a result of Jerry Tarkanian's lengthy legal battle with the NCAA.

The enduring image of Jerry Tarkanian is that of a droopy-eyed, towel-chewing coach exhorting his team to run-and-gun and play stifling defense. Oh, what a fun team to watch! UNLV played an exciting brand of basketball, with the kind of success that would be envied by nearly any program, let alone one in a midlevel conference. Tark the Shark finished his nineteen-year run at UNLV with a phenomenal 509-105 record, including a 103–73 thrashing of Duke to win the national championship in 1990. The team returned to the Final Four the following year but lost to Duke, 79–77, in a national semifinal rematch, finishing the season at 34-1. Many would say the UNLV teams to play in those years were among the best ever to play the college game.

A competing image of Tarkanian is that of a perpetual thorn in the side of the NCAA enforcement division. One could write an entire book detailing proceedings related to Tarkanian, both at the NCAA level and in court. We'll only scratch the surface here; the main point is that for all the aggravation he caused the NCAA, Tark made its enforcement procedures stronger and fairer.

The story begins in 1968 when Tarkanian became head coach at Long Beach State. Five years later, in March 1973, he accepted the head coaching job at UNLV, but a month after his departure the NCAA sent an official inquiry letter to Long Beach, announcing an investigation into alleged rule violations in the men's basketball program during Tarkanian's tenure as head coach. In January 1974 the Committee on Infractions handed down penalties against the Long Beach program that included a postseason ban and scholarship reductions in men's basketball. Tarkanian denied knowledge of violations and complained that the committee had made its findings without affording him an opportunity to participate in the infractions hearing. For its part, Long Beach State unsuccessfully lobbied for NCAA legislation in 1975 to allow punishment of a coach who had committed violations at one school and then moved on to another school.

In 1976 the NCAA investigated alleged violations in the UNLV men's basketball program, both before and after Tarkanian's hiring as head coach. The following year, the Committee on Infractions found numerous major violations, including some involving Tarkanian. The penalties were harsh—scholarship reductions and bans on both postseason competition and TV appearances for two years. What really caused problems, however, was a show-cause penalty requiring UNLV to show cause why it should not be penalized further if it did not suspend Tarkanian from all coaching activities for two years.

The show-cause penalty was the genesis of a legal odyssey that lasted over twenty years. Tarkanian filed a lawsuit in Nevada state court in 1977 to prohibit UNLV from suspending him. Not surprisingly, he found a sympathetic local judge, perhaps one who enjoyed the on-court success of the home team. The judge granted a permanent injunction prohibiting UNLV from suspending Tarkanian.

The NCAA has lost numerous cases in court. Often, though, those losses come in lower-level state courts, where plaintiffs have a built-in home-court advantage—sometimes with judges and certainly with juries. Because the NCAA has a national reach, it typically can be sued anywhere in the United States, so those with a legal complaint against the NCAA would be foolish *not* to employ the advantages of their home court, portraying the big, bad, outsider NCAA as an out-of-control monster. But the further one is removed from local passions, the less likely the NCAA will lose in the end.

While the NCAA has lost some important battles (the legal fight over control of college football TV broadcasting in the early eighties comes to mind), overall it has had a strong record of ultimate success in litigation. Following the 2002 Alabama infractions case, for example, one of the disassociated boosters filed a $35.5 million defamation suit against the NCAA, alleging, among other things, that the Committee on Infractions went overboard in calling the boosters such things as "parasites." The $35.5 million was a little steep even for a local Alabama jury, which returned a verdict for $5 million. The NCAA calmly asked the presiding judge of Jackson County to overturn the jury's decision, noting that it would appeal to the Alabama Supreme Court if necessary. It didn't have to appeal; the circuit judge threw out the verdict, concluding that it was "the product of passion or prejudice."

Tarkanian's 1977 judgment, however, held until he resigned fifteen years later. (For law aficionados, the case had plenty of twists and turns, including a reversal by the Nevada Supreme Court on the ground that Tarkanian had failed to join the NCAA as an indispensable party and a 1988 ruling by the U.S. Supreme Court that the NCAA could not be liable for constitutional claims because it was not a state actor.) Ultimately the parties resolved the matter with a penalty that included a postseason and TV ban in 1991–92, Tark's last season as coach. Later in 1992 Tarkanian filed another suit against the NCAA, which finally was resolved through a settlement in 1998.

Along the way, Tarkanian's litigation led to significant changes in NCAA enforcement procedures and policies. In 1978 a U.S. congressman from Nevada named James Santini took on Tarkanian's cause and pressed the House Subcommittee on Oversight and Investigations to conduct hearings on the NCAA's enforcement program. A subcommittee report recommended changes to enforcement procedures, some of which the NCAA adopted. Even more changes came in the early 1990s, again partially in response to the Tarkanian litigation.

Tarkanian's principal allegation was that he was denied

"due process." Due process is guaranteed under federal and state constitutions, which constrain *government* actors. The U.S. Supreme Court's 1988 decision holding that the NCAA was not a government actor effectively put an end to Tarkanian's due process claims, but the attention drawn to his claims led to a renewed focus on basic fairness in NCAA proceedings.

Soon after the Supreme Court's decision, the NCAA appointed an outside Special Committee to Review the NCAA Enforcement and Infractions Process. The committee was high powered and high profile. Rex Lee, a former U.S. solicitor general, chaired the committee, which also included such luminaries as Warren Burger, former chief justice of the U.S. Supreme Court, and Benjamin Civiletti, a former U.S. attorney general. The committee issued its report, generally known as the Lee report, in 1991. The report made numerous recommendations for changes in the process, all but a few of which the NCAA adopted. One of the recommendations the NCAA membership did *not* adopt was to replace the Committee on Infractions as fact-finder in infractions proceedings with a hearing officer completely independent from the NCAA. The membership instead responded by adding two public members to the committee. Another rejected recommendation was to make all infractions hearings open and public.

Among the Lee report recommendations the membership did adopt was the creation of an appeals process overseen by "a special review body of three to five members." That body became the Infractions Appeals Committee. The new committee, comprised of five volunteer members, including one public member (not affiliated with a particular NCAA institution or athletics conference), would exercise its own independence in reviewing decisions of the Committee on Infractions. The appeals committee heard its first appeal in 1993, and since then, it has decided dozens more.

So it was this relatively new body before whom UNLV argued its case on appeal in 2001 in the matter of Dr. David Chapman's "hundred-dollar handshakes" with Lamar Odom—an appeals committee created out of the ashes of litigation brought by UNLV's only *great* basketball coach. I had been appointed as the infractions committee's first coordinator of appeals only months before, but I was recused from the case because UNLV and my employer, the University of Wyoming, were in the same newly formed conference, the Mountain West. So I was only an observer at my first appeals hearing. Committee chair Jack Friedenthal argued the case on behalf of the infractions committee. The king of institutional representatives in infractions matters, Mike Glazier of the Kansas City office of the Bond, Schoeneck, and King law firm, represented UNLV, along with the university president, athletics director, senior associate director of athletics, and faculty athletics representative.

UNLV had accepted all the infractions committee's findings of violations and all but one of the penalties. The sole issue on appeal was whether the one-year postseason ban was "excessive or inappropriate," the appeal standard set forth in the NCAA bylaws at the time. UNLV argued principally that the ban would punish innocent student athletes who remained at the institution and who had no involvement in any wrongdoing. That is a common argument on appeal, and the impact on innocent student athletes certainly is a consideration both committees must consider in determining whether penalties are fair and appropriate. But the NCAA membership considers the postseason ban to be one of the few weapons in the infractions committee's arsenal that has a chance to be an effective deterrent. And unless one takes the ban completely off the table, it nearly always affects innocent competitors.

The appeals committee emphasized UNLV's repeat-violator status and the fact that both cases (in 1993 and 2000) involved similar booster infractions, in the same sport of men's basketball. The committee upheld the postseason ban and addressed the NCAA's goal of deterrence: "The imposition of penalties always involves a balancing of interests. Almost every ban on competition impacts some innocent individuals. We hope the regrettable consequences of this penalty are appreciated fully by representatives of the institution's athletics interests [boosters] so that there will not be a recurrence of the facts that gave rise to the violations in the 1993 case and this case."

The appeals committee handed down its decision in the UNLV case on February 16, 2001. By that time, the Alabama football investigation was in full swing. Trezevant High School assistant coach Milton Kirk began talking to NCAA investigators in July 2000. In December the enforcement staff invited Alabama officials to join in an interview with Kirk, and the investigation became a truly joint investigation conducted by NCAA investigators and representatives from both the University of Alabama and the Southeastern Conference. Alabama officials paying attention to the UNLV case would have cause for concern; if UNLV received a postseason ban for being a repeat violator with successive booster cases, surely the infractions committee would be even more troubled by a double repeat violator with three booster cases, particularly when the dollar amounts in the UNLV case paled in comparison to the recruiting inducements involved in the latest Alabama case.

As the Alabama case became public (the enforcement staff issued its letter of official inquiry to the university in September 2001, and at that time the university publicly released the enforcement staff's formal allegations), I received a thoughtful email message on October 3, 2001, from a military officer and apparently acute observer of the NCAA infractions world:

Professor Parkinson,

I am writing to express my concern that the NCAA Infractions Committee conduct enforcement and infractions hearings and implement punishments in a fair and equitable manner. There is a widespread public perception that there are 2 sets of punishments considered for member institutions: a harsh standard for the UNLVs of the world, and even schools like Ole Miss that, while major, are not marquee names, and a second standard for the Notre Dames and Alabama's of the world. Unfortunately, the non-sanctions recently assessed against Notre Dame only serve to reinforce the notion that there are "Sacred Cows."

The allegations against the University of Alabama recently released are, as a set, the most appalling and outrageous acts of blatant cheating and violations of NCAA rules that I have seen since the days of SMU. The cheating and immorality contained in these allegations, if true, cannot and must not be tolerated and must be answered with timely and meaningful punishment. Anything less than very significant punishments for such outrageous violations will be to undermine the deterrent effect that is vital in maintaining order among NCAA member institutions. As a military officer and 1988 graduate of the United States Military Academy, I am reminded of our West Point Motto: "We will not Lie, Cheat, or Steal, nor Tolerate Those Who Do." Cheating cannot be tolerated.

Major Alan W. Hester

USMA 1988

I don't know Major Hester, but I appreciated his message and kept it in part because it was so much better written (and far less nasty) than most of the unsolicited correspondence sent to members of the Committee on Infractions. Of course, I would take issue with the notion that there are two sets of punishments, depending on the prominence of the athletics program. Jerry Tarkanian also contended that the little guys got picked on. In his ever-colorful way, he famously stated in the late 1980s that "the NCAA is so mad at Kentucky that it put Cleveland State on two more years' probation." A look at the NCAA's major infractions database, however, suggests otherwise—the "big boys" have had more than their fair share of major infractions cases and severe sanctions.

On the other hand, Major Hester may be right that there is a *public perception* of differential treatment. And if that is the case, the NCAA leadership, including the infractions and infractions appeals committees, must be continually vigilant about ensuring well-reasoned, consistent results. One way to help achieve that goal, of course, is to do precisely what Major Hester suggests: answer "cheating and immorality . . . with timely and meaningful punishment," including "very significant punishments for . . . outrageous violations."

The violations in the 2002 Crimson Tide case were pretty outrageous. Four months after Major Hester wrote, the Committee on Infractions leveled harsh sanctions on Alabama, which certainly wasn't feeling like a sacred cow after the committee released its report. Indeed, university officials felt quite aggrieved and almost immediately announced their appeal of both findings and penalties. Then they called in their big guns to prepare and argue the case.

Fortunately, Charles J. Cooper was an Alabama law graduate and Crimson Tide through and through. After earning a business degree with honors from the University of Alabama, Cooper moved on to the university's law school, where he finished first in the class of 1977 and served as editor in chief of the *Alabama Law Review*. His legal career soared, undoubtedly aided by a prestigious clerkship with Justice William Rehnquist of the U.S. Supreme Court. Before founding his own law firm in Washington DC, Cooper worked for the U.S. Department of Justice, where he rose to be assistant attorney general for the Office of Legal Counsel in the Reagan administration. He has had a stellar career as both trial and appellate lawyer and has been named one of the top-ten civil litigators in Washington by the *National Law Journal*. In perhaps Cooper's most prominent case, he defended California's Proposition 8, the referendum by which California voters banned gay marriage in 2008. The case is one of several Cooper has argued before the U.S. Supreme Court.

Also at the ready was Robert T. Cunningham, a perennial "Super Lawyer" from Mobile with a career rivaling Cooper's. His most prominent case probably was *Alabama v. Exxon*

Mobil, in which a jury returned the largest verdict in Alabama history—$11.9 *billion* for the State of Alabama for Exxon Mobil's underpayment of gas royalties. The jury award, comprised primarily of punitive damages, later was reversed on appeal, but the case nonetheless solidified Cunningham's reputation. At the time this book went into production, he was serving as lead counsel for the state in Alabama's suit against BP for economic damages resulting from the Deepwater Horizon explosion in the Gulf of Mexico. For the Alabama appeal, Cunningham offered his services and those of his firm, pro bono, saying later that "the university is an important institution in the state. An awful lot of Alabama alumni and fans felt that the sanctions were grossly unfair. We agreed with them and wanted to help the university in any way we could."

Needless to say, the University of Alabama was in able hands when Charles Cooper and Robert Cunningham answered the university's call for help. They put together a strong case, and their legal team, including four other lawyers and one paralegal, came with guns blazing in August 2002 to Chicago, the site of the hearing before the Infractions Appeals Committee. Appeal hearings typically are held in a modestly sized hotel meeting room, and typically the university delegation is modestly sized as well. This was the only one of about two dozen hearings I attended in which bleachers (two tiered rows) had to be installed to accommodate Alabama's ten-person delegation. The others present, besides the seven-person legal team, were the current and former university presidents and the athletics director. From the other side of the room, I represented the Committee on Infractions, accompanied by Shep Cooper, the director of the NCAA infractions committees, and Tom Yeager, the chair of the Division I infractions committee.

Unlike most appeal hearings, where the sole focus is on the severity of the penalties, the Alabama attorneys argued that some of the infractions committee's findings of violations were erroneous. Their arguments were fairly technical. They did not dispute that the violations occurred, but they argued that the NCAA's statute of limitations and the committee's reliance on a confidential source precluded the findings. In its later report, the appeals committee rejected those arguments and went on to the real issue—whether the penalties as a whole, and particularly the two-year postseason ban, were excessive or inappropriate.

Not surprisingly, the appeals committee cited the most relevant precedent—the UNLV decision it had handed down just the year before. That case, of course, also involved a repeat violator with significant booster troubles. The committee agreed with the Committee on Infractions that boosters with "favored access and insider status created 'greater university responsibility for any misconduct in which they engage.'" Upholding all the findings and penalties, the appeals committee noted that "the violations in this case were numerous and particularly egregious."

Alabama fans, naturally, were not convinced. Most of them probably agreed with the sentiments of one Dewayne McCann, who sent the following love note (capitalization and grammatical errors intact) to the infractions committee earlier in the year:

> You guys are "screwed up", your sanctions given to alabama are ludicrous! they do NOT fit the crime! you want to compare the kentucky case to alabama's? well it doesnt compare, NOT at all, alabama's charges are way less! but the penalties are more, and do NOT give me this "repeat offender" bull! wisconsin was a 3 time offender, who the hell do you think you are fooling? AND WHO THE HELL DO YOU THINK YOU ARE! YOU THINK YOU DONT HAVE TO FOLLOW GUIDELINES? I HOPE EVERYONE OF YOU IDIOTS GETS THE SHIT SUED OUT OF YOU AND YOU ALL HAVE TO LIVE ON WELLFARE, AND EAT OUT OF TRASH CANS LIKE THE RATS YOU ARE!

Ahh, the rats we were . . . but at least the members of the infractions committee could take solace this time in the fact that the appeals committee (the rats!) agreed with us.

Bile from fans is part of the NCAA landscape. But what catches some of us off guard occasionally are the reactions of NCAA member universities and their representatives—those who supposedly are engaged in a common endeavor to keep college sports clean. We all know, of course, that gracious loser is an oxymoron in many quarters of the sports world. And as the saying goes, where one stands depends on where one sits. In my experience, school or conference officials who are the first to criticize others for wrongdoing—and clamor for harsh penalties—often are also the first to criticize the NCAA when their own schools are sanctioned for similar misbehavior.

Some Alabama supporters undoubtedly exhibited grace in the face of this setback, which would have been infinitely worse had the Committee on Infractions pulled the trigger on the death penalty. But other reactions disturbed me, because people sometimes seem to be able to get away with saying anything about the NCAA without being challenged. And if assertions go unchallenged, they often are accepted as fact, leaving readers with a jaundiced view of the rule enforcers.

For example, in an interview years after the case, one of Alabama's lead appellate attorneys, Robert Cunningham, was quoted as saying, "Unfortunately, the main thing I took away from that experience was that it made me appreciate the rare, bad judges I've been in front of. We went up to Chicago to orally argue the case in front of the NCAA panel. About three to four minutes into the oral argument, they started asking questions, and it rapidly became apparent that they hadn't even read the brief." I was there. It was not my experience, either that day in Chicago or at any of the other twenty-one appeal hearings in which I actively participated, that the Infractions Appeals Committee was unprepared. Indeed, despite my own travails with the appeals committee, one thing I could *always* count on was a vigorous, well-informed, and challenging conversation with the committee members.

That doesn't mean they didn't torment me. Lest one think that the UNLV and Alabama results—full affirmance on appeal of the infractions committee's findings and penalties—were par for the course, the reader should know how truly independent the appeals committee is. I purposefully referred at the end of the last chapter to the "wonderland of infractions appeals" because the appeals committee historically has been aggressive, unpredictable, and fiercely independent.

Since the Infractions Appeals Committee began its work in 1993, following the Tarkanian litigation and the Lee report, there have been a *lot* of appeals, including two dozen in the early years from 1993 until January 2000. During the decade from January 2000 through December 2009, the Committee on Infractions considered ninety major infractions cases at a hearing, and appeals were made in thirty-four of those cases. Some of those cases involved multiple appeals—for example, appeals by both the institution and a coach or by two coaches—so overall in that ten-year period there were forty-six appeals.

One reason for the high number of appeals undoubtedly is the fact that appealing parties often realized considerable success before the Infractions Appeals Committee. Had the committee been merely a rubber stamp for the Committee on Infractions, the incentive to appeal would be low. As suggested previously, virtually all the action on appeal relates to penalties rather than findings of violations. Occasionally findings are challenged, but seldom are they overturned, in part because of a high standard imposed on the appeals committee. Under NCAA bylaws, findings of violations are not to be overturned unless the appeals committee concludes that the findings are "clearly contrary" to the evidence presented to the infractions committee. The fact that findings rarely are reversed or, for that matter, even appealed is an indication that the Committee on Infractions truly does consider the evidence carefully and base its decisions on that evidence.

Penalties, on the other hand, have been fair game. Before 2008 the standard for reviewing penalties was far less stringent; the bylaws allowed the appeals committee to overturn a penalty if the committee found the penalty to be "excessive or inappropriate." And as it turned out, appellants often were successful in claiming a particular penalty was inappropriate, particularly to a body that relished (flaunted?) its role as an independent check on the Committee on Infractions. Appellants won some relief from penalties in 43 percent of the appealed cases from 2000 through 2009. During one five-year stretch from 2003 through 2007, only four of thirteen appealed decisions were upheld in their entirety by the Infractions Appeals Committee.

Those kinds of results, of course, naturally created significant tension between the two committees and within the NCAA leadership. Myles Brand, president of the NCAA from 2002 until his death in 2009, regularly received complaints that cheating was out of control and that penalties were too weak to deter wrongdoers. The NCAA membership in particular was sending a "get tough" message to Brand. It was hard to get tough, though, if the Infractions Appeals Committee regularly reversed penalties on appeal because the committee deemed them to be excessive or inappropriate. The appeals committee, after all, had authority only to *reduce* penalties, not to enhance them.

In May 2005 Brand engaged a prominent Washington DC lawyer named James Duff to conduct an independent review of Division I enforcement and infractions processes. In a sense, the review was a follow-up to the Lee report that examined the same processes in the early 1990s, but it also was an outgrowth of litigation against the NCAA (in part, litigation spawned by the Alabama infractions case) and an effort to manage litigation risk. Like Rex Lee, Duff was highly respected, and the recommendations generated by his review surely would carry weight. At the time of his hire, Duff was the managing partner of the Washington DC office of the Baker Donelson law firm, founded by the grandfather of Howard Baker, former U.S. senator, White House chief of staff, and ambassador to Japan. In 2006, while wrapping up work on the NCAA assignment, Duff was named by U.S. Supreme Court chief justice John Roberts to direct the Administrative Office of the U.S. Courts.

Duff spoke with numerous stakeholders, including members of the infractions and appeals committees, and submitted his final report to NCAA leaders on June 12, 2006. Among about fifty recommendations were nine related to the appeals process. Perhaps most significant was a recommendation that the NCAA "confirm and articulate more clearly standards for alterations on appeal, such as 'abuse of discretion,' that encourage deference to the fact finder." That legalese represented a watershed moment for infractions appeals. Duff was recommending the demise of the loose "excessive or inappropriate" standard, which allowed the appeals committee essentially free rein to do what it wished with regard to penalties. If Duff's recommendation was adopted, the appeals committee would have to *defer* to the judgment of the infractions committee, reversing penalties only if it could articulate how the infractions committee *abused* the *discretion* it had in assessing penalties.

Various stakeholders vetted the Duff recommendations thoroughly, but finally, in January 2008, the NCAA membership accepted a bylaw change that incorporated a new "abuse of discretion" standard: "A penalty determined by the Committee on Infractions shall not be set aside on appeal except on a showing by the appealing party that the penalty is excessive such that it constitutes an abuse of discretion." The standard remains the same today, but the bylaw language now refers to the new hearing panels of the committee: "A penalty prescribed by the hearing panel . . . shall not be set aside except on a showing by the appealing party that the panel abused its discretion."

The significance of the 2008 amendment cannot be overstated. The members of the Infractions Appeals Committee, nearly always lawyers, now knew that they were constrained by a much stricter standard. The assessment of penalties is committed to the discretion of the infractions committee, and only if the committee abuses that discretion can its penalties be overturned. In the twenty appeals I had handled for the infractions committee up to that point, the appeals committee had granted some penalty relief to appealing parties in fully half the cases. My last eight cases, from 2008 to 2010, were affirmed in their entirety.

But this greater consistency came years after the Infractions Appeals Committee affirmed the penalties in the Alabama case in September 2002. At that point, the committee was in full wonderland mode, so its full affirmance should have sent a strong message to Alabama fans that the penalties were not out of whack. The fans—and the University of Alabama—got the last word, however.

Did I mention graceful responses? The Committee on Infractions' postseason ban said that the Crimson Tide football team "shall end its 2002 and 2003 seasons with the playing of its last regularly scheduled, in-season contests and shall not be eligible to participate in any bowl game." The language left a loophole. During the summer of 2002, while the appeal was still pending, a headline in one Alabama newspaper screamed, "IN YOUR FACE BOWL." Alabama athletics officials had just announced the addition of a thirteenth game at the end of the 2002 regular season; the team would be headed to Hawaii—the first time an SEC team had played in Hawaii since 1975. Seems the University of Hawaii had an open date, and technically a trip to sunny Oahu in late November would be a "regularly scheduled, in-season contest" and certainly not a bowl game.

Hawaii was a top-twenty-five team in 2002 and gave the Crimson Tide a tussle before falling 21–16. The Warriors— now the Rainbow Warriors—had a high-powered passing offense but could not overcome Alabama's vaunted defense, which held Hawaii to -12 yards rushing. Without the thirteenth game in Hawaii, the Tide would have finished the season with nine wins; the added game allowed Alabama to extend its NCAA record of double-digit-win seasons (ten wins or more) to twenty-seven.

THE RATS YOU ARE

After the game, a Honolulu newspaper quoted Alabama offensive lineman Justin Smiley (later to be drafted in the second round by the San Francisco 49ers) as saying, it "came to mind" that the Hawaiian vacation was viewed as an opportunity to "stick it" to the NCAA. A more colorful quote came from a Tide fan named Darrell McIntyre, front man of a band known as Darrell McIntyre and Mojojuce. He twisted the famous jab at Neil Young in Lynyrd Skynyrd's "Sweet Home Alabama" to the following: "I hope the NCAA will remember, Alabama don't need those sons-of-bitches around anyhow."

The Alabama players, coaches, and fans had such a good time in Hawaii that the athletics administration decided to do it again in 2003, the second year of the football program's postseason ban. Perhaps they had too good of a time on the beaches of Waikiki. The Tide lost to Hawaii 37–29 to finish the season at 4-9.

One might hope that the 2003 season is an indication that NCAA sanctions do have a bite. Perhaps they do in the short run, but teams typically rebound pretty quickly, even after harsh sanctions. Even Penn State was 8-4 the year after its remarkable set of sanctions. SMU, of course, is the exception, which indicates why the death penalty is so scary. In no time, the Crimson Tide football program returned to its tradition of dominance, winning five national championships in the next thirteen years and steamrolling to double-digit-win seasons every year from 2008 to 2017. Of course, the addition of the Hawaii games in 2002 and 2003 helped to blunt the impact that the 2002 sanctions may have had on recruiting.

In response to the In-Your-Face Bowls, the Committee on Infractions changed the language of its postseason penalty. To avoid rewarding bad actors, the committee's boilerplate language now would add the following: "Moreover, during the two years of this postseason ban, the football team may not take advantage of the exceptions to the limit in the number of football contests that are provided in Bylaw 17.10.5.2." Among those exceptions is an allowance for a thirteenth game in Hawaii, expanding the typical limit of a twelve-game regular season.

In 2009 the University of Alabama was back before the Committee on Infractions. The committee report summarized the problem: "Beginning in at least the 2005–06 academic year and continuing through the fall of 2007, the institution's textbook distribution system allowed approximately 200 student-athletes to obtain impermissible textbooks and supplies, with a total retail value of approximately $40,000. Approximately $21,950 of this total was obtained by student-athletes identified by the institution as 'intentional wrongdoers.'" This time the university admitted institutional responsibility—it failed to monitor adequately its textbook-distribution program to ensure that its student athletes were not stealing, primarily by obtaining free books and providing them to friends. The violations were systemic within the athletics department, stretching across sixteen separate sports, and only seven of the "intentional wrongdoers" were football players. Thus, despite the infractions committee's concern about the university's "extensive recent history of infractions cases," the committee decided against harsh sanctions such as another postseason ban.

Football players, however, accounted for some of the largest values of improperly obtained books. (The top four violators, accounting for thefts of over $13,000, were all football players.) The university had declared all the intentional violators ineligible to compete, so the committee vacated the wins in which the ineligible football players competed, wiping out a ten-win season in 2005. Naturally, the university appealed the penalty, but that pesky triple-repeat-violator status got in the way, and the Infractions Appeals Committee denied relief.

7

Cooperation

The only thing that will redeem mankind is cooperation.

BERTRAND RUSSELL

We've noted the importance of institutional cooperation previously. In 2002 Alabama was "staring down the barrel of a
gun," facing the possibility of the death penalty as a two-time
repeat violator. In 2005 Baylor, also a two-time repeat violator,
was even closer to the death penalty, considering what went
down in Waco under Dave Bliss. What saved both institutions
was their exceptional cooperation with the NCAA.

So SMU remains the only Division I program to have received
the death penalty from the Committee on Infractions. No one
ever talks about the *Division III* infractions committee leveling the death penalty against the tennis program at Mac-
Murray College in 2005 or about the *Division II* committee's
three-year extension of a soccer program suspension at Morehouse College in 2003. There's some good trivia for your next
dinner party. And if you really want to impress, you can add
two other Division I programs to the de facto death penalty
list: the 1952–53 Kentucky and 1973–75 Southwestern Louisiana men's basketball programs. Both programs were prohibited from outside competition, but through processes that
predated committee-imposed penalties and long before the
NCAA legislated the death penalty in 1985. Kentucky's one-
year "ban" resulted from an NCAA-imposed boycott by other
member institutions.

Lest one misunderstand, SMU clearly was not alone in its shenanigans of the late seventies and early eighties. Indeed, if the accounts of former recruited athletes are to be believed, SMU may even have been on the low side in the payment-to-players game. In David Whitford's book, for example, he quotes one former student athlete as saying that SMU recruiters were "pikers" compared to some of the competition. Another recruit said that SMU was no more than "competitive in the Southwest Conference. SMU wasn't the bad guy on the block."

In fact, SMU may have been motivated to cheat even by what its nearest rival was doing. Across town in Fort Worth, another religiously affiliated school, Texas Christian University (TCU), was engaged in similar misconduct, right at the heart of the time when SMU was achieving its greatest success . . . and facing its biggest challenges in trying to stay on top. In 1986, a year before SMU received the death penalty, the Division I Committee on Infractions imposed severe sanctions on TCU—a one-year postseason ban, the loss of thirty-five scholarships over two years, forfeiture of $343,203 in television revenue from the 1983 and 1984 seasons, and disassociation of six boosters—for payments to seven players. The payments were every bit as egregious as those being paid at SMU: up-front cash payments ranging up to $15,000, monthly payments up to $1,100, cash bonuses of several hundred dollars, and up to $5,000 for down payments on cars. Moreover, some of TCU's violations were downright ungodly. Not only did the committee find regular booster payments to players, but it also tagged the institution for "excessive entertainment" that included providing prostitutes to high school recruits.

It was TCU's first major case in football, though, so the death penalty was off the table. Although TCU did have a major case in men's basketball in 1981, within five years of the infractions in the 1986 case, the death penalty was new, and it hardly would have been imposed for the first time on a sport that had not been involved in a prior case. In addition, the infractions committee explicitly lauded the TCU chancellor's "lead-

ership and forthright approach in resolving the issues in the
case and the full cooperation extended by university officials,
coaching staff members and numerous student-athletes in all
phases of the processing of this case." Had it not been for that
cooperation and "forthright approach," the committee made
it clear the penalties would have stung a lot harder. Indeed,
the most remarkable aspect of the TCU infractions report
is that the committee explicitly set forth a set of penalties it
would have imposed in the absence of those mitigating factors: *three-year* postseason and television bans and *no* new
scholarships for two years.

The SMU and TCU cases from the mid-1980s are as relevant today as they were then. The SMU experience still should
send a strong message to any school receiving major sanctions: don't come back; stay out of repeat-violator status. The
TCU case similarly should serve as a deterrent to committing
major violations. But the TCU decision also offers a significant
carrot in addition to the big stick: if you *are* caught in major
violations, be cooperative, honest, and forthcoming.

Cooperation is something we teach our children and something
our politicians and leaders espouse. But when one is in trouble,
a habitual, deep-seated instinct toward self-preservation often
kicks in. When it does, the truth comes second; cooperation,
a distant third. And it is this instinct toward self-preservation
that makes NCAA investigations so difficult. As we'll explore
more deeply in the next chapter, the NCAA enforcement staff's
investigative powers are quite limited. With no subpoena power
or other tools to *compel* cooperation, the staff must rely on
the voluntary participation of witnesses. And witnesses know
that, so stonewalling, denial, and delay are all too common
during investigations.

The NCAA certainly has leverage over its member institutions, which are bound by governing legislation to cooperate. Bylaw 19.2.3 states in part, regarding the responsibility
to cooperate, "Current and former institutional staff mem-

bers or prospective or enrolled student-athletes of member institutions have an affirmative obligation to cooperate fully with and assist the NCAA enforcement staff, the Committee on Infractions and the Infractions Appeals Committee to further the objectives of the Association and its infractions program. The responsibility to cooperate requires institutions and individuals to protect the integrity of investigations and to make a full and complete disclosure of any relevant information, including any information requested by the enforcement staff or relevant committees."

That is relatively new language. Prior to 2013 the bylaw imposed the responsibility to cooperate only on "institutional representatives," in recognition of the practical limitations on both NCAA and member institution authority. University officials can exert pressure on people under their control, including *current* coaches and student athletes, and they often do—for instance, deciding who must fall on the sword for the greater good of the institution. But many infractions cases must be built on knowledge possessed by individuals who are *not* or are no longer under the control of the institution—fired coaches; former student athletes who have graduated, transferred, or otherwise used up their eligibility; or boosters. And if those individuals choose not to cooperate, no NCAA investigator, committee, or university can compel them to do so. Even *prospective* student athletes fall into this category, although the NCAA conceivably could withhold eligibility certification for failure to cooperate.

So the legislative language imposing a responsibility to cooperate on *former* institutional staff members seems like wishful thinking. While the NCAA would *like* all involved individuals to cooperate, only current staff members or student athletes are really on the hook; others with relevant information simply may refuse to cooperate. (Current employees or student athletes include those who have moved on to another NCAA institution, over which the NCAA does have authority.)

Even if the enforcement staff does obtain the voluntary

cooperation of a witness, corroborating that individual's testimony or evidence often is difficult, unless others are willing to come forward as well. Far too many cases are based, and resolved, on the testimony of witnesses whose credibility cannot be adequately tested, either by corroborating evidence or through forceful cross-examination. Just as ex-employees or boosters, for example, are outside the control of a university, they also are outside the control of the Committee on Infractions, which has no means of compelling their testimony at a hearing. So the committee is left to assess credibility in many cases on the basis of a cold record . . . and to ask unanswerable questions: What is the witness's angle? Does the person have an ax to grind because of a lost job, ruined career, or athletic promise cut short? Is the witness motivated by vengeance? If so, does that make the witness unreliable, or is he or she honestly trying to right perceived wrongs, to bring to light perceived injustices?

These challenges highlight the importance of securing cooperation in infractions cases. With all the competing interests involved, the only way to achieve any real sense of justice is for all the actors to work together. That is why cooperation typically is the single largest mitigating factor during the investigative phase of a major infractions case. The enforcement staff comments on the institution's level of cooperation at virtually every infractions hearing. Under the bylaws, "exemplary" cooperation can be a substantial mitigator in the penalty phase as well.

As important as cooperation is to an effective rules-enforcement program, it also presents some interesting quandaries. How much credit, for example, should an institution involved in egregious misconduct expect for its cooperation after the misconduct is exposed? Should the university's *obligation* to cooperate minimize such credit? These questions will be considered in the context of a prominent case in which institutional cooperation may have played an outsized role. The case, involving the Michigan men's basketball program, was similar to the Alabama case in that it involved a bad-actor booster engaged not only in NCAA violations but also in *criminal* behavior. In such a case, university and NCAA investigators may be able to leverage the tools *prosecutors* have in putting together criminal cases—subpoena power and credible threats of contempt of court, perjury, fines, or jail time.

February in Miami . . . a welcome escape from the bitter cold for many members of the Committee on Infractions. The date was February 14, 2003—Valentine's Day. The committee had worked hard all day ensconced in a hotel meeting room, hearing a major infractions case involving the University of Michigan men's basketball program. It was time to relax. One of the committee members was a local—Paul Dee, the athletics director and general counsel at the University of Miami—and he had arranged to host the committee at one of his favorite Cuban restaurants. Because it was Valentine's weekend, several spouses and partners had joined the group on this trip. The food was incredible, the conversation light, until one of the committee members delivered sobering news that Ed Martin had died earlier that day, back in Detroit. His death was sudden and unexpected—apparently the result of a pulmonary embolism, according to a spokesperson for Henry Ford Hospital.

February in Michigan . . . not so nice; one has to be careful on the roads. The Michigan infractions case—at the heart of which was booster Ed Martin—began seven years earlier, at roughly 5:00 a.m. on February 17, 1996. On a stretch of State Highway 14 between Ann Arbor and Detroit, a sport-utility vehicle carrying six young men was involved in a rollover accident. The first officer on the scene, a Washtenaw County deputy sheriff, said the road actually was dry; the SUV hit snow and ice as it left the roadway. "The driver must have fallen asleep," he said. "The car kept going straight where there was a curve in the road. The tire marks showed that."

The driver, Maurice Taylor, denied falling asleep, perhaps out of pride since he had no other explanation for losing control of the vehicle. Taylor was a sophomore on the University of Michigan men's basketball team, and not just any player. A starter, Taylor had been named Big 10 Freshman of the Year in 1995. Four teammates, including three other starters, were in the vehicle with Taylor—Louis Bullock, Willie Mitchell, Ron Oliver, and Robert Traylor. The sixth occupant was a blue-chip recruit, Mateen Cleaves of Flint, who was on his official recruiting visit to Ann Arbor.

Robert "Tractor" Traylor, a 320-pound behemoth and starter that year at center as a freshman, broke his arm in the accident and was lost for the remainder of the season. Remarkably, the others all walked away, shaken and bruised but otherwise fine. Shortly thereafter, Willie Mitchell transferred to the University of Alabama–Birmingham, and Mateen Cleaves signed with cross-state rival Michigan State. Four of the six players, including Cleaves, eventually would go on to be drafted into the NBA. Such was the power of the Michigan program at the time, following a 1989 national championship and the subsequent wonder years of the Fab Five.

Few sports fans alive at the time will forget the 1991 class of the Fab Five—Juwan Howard, Ray Jackson, Jimmy King, Jalen Rose, and Chris Webber. In 1993 Mitch Albom labeled them "the greatest class ever recruited," and the moniker has stuck ever since. They had the swagger, and they could back it up. To date, they remain the only NCAA Division I men's basketball team to reach the national finals with an all-freshman starting five. They reached the finals in both 1992 and 1993, the Fab Five's freshman and sophomore years. Four of the five went on to play in the NBA.

The SUV accident in 1996 naturally drew the attention of the media. Sports fans everywhere, and particularly Wolverines fans, shuddered to think about what *could* have happened. But as the story unfolded, attention shifted from the relief of avoiding tragedy to other details, such as why the players were out on the highway at 5:00 a.m. And who owned that new Ford Explorer, *Limited Edition*? And if they were coming from Detroit, wasn't that a problem? Detroit is only about forty miles east of Michigan's Ann Arbor campus; as it turns out, though, that's ten miles past the thirty-mile radius permissible for entertaining a prospect (Cleaves) on an official visit.

The initial news from the university was pretty innocuous. The players had attended a party in Detroit; Taylor, the driver and Cleaves's designated host, said they had lost track of time. The officer on the scene did not administer a breathalyzer or field sobriety test on Taylor, because "there was no smell of alcohol on him or any of the others, and no sign of alcohol in the van." Head coach Steve Fisher saw no reason for any player suspensions. He had told them, "Use good judgment. Don't stay out all night." That they disregarded his instructions "tells you they're 18-year-old kids, doing what a lot of them do."

Even the vehicle checked out. The SUV was coleased by Taylor's grandmother and aunt the previous September, and they let Taylor drive it while he was in school. However, skeptics later would wonder if the two women, who lived together in a modest Detroit home with a reported fair market value of $20,000, considerably less than the SUV's $30,000 price tag, might be unduly strapped by the monthly lease payments. Taylor's aunt, an employee of the Ford Motor Company, did get the Plan A discount on the Explorer, but that still left payments of roughly $600 a month.

All in all, no big deal—essentially a trip to Grandma's house, an after-party that ran late, a bit of bad luck on the road. The Michigan sports information office summarized the matter this way: "The group in the van drove 38 miles from campus to Robert Traylor's grandmother's home, and then a couple miles farther. Technically, it does exceed the 30-mile radius." An NCAA spokesperson concurred: "Going to a party a few miles over the 30-mile limit is considered a secondary, not a major, violation." She added that the likely punishment would be "educating the host [Taylor] of the error, perhaps removing the host from that duty for a while."

Except it wasn't just a trip to Grandma's house; they went "a couple miles farther" to the home of Ed Martin. Martin reportedly provided cash to all the players, including the recruit, Cleaves, before they headed off to a party at a room in the Westin Hotel in downtown Detroit. Media accounts reported alcohol, drugs, and strippers at the party, but those details would all come later too. Initial university investigations following the accident, stymied by Martin's refusal to cooperate, came up nearly empty-handed, despite the fact that Martin was well known within the Michigan athletics department.

Ed Martin was a retired Detroit autoworker and a rabid basketball fan and supporter in the Detroit area. For many years, he also ran an illegal gambling operation out of the Ford plants in the area, grossing hundreds of thousands of dollars. According to a later federal indictment, he laundered a good deal of that money, approximately $616,000, by "loaning" it to four University of Michigan basketball players, including a total of $336,000 to Louis Bullock, Maurice Taylor, and Robert Traylor—all occupants of the suv that cold February night.

To understand Ed Martin is to understand his influence on basketball in the Detroit area, from middle school all the way to the NBA. Chances are, if you were involved in basketball in the Detroit area in the 1980s and 1990s, you knew Ed Martin. There's also a good chance that if you were a basketball player of a certain caliber and you needed something—a pair of shoes, a hot meal, a ride—Ed Martin provided it. As Gregory Lord, one of Martin's one-time lawyers, put it, "Eddie had the best of intentions. He was a one-man equal opportunity office."

Yes, Ed Martin was the man on the scene for Detroit basketball, and despite some serious flaws, he was an extremely generous man who did a lot of good in his community. Lord said Martin had financially helped between five hundred and one thousand Detroit-area athletes over the years, including at least a dozen who made it to the NBA. According to Lord, "If you were getting drafted or announcing your college choice and you needed a suit, Eddie would help you."

The recipients of Martin's largesse included men and women and even athletes in other sports—Lord mentioned volleyball as well—but men's basketball was in his blood, in the marrow of his bones. Martin was invariably described (even by himself) as a "basketball junkie." And like a junkie to the spike, he could not stay away. He needed more. He needed access.

Martin was a good friend of Perry Watson when Watson was the head coach at Detroit's Southwestern High School, and Martin often could be seen sitting on the bench with the assistant coaches during high school games. Martin literally had a front-row seat to the up-and-coming basketball talent in the Detroit area . . . and perhaps a place in their mamas' hearts by providing "meals, clothing, money and other benefits" to players and their families (in the words of the eventual infractions report). One of Perry Watson's best at Southwestern was Jalen Rose, who joined the rest of the Fab Five at Michigan in 1991, the same year Watson became a Wolverines assistant coach. (Watson spent only two years at Michigan before moving on to a very successful head coaching career at Detroit Mercy.)

Martin also went way back with Scott Perry, who also served as an assistant coach at Michigan from 1993 to 1997. Their relationship began during Perry's playing days at St. Cecilia, a high school basketball powerhouse in Detroit. (Martin's son, Carlton, later would play with Perry at the University of Detroit Jesuit High School.) It was actually Perry who had arranged for Cleaves's recruiting trip that fateful night in 1996. He later told university investigators that the Michigan players on the trip must have viewed Cleaves "as a kid that we really wanted to sign, and I guess that was their way of showing him a good time to get him here to Michigan. Obviously it was poor judgment." Perry went on to have an illustrious career in basketball, including high-level management positions with the Seattle Supersonics, Detroit Pistons, Orlando Magic, and Sacramento Kings. Cleaves was indeed one they wanted to sign; he ended up as a two-time Big 10 Player of the Year at Michigan State, leading the Spartans to a national championship in 2000 and earning a first-round NBA draft selection.

So Ed Martin had close connections—and access—to the University of Michigan program, not only through Watson and Perry, but also through head coach Steve Fisher and his predecessor, Bill Frieder. Martin was present in the home of another Southwestern star in the early eighties when Frieder visited the prospect's home. After the athlete enrolled at Michigan, Martin began attending Michigan games and practices in the mid-1980s, becoming "a fixture at Michigan's basketball arena," including the locker room, according to the later infractions report. When Frieder left Michigan in 1989 for Arizona State and Steve Fisher was elevated to head coach, Martin cultivated a personal relationship with Fisher, including providing the barbecue for a wake at Fisher's home following the death of Fisher's father. By 1991 Martin was a regular on the Michigan coaches' complimentary-pass list, receiving dozens of free tickets to home games over the next few years. In 1992 he stayed at the team hotel at the Final Four in Minneapolis.

In essence, the Michigan basketball coaches afforded Martin the same kind of insider status that Alabama, around the same time, was providing Logan Young. Fisher, the infractions committee would say later, included Martin "in the innermost circle around his teams." Nothing wrong with boosters in the fold, as long as they're monitored and keep their noses clean. But ultimately Martin's insider status would lead to Fisher's demise at Michigan. Fisher was a hero to Wolverines fans after leading Michigan to a national title in 1989 (after taking over the team from Frieder on the eve of the tourney) and then the Fab Five to consecutive Final Four appearances. In the aftermath of the 1996 automobile accident, however, things just smelled too bad.

Rumors swirled about Martin giving money and other benefits to star players, but an internal university investigation following the accident yielded no hard evidence that the rumors were true. Martin refused to cooperate with investigators; as a consequence, the university formally disassociated him from the athletics program in March 1997. Further investigation by an outside law firm, Bond, Schoeneck, and King, with a team led by go-to guy Mike Glazier, substantiated only minor infractions, including Martin being present in Robert Traylor's home when coaches Fisher and Perry came recruiting and Martin providing food and improper transportation to Traylor and his grandmother.

The independent report, though, made clear that the investigators were not absolving the university; instead, they were simply saying no major violations could be *proven*. In doing so, they clearly expressed frustration about the limits on their investigative reach, particularly in light of reports in the *Detroit Free Press* quoting anonymous sources saying they knew of Martin providing cash to Michigan players:

> This is a most unique case in that virtually all of the allegations that spawned and fueled the investigation were made by sources the media, which brought the allegations to light, did not name. In fact, there have been no published allegations by an identified individual who claimed to have firsthand knowledge that Ed Martin either assisted in the recruitment of prospects to Michigan or provided impermissible benefits to Michigan student-athletes. . . . Without the opportunity to identify and question the individuals who claim to have direct knowledge and information about Martin's provision of benefits to prospective and enrolled student-athletes, it is not possible to conduct a complete investigation.

So the odor lingered, and even though the report did not implicate Fisher directly in any violations, he was out as head coach within the week, just days before the start of practice for the 1997–98 basketball season. "I just felt we needed a new direction in Michigan basketball," said new athletics director Tom Goss in announcing Fisher's firing. Goss did not cite anything specific from the report, but a careful reading of the report suggested two potential problem areas beyond Fisher's general relationship with Martin. The report indicated that Fisher, to his credit, actually had headed off two potential major violations by Martin, involving a deposit on an apartment for Traylor and Bullock and an offer to buy airline tickets for Bullock's parents to attend a tournament in Puerto Rico. Fisher effectively stopped both violations but failed to report the incidents to the compliance staff. A question also arose about whether Fisher had been completely forthcoming about his involvement in providing complimentary game tickets to Martin.

The university's investigative limits, of course, were shared by the NCAA. The witnesses who stiffed the university's investigators were not going to talk to the NCAA, and without subpoena power, the enforcement staff likely would be unable to make a stronger case. So, perhaps reluctantly, the NCAA announced in December 1997 its acceptance of the Michigan report. While it added an additional secondary violation—Martin's contact with recruit Mateen Cleaves on the night of the accident in 1996—it was satisfied that no major violations could be proven. The NCAA would investigate no further; aside from a slap on the wrist for secondary violations, the case was closed . . . until May 1999. Out of a clear blue sky, the FBI came calling. Things were about to get interesting.

On April 28, 1999, agents from the FBI and the IRS had conducted simultaneous raids on the Detroit-area homes of individuals suspected of participating in an illegal gambling operation in the area's Ford plants. One of those homes belonged to Ed Martin, the purported ringleader of the operation. According to a May 14 account in the *Detroit Free Press*, the agents' search warrants were supported in part by wiretaps that recorded conversations between Martin and several former University of Michigan basketball stars. The agents executed the warrants on Martin's home, ten other homes, an office, and a safe-deposit box. The *Free Press*, citing an unnamed source "close to the investigation," reported that the agents confiscated several loaded handguns, over $165,000 in cash, and a trove of gambling records. The gambling did not involve sports gambling but, instead, revolved around gambling on numbers picked by the Michigan lottery. "Martin ran a numbers operation, not a sports book," said John Bell, the special agent in charge of the local FBI office.

The seized records, including evidence of a Western Union transaction between Martin and Robert Traylor, indicated that Martin had given cash payments and other benefits to several Michigan players, as well as to other Detroit-area college prospects. The payments went back to the 1980s and, according to the *Free Press*, implicated not only Louis Bullock, Maurice Taylor, and Robert Traylor but also two members of the Fab Five—Jalen Rose and Chris Webber.

The University of Michigan was back on the hot seat, and if Rose and Webber were implicated, the glorious Fab Five records were in jeopardy. Certainly the allegations were not far-fetched, given Martin's reputation for taking care of top Detroit talent. Martin long had been known to be a friend of the Webber family. He had known the Webbers since Chris was in middle school, and he had attended church where Chris's father was a deacon. Rose, as noted previously, was one of Perry Watson's stars at Southwestern High School, at a time when Martin had deep connections to that program (although at the end of Watson's high school coaching career, he effectively disassociated Martin from his program for being "too close" to some of his players).

The infractions investigation would begin anew, but first it had to take a back seat to the criminal investigation. The *Free Press* had noted in its May 1999 report that a federal grand jury already had subpoenaed several Michigan players and coaches. They would have to talk . . . under oath and under threat of criminal sanctions if they failed to cooperate or lied.

Grand jury testimony, of course, is secret, so we don't know what the witnesses said. But their statements, along with the documents seized in the raid, were enough for Martin to sign a plea agreement with federal prosecutors in March 2000. Martin and his son, Carlton, were facing multiple charges, with the possibility of lengthy prison sentences. Under the plea agreement, they would each plead guilty to one count of illegal gambling and one count of tax evasion, for which they would receive no more than fifteen months in federal prison. In exchange for the reduced prison time, each man agreed to cooperate not only with the ongoing federal gambling investigation but also with any university investigation related to the men's "associations with representatives, associates, employees, athletes, and/or those affiliated with the University of Michigan."

The plea bargain held for only two months; in May 2000 Martin and his son both backed out of the deal. Ever the gamblers, they essentially opted to roll the dice at a trial. Presumably, Martin did not want to detail his relationships with former players and coaches, but he should have known what was coming. The federal prosecutors, left at the altar, upped the ante. They subpoenaed more witnesses to testify before the grand jury and expanded the scope of the investigation. Nearly two years later, on March 21, 2002, the grand jury handed up an *eight-count* indictment against Martin, including charges of illegal gambling, laundering money, and conspiracy to launder money. And to really up the ante, prosecutors charged Martin's wife, Hilda, with conspiracy as well. She now faced prison time along with her husband. Son Carlton already was incarcerated; he had had a change of heart and pled guilty to gambling charges. He was sentenced in June 2001 to eighteen months in federal prison.

With respect to the money laundering and conspiracy counts, the indictment alleged that Martin made payments to players as a way to conceal the profit he was making from the gambling operation. The specific allegations surely shocked a lot of observers: Ed Martin had either given or "loaned" a total of $616,000 to four former Michigan ballplayers—$280,000 to

Chris Webber, $160,000 to Robert Traylor, $105,000 to Maurice Taylor, and $71,000 to Louis Bullock. The indictment did not allege payments to Jalen Rose. Rose later would admit publicly that he accepted money from Martin, but not in substantial amounts: "He gave me money before, but it wasn't in excess—you know—trying to allow me to be rich. You know, it was allowing me to have a couple of dollars in my pocket . . . just something to make me feel like I can go to a movie, go to a show, I can get a pair of gym shoes, I can get—you know—a fresh outfit."

Martin had told others that he truly viewed the payments as loans, part of his retirement plan and a win-win for everyone. He would loan money to these top players, local boys at that, to help them through lean times, and then, when they went pro, they would remember Uncle Ed and pay back the loans. Of course, it also gave him somewhere to put all that cash he'd been making through his numbers game. Whether he *really* expected repayment is unknown; if he did, it turned out to be a lousy investment strategy. Later reports suggested that only Chris Webber paid back any of the funds—a total of $38,200, which would be a terrible return on $280,000 (if that's what was "loaned"; Webber admitted to accepting $38,200 from Martin, but no more). As a return on $616,000, it's like burning money. But basketball was coursing through Martin's veins, and in the throes of a habit, the habit can start making the decisions.

In May 2002, two months after Ed and Hilda Martin were indicted and arrested, they were facing sobering realities. Trial was set for June 17, the prosecutors had a new wave of evidence, and the Martins faced the prospect of lengthy prison terms. Basketball was one thing, freedom quite another . . . and the latter seemed increasingly in jeopardy. And so at age sixty-eight, Martin took a new plea deal: plead guilty to one count of conspiracy to commit money laundering and the other seven counts are dropped; your wife walks and you get to keep your house; cooperate fully with ongoing investigations, including both the federal prosecutors' and the university's, and the judge *might* go easy in sentencing. Even standing alone, the conspiracy count carried a maximum of twenty years and a fine that doubled that of the laundered money, or up to roughly $1.2 million. Prosecutors suggested the possibility of a prison term of thirty to thirty-seven months, but the judge made it clear that his ultimate sentence would depend in large measure on the value of Martin's information.

University of Michigan officials reacted to the plea agreement by pledging a renewed commitment to unearthing the full truth of Martin's relationship with the men's basketball program. The investigative focus would not be on the players and the "loans"—that was covered in the indictment. Instead, the university, in cooperation with the NCAA, would focus on the administration of the men's basketball program. "There are a lot of factors not relevant to the criminal case," said the university's general counsel. "What did [university officials] know or what did the institution do about it?"

Over the next few months, the university conducted that renewed investigation, ultimately announcing its conclusion at a press conference on November 7, 2002. University president Mary Sue Coleman, acknowledging "a day of great shame for the University," said the university's investigation, conducted jointly with NCAA enforcement staff representatives, included additional interviews with former athletics department personnel and a July 26 meeting between attorneys representing both the university and Ed Martin (together with NCAA enforcement staff members, an FBI agent, and an assistant U.S. attorney). A university report to the NCAA confirmed the $616,000 in payments detailed in the federal indictment. Finally, President Coleman announced a set of self-imposed sanctions:

> Forfeiting all games won while the four players were ineligible, including the 1992 and 1993 Final Fours, the entire 1992–93 season, and the seasons from fall 1995 through

spring of 1999. The University has removed four championship banners that were hanging in Crisler Arena, and
will excise mention of any victories from all programs and
written materials

Repaying to the NCAA about $450,000 the University received
for postseason play with those ineligible players

Declaring the men's basketball team ineligible to participate
in the 2003 NCAA Division I Men's Basketball Championship Tournament, as well as the 2003 National Invitational
Tournament

Placing the basketball program on probation for two years . . .

An investigation that had begun nearly seven years earlier,
after the February 1996 rollover accident, was finally over.
Everyone was in agreement with the essential facts, so the
infractions hearing could be fast-tracked. It was too late to put
the matter on the infractions committee's December agenda,
but the case could be heard at the committee's next scheduled
meeting in February 2003. University and NCAA representatives appeared before the committee on February 14, 2003,
the same day Ed Martin died. At the time of his death, Martin was awaiting sentencing for "conspiracy to launder mon-
etary instruments."

The Committee on Infractions released its public report on
May 8, 2003. The report made clear that the infractions hearing was straightforward: "There was universal agreement with
regard to the facts." And the principal facts came straight out of
the federal indictment: Ed Martin had paid Webber $280,000,
Traylor $160,000, Taylor $105,000, and Bullock $71,000. The
only thing left to do with respect to the findings was to couch
them in NCAA "infractions speak," rather than in terms of
criminal activity. So the violations became "impermissible
recruiting inducements and extra benefits by an athletics representative." Ed Martin, of course, was the "athletics representative," and Michigan did not contest the enforcement staff's

allegation that Martin had become a booster of the University of Michigan, at least since the spring of 1992. Nor did the university contest the fact that some payments were made while at least one of the players was still a prospect (i.e., recruiting inducements), while other payments came after the players' enrollment at Michigan (i.e., extra benefits).

One other university concession was critical. Ordinarily, the NCAA operates under a four-year statute of limitations, and some of the violations, particularly with respect to Chris Webber, went back a decade or more. But the NCAA bylaws provide for exceptions to the statute of limitations in two circumstances that could be relevant to the Michigan case: (1) "a pattern of willful violations on the part of the institution or individual involved, which began before but continued into the four-year period," and (2) "a blatant disregard for . . . fundamental recruiting, extra benefit, academic or ethical-conduct bylaws or . . . an effort to conceal the occurrence of the violation." By self-imposing a forfeiture of games dating back to 1992, the University of Michigan implicitly was conceding that the statute of limitations did not preclude "dated" findings. The university did not press the statute of limitations at the infractions hearing; nonetheless, the committee addressed the issue in its report: "While some of the violations did occur several years ago, the actions of the athletics representative [Martin] continued through most of the [1990s] and constituted a continuing pattern of NCAA violations until 1999."

The four-year statute of limitations dates back from the time the NCAA enforcement staff sends a notice of inquiry to the institution. In the Michigan case, that notice occurred in October 2002, following the federal indictment, Martin's plea agreement, and the brief ensuing investigation. So the four-year time period would date back to October 1998, and Martin's continuing pattern of violations extended into 1999. Remarkably, his payments to players continued even *after* the university disassociated him in 1997 and after the university closed its independent investigation that same year.

With full agreement on the facts, the infractions committee focused its attention on two remaining issues: (1) "the
extent, if any, of institutional culpability and responsibility"
and (2) whether additional sanctions, beyond those already
self-imposed by the university, were warranted. Interestingly,
the enforcement staff did not allege either lack of institutional
control or failure to monitor, the most serious *institutional*
violations. Perhaps that was a reflection of several factors,
including the dated nature of the infractions, the university's
cooperation in the investigation, and the recurrent difficulty
of assessing institutional blame for the actions of boosters.
(This case came before the infractions committee one year
after the Logan Young booster case involving Alabama football.
In that case the committee similarly found neither failure to
monitor nor lack of institutional control.) So the committee's
focus on institutional culpability and responsibility seemed
intertwined with the second question: Were additional penalties warranted *because* the university bore some responsibility for the violations?

Ultimately the committee answered that question: yes. In
something of an understatement, the committee said, "The
fact that the athletics representative was influential with talented men's basketball recruits in the Detroit area was not
lost on the men's basketball coaching staff at the university."
Just as Ed Martin, or any other booster, craves access and
influence with a particular institution and its players, so too
do college coaches crave access and influence with talented
recruits. And if that means snuggling up to individuals with
the juice to steer top talent (or keep talent happy), so be it. But
the relationship with these boosters is like dancing with a ven-
omous snake—the dancer never knows when, or if, the snake
will bite, but if it does, the dancer is in big trouble. If it doesn't
bite, though, the snake can bring the dancer riches—in the
college athletics world, named arenas and glory on the court.

The University of Michigan acknowledged this enticement
during the first investigation, in a 1997 report to the NCAA that

the infractions committee quoted in its 2003 report: "There are individuals who, like [Ed Martin], closely follow prep basketball in their communities and develop relationships with the prospects long before colleges begin recruiting them in their senior year of high school. Whether accurate or not, many college coaches perceive individuals like [Martin] to be influential in a prospect's decision on which school to attend. The coaches believe that if they want to successfully recruit prospects, they must be courteous to those individuals and treat them with respect."

Surely this situation is understandable. (And Michigan certainly wasn't alone. George Raveling, when he coached at Iowa, also recruited heavily in the Detroit area. He recognized Martin's value and paid the requisite tribute, including complimentary tickets to Hawkeyes games. Martin, Raveling said, "was a person you did not want to alienate.") The relationship also is difficult to navigate. But the infractions committee said the Michigan coaching staff had gone well beyond showing respect and courtesy; the basketball staff treated Martin "with great deference, extending privileges and benefits that are usually reserved for only the most highly regarded individuals associated with the university's athletics program. . . . Such treatment only served to encourage [Martin] in his illicit activities relative to prospects and student-athletes."

The committee detailed the relationship between the Michigan coaching staffs and Martin, noting that despite plenty of red flags, the coaches "continued to tolerate, if not embrace him." That embrace resulted in the same kind of insider status that proved problematic in the Alabama–Logan Young case. Insider status elevates an institution's responsibility to monitor and control the activities of its boosters.

The committee commended the university and its president for taking decisive action and implementing meaningful self-imposed penalties. And indeed, the penalties were substantial. While a vacation of records is par for the course when schools compete with ineligible student athletes (the athletes became ineligible when they accepted illicit payments), few schools self-impose a postseason ban. The committee also commended Michigan's cooperation in the case, "including its efforts in conjunction with federal authorities to develop complete information in the case beyond the reach of the NCAA's investigative abilities." That cooperation was an important mitigating factor, to which the committee accorded "significant weight in its determination of appropriate penalties."

The committee's job ultimately is to balance the mitigating factors, which counsel toward leniency, against the aggravating factors that weigh in favor of harsh penalties. In the Michigan case, the aggravating factors were exceptional:

> Despite this mitigation, however, the case remains one of the most serious ever to come before the committee. It represents the largest acknowledged cash payments ($616,000) in the history of NCAA infractions cases, to some of the most prominent men's basketball student-athletes of an era. These student-athletes led the university to NCAA Tournament appearances in four of the six years in which the violations occurred, including two consecutive Final Four appearances in 1992 and 1993 and the NIT championship in 1997. . . . The violations provided a staggering competitive and ancillary recruiting advantage over other member institutions. The fact that the university's men's basketball coaching staffs embraced the representative and accorded him insider status within their programs further elevated the seriousness of the case.

In the final analysis, the committee concluded that the balance favored stronger sanctions than those self-imposed by the university. The committee added a second year to the ban on postseason competition; reduced the total number of scholarships in men's basketball by one (thirteen down to twelve) for each of four years; increased the period of probation from two to four years; and effectively directed the university to disassociate for ten years the four former athletes involved in the violations (Bullock, Taylor, Traylor, and Webber), in part because of "some of the student-athletes' refusal to cooperate with university and NCAA investigators." The disassociation was in the form of a show-cause penalty; the committee did not explicitly *direct* the disassociation, but it would require the university to show cause why it should not be punished further if it did *not* disassociate.

Surely, for a case involving such serious violations, the four-year probation was not a surprise, and as noted previously, it's not a substantial penalty anyway. Probation requires a rededication to compliance, annual compliance reports, and keeping one's nose clean, but the university was subject to a *five-year* repeat-violator window anyway. The scholarship reduction probably was irksome, because of its four-year length, but certainly manageable; a team ought to be able to have success with a twelve-man roster. The disassociation was lengthy, but some disassociation was to be expected, particularly in light of some players' lack of cooperation. The additional year of a postseason ban, however, stuck in the craw of Michigan officials. "The additional postseason ban is unfair and counter to the core mission of NCAA enforcement," said athletics director Bill Martin. President Mary Sue Coleman, announcing an appeal of the postseason ban, echoed Martin's comments, adding, "I am deeply disappointed that the committee is punishing our current, uninvolved student-athletes."

A postseason ban always presents an interesting dilemma. It invariably punishes "current, uninvolved" student athletes. *Involved* student athletes (at least those involved in serious infractions) typically are rendered ineligible to compete, and by the time an infractions case works its way through the investigative and hearing processes, involved individuals often are long gone. NCAA transfer rules attempt to ameliorate the impact on innocent student athletes by allowing them to transfer to another school and play immediately, without sitting out the one year that typically applies to transfers, when their school becomes subject to a postseason ban. But that certainly is not a viable option for many student athletes, particularly if they are invested in their education at their current institution. So the postseason ban undoubtedly works a hardship on innocents. On the other hand, the ban has become one of the few tools the NCAA enforcement system has for punishing the most serious violators (and hopefully deterring others from committing serious violations). This is particularly so in the absence of a viable death penalty.

A body of NCAA case law has developed, primarily through the infractions appeals process, that requires both committees (infractions and infractions appeals) to consider "the impact on innocent student-athletes and coaches" in the assessment and imposition of penalties. This factor seems tailor-made to postseason bans. But it is only one of several factors to be considered: the others are the nature, number, and seriousness of the violations; the conduct and motives of the individuals involved in the violations; the corrective actions taken by the institution; a comparison of the penalties with those in other cases; the cooperation of the institution in the investigation; and a catchall—NCAA policies regarding fairness in, and equitable resolution of, infractions cases.

The reader can readily see that the determination of penalties is far from an exact science. A new penalty matrix, akin to sentencing guidelines, attempts to channel the committees' discretion, but ultimately the committees still must assess the weight of aggravating and mitigating factors. In the Michigan case, the infractions committee credited several significant mitigation factors, including the university's cooperation in the investigation, its meaningful self-imposed penalties, the age of the violations (and thus the fact that all involved parties were no longer with the institution), and the impact on current student athletes and coaches. On the other hand, the committee faced five primary aggravating factors: (1) the extraordinary level of cash payments (the largest in NCAA history); (2) the extended period of time (1992–99) over which the payments occurred; (3) the fact that the violations involved four student athletes of star quality who voided their amateur status by accepting the payments; (4) the enormous competitive advantage gained by using those ineligible student athletes; and (5) the university's embrace of Martin into the coaches' and teams' innermost circle, which served only to encourage his actions.

The infractions committee strives for consistency with its penalties, which always requires a comparison to other cases. The readiest comparison in the Michigan case was to the Alabama football case of the year before, which also involved very large payments by a booster granted insider status. (Recall that the appeals committee upheld a two-year postseason ban in the Alabama case.) The two cases had several parallels but one very significant difference—Michigan was not a repeat violator; Alabama was a two-timer.

In the end, Michigan won its appeal, and perhaps it should have, given the fact that it was not a repeat violator. On the other hand, the committee had imposed two-year postseason bans in eleven cases during the prior decade, and not all involved repeat violators. The infractions committee chair, Tom Yeager, had over twenty-five years of NCAA enforcement experience, including many years as an NCAA enforcement staff member. In his public comments announcing the Michigan decision, he characterized the case as "one of the three or four most egregious" in the history of the NCAA. Nonetheless, the Infractions Appeals Committee deemed the second year of Michigan's postseason ban excessive and vacated the penalty. In doing so, the committee highlighted the importance of institutional cooperation:

> We have indicated that institutional cooperation is a factor that must be considered when fashioning penalties. In its decision, the Committee on Infractions did commend "the university's cooperation, including its efforts in conjunction with federal authorities to develop complete information beyond the reach of the NCAA's investigative abilities." We

believe, however, that the Committee on Infractions did not accord sufficient weight to the institution's unique level of cooperation. In this case, the institution's and NCAA's investigations were stymied for several years by the investigators' inability to interview any of the parties directly involved in the violations. In order to uncover the facts, the institution insisted that [Ed Martin] agree, as part of his federal criminal plea agreement, to cooperate with the institution's and NCAA's investigations. And, when the institution's request threatened the plea agreement, the institution successfully pressed the U.S. Attorney's office to insist on [Martin's] cooperation. Without [Martin's] cooperation pursuant to the plea agreement, the identities of the individuals involved and the amounts of the loans never would have been established, and there likely would have been no NCAA enforcement case. The institution's extraordinary efforts transcended "cooperation," and strongly militate against imposition of the second year of the postseason ban.

With all due respect, a couple of these statements bear further examination. The institution was stymied by its "investigators' inability to interview any of the parties directly involved in the violations"? True, Martin was a clam, but three of the others "directly involved in the violations" were current student athletes, at least at the time of the first investigation—Bullock, Taylor, and Traylor. Did the university not have significant leverage over them to elicit the truth? According to the infractions report, all three of them continued to accept payments from Martin after the first investigation ended and Martin was disassociated—Taylor and Traylor into 1998 and Bullock into 1999.

And is it true that without Martin's "cooperation pursuant to the plea agreement," insisted on by the university, "the identities of the individuals involved and the amounts of the loans never would have been established, and there likely would have been no NCAA enforcement case"? Martin did not cooperate until *after* the federal indictment, which detailed publicly "the identities of the individuals involved and the amounts of the loans." Indeed, all the relevant information on the actual NCAA violations was out in the open. And if it had not been out in the open by way of the indictment, it all would have been on display at a public trial. The prosecutors handed the NCAA its case on a silver platter, which is why the enforcement staff's allegations, and the Committee on Infractions' report, used the federal indictment as their template. Martin's cooperation following his plea agreement, which didn't even involve him directly (the meeting was with his attorneys, who confirmed the accuracy of the payments alleged in the indictment), *may* have been relevant to the university's effort to assess what *university officials* knew, when they knew it, and what they did about it. (Recall the university counsel's stated focus of the postplea investigation.) If so, that information also was within the knowledge of institutional actors (or former institutional actors).

This is not to reargue the Michigan case—as appeals coordinator in the case (arguing to uphold the infractions committee's penalties), I had my shot and I lost. Nor is it to diminish the university's cooperation—the infractions committee rightly praised the university's cooperative efforts and accorded them significant weight in determining penalties. What troubled me—and the full infractions committee—was the singular importance the appeals committee placed on cooperation, one factor in a nuanced, multifactor analysis. And it was not the first time, so perhaps I should have been prepared for the laser focus. In the Howard case mentioned in chapter 4, the appeals committee reduced a five-year probation to three years, despite an unprecedented scope of violations: five separate sports with major violations, including academic fraud, recruiting violations, and improper benefits to student athletes; unethical conduct by five different coaches, including not only deliberate violations but also lying to investigators; and lack of institutional control over the athletics program.

Why the reversal? The Committee on Infractions had not provided a sufficient "analysis of the mitigating factor of institutional cooperation/self-investigation."

The Howard and Michigan appeals decisions were the beginning of a trend, with more decisions over the next few years highlighting the infractions committee's failure to fully explain the impact of cooperation on the determination of penalties. Ironically, all of this occurred at a time when the infractions committee was being told by NCAA leaders that it was not tough enough on major violators.

In 2007 I was asked to chair a penalty subcommittee of the Committee on Infractions. Half (five) of the committee members served on the subcommittee; a member of the Infractions Appeals Committee also participated in the discussions, along with two enforcement staff representatives. Among many items on the subcommittee's agenda was clarification of the role of cooperation in major infractions cases. After more than a year of discussion, the subcommittee, with the support of the appeals committee member, recommended a bylaw change specifying that "full and complete cooperation in investigations and in disclosure of violations is an obligation of membership and does not mitigate sanctions imposed on either institutions or their staff members." The full infractions committee adopted the recommendation, agreeing that the bylaws already required all members of a university to "cooperate fully" in an investigation and that providing penalty relief for cooperation effectively minimized the gravity of some violations and was not fair to rules-compliant schools. *Failure* to cooperate fully, in the committee's judgment, should be an aggravating factor that *enhances* penalties, but credit should not be given to schools for doing what they are obligated to do.

Several more months of discussion, however, resulted in an about-face by the committee. Enforcement staff members ultimately convinced the committee that providing *no* credit, at least in exceptional cases, would undermine staff efforts to secure cooperation. And incentivizing schools and involved individuals to cooperate was critical in light of extreme limits on the enforcement staff's investigative powers. So the committee withdrew the proposed bylaw change before forwarding its recommendations to the NCAA Board of Directors in 2009. In its place, the committee added a couple of comments: (1) if a school or involved individual *did not* cooperate, the enforcement staff should bring an additional charge of failure to cooperate (which, of course, could enhance penalties if the committee made such a finding), and (2) if a school or involved individual *did* cooperate, the enforcement staff should categorize that cooperation at one of two levels— either the party simply did what was expected in meeting its obligation to cooperate or it provided "extraordinary" cooperation. One factor in assessing whether cooperation was extraordinary would be whether a school's investigative efforts or an involved individual's statements led to information that otherwise would not have been discovered by the enforcement staff. Only extraordinary cooperation would serve to mitigate penalties.

This essentially is the approach the infractions committee employs today, though the NCAA bylaws now speak of "exemplary," rather than "extraordinary," cooperation. In its public infractions reports, the committee typically will note only that the institution "met its obligation" under the relevant bylaws that require cooperation. But if the school has engaged in exemplary cooperation—typically by digging deeper than expected and unearthing information that would have been unavailable to the enforcement staff in its own investigation— the committee will recognize those efforts and give weight to them in the imposition of penalties. That does *not* mean, though, that a school will escape harsh penalties if egregious violations occurred.

Ultimately, then, the "new" regime is not significantly different from what it was at the time of the Michigan case. The committee considers the level of the school's cooperation and accords it appropriate weight, along with numerous other factors, in determining a set of penalties. Today the committee would be obligated to determine whether Michigan's cooperation was "exemplary," and I'm not sure the answer to that question is clear, even with the benefit of hindsight.

The Michigan case provides a reminder both of the investigative limits schools and NCAA enforcement staff members face and of the enhanced information-gathering tools available to prosecutors in a criminal investigation. When asked to speak to university or NCAA investigators, many witnesses simply can refuse to cooperate. If subpoenaed by a grand jury, however, a witness has to cooperate fully and truthfully. Otherwise, as Chris Webber discovered, the witness may face his own criminal charges. In September 2002, federal prosecutors indicted Webber—at the time, an NBA All-Star—on charges of obstruction of justice and lying to a federal grand jury in August 2000. All the charges, which also were made against Webber's father and aunt, stemmed from alleged misrepresentations about Webber's relationship with Ed Martin and whether or not he had accepted money or gifts from Martin.

Martin's death in February 2003 complicated the prosecutors' case. Obviously, Martin, who had already confessed to "loaning" Webber $280,000, would have been an important witness in the government's case against Webber. Prosecutors announced after Martin's death that their case against Webber would continue, but in early July 2003, a week before jury selection was to begin in Webber's trial, the judge in the case ruled that the government could not use Martin's handwritten notes detailing the "loans," money, or gifts that he had given to various players—all evidence seized when federal agents raided Martin's home in 1999. The judge also ruled that prosecutors could not use Martin's testimony about loaning Webber $280,000, nor could they call Bullock, Taylor, or Traylor to testify about money Martin may have given to them. Shortly after this evidentiary ruling, with both sides bruised and weary,

Webber and federal prosecutors came to an agreement. Webber pled guilty to one count of criminal contempt and, for the first time, publicly admitted to accepting money from Martin over the years, dating back to when he was in junior high school. As part of his admission, Webber also stated that he paid back $38,200 to Martin after Webber turned pro. (Webber left Michigan after his sophomore year as the number-one NBA draft pick in 1993 and went on to a stellar NBA career.)

As a result of the plea bargain, Webber avoided any jail time. (Prosecutors dismissed charges against his father and aunt.) The judge deferred sentencing—and a decision on whether the criminal-contempt plea would be considered a misdemeanor or a felony—for two years, ordering Webber to spend three hundred hours of community service reading to middle school students in a Detroit summer literacy program. Webber successfully completed his service (earning accolades for his work with the kids), and in August 2005 the judge determined that he would be guilty of only a misdemeanor and imposed on him a fine of $100,000.

Ed Martin's legacy still leaves a stain on the Michigan men's basketball program, but his love for the program remained within his blood until his death. Asked to comment after his plea bargain in May 2002, Martin uttered two of his last public words on the matter: "Go Blue."

8

The Investigators

There is a way around it.

AMEEN NAJJAR

"No team inspired more headlines in college sports than the
NCAA's enforcement division." So said an ESPN writer in a
May 2011 article cataloguing a series of college sports scandals during the 2010–11 academic year. How prophetic he was
in his smart-ass title: *The Most Scandalous Year Ever in College Sports . . . Until Next Year.*

In January 2011 Auburn and Oregon squared off in the BCS
football championship, following allegations that Auburn's
Heisman Trophy–winning quarterback, Cam Newton, was
shopped for cash by his father and that Oregon had essentially bought running back Lache Seastrunk with a $25,000
payment to Seastrunk's friend and mentor Willie Lyles. The
same week, Ohio State, led by star quarterback Terrelle Pryor,
competed in the Sugar Bowl, on the heels of findings that
Pryor and other football players had impermissibly traded
memorabilia for tattoos and other benefits. The bowl game
was played before NCAA investigators learned that head coach
Jim Tressel knew about possible violations but kept the information to himself. The Fiesta Bowl was played under a cloud,
because bowl executives were under federal and state investigation for illegal campaign contributions, not to mention a
bit of frivolous spending at strip clubs.

In April 2011, UConn won the men's basketball championship even though it had just gone on probation for major violations. The week after the Final Four concluded, allegations of a point-shaving scandal at the University of San Diego became public. And in May 2011, just days before the ESPN article appeared in print, the NCAA Infractions Appeals Committee upheld a two-year postseason ban and other major penalties on USC for infractions during the Reggie Bush and O. J. Mayo era. That ruling led to the BCS's vacation of USC's 2004–5 national football championship.

So the ESPN writer was justified in labeling the previous academic year as the most scandalous year ever in college sports. Little could he know in May, however, that 2011 would end with an enormous bang, with revelations of Jerry Sandusky's sexual abuse of children in the showers at Penn State.

Amid all those messes, NCAA investigators also were deep in the dirt of Miami—a case that would shine an unflattering light on the enforcement staff itself. Nevin Shapiro, a University of Miami booster serving a twenty-year sentence in federal prison for running a $930 million Ponzi scheme, reportedly told the NCAA enforcement staff early in 2011 that he had provided impermissible benefits, including cash, booze, hookers, Cadillac Escalades, and party cruises on his yacht, to at least seventy-two current and former student athletes at Miami.

Needless to say, the NCAA investigators, who numbered in the twenties, had a lot on their plates in 2011. Further handicapping those investigators was a lack of subpoena power. As noted previously, to do its work, the enforcement staff must rely on the voluntary cooperation of individuals involved in an infractions case. If those individuals are student athletes or employees of NCAA member institutions, the enforcement staff has leverage over them, because NCAA bylaws demand cooperation from student athletes and institutional staff members. Failure to cooperate can result in the loss of one's scholarship or job. *Former* student athletes and employees, however, can essentially tell investigators to go to hell. So can other witnesses with relevant information, such as boosters like

Nevin Shapiro. They fall outside the jurisdiction of the NCAA and cannot be forced to cooperate with investigators, either through a subpoena or through other legal means.

Nevin Shapiro, though, was quite willing to cooperate, in part to get back at the University of Miami, whose coaches and student athletes, in his perception, had turned their backs on him and made him a pariah. (*After all the fun and games we had, how could you?*) Indeed, his cooperation led an NCAA enforcement staff member in the Miami case, a director of enforcement, Ameen Najjar, to submit a letter on Shapiro's behalf at Shapiro's sentencing in June 2011 for the crimes of securities fraud and money laundering. (Shapiro had admitted to the charges in a plea agreement in September 2010.) On NCAA letterhead, Najjar praised Shapiro's assistance to the NCAA enforcement staff in its investigative efforts and raised the possibility that the NCAA could use Shapiro "in the future as a consultant and/or speaker to educate our membership." "Throughout the course of our interactions," Najjar wrote, "it is my belief that Mr. Shapiro possesses a unique depth of knowledge and experience concerning representatives of athletics interests ('Boosters'), agents and the provision of extra-benefits to student-athletes." Indeed, he did.

Nevin Shapiro may have been eager to cooperate, but others with knowledge of his shenanigans were not so willing. Investigators, for example, wanted to interview Shapiro's former bodyguard, Mario Sanchez, and a former assistant equipment manager for the Miami football team, Sean "Pee-Wee" Allen. Both, however, refused to cooperate. Other witnesses agreed only to unsworn interviews and provided incomplete or patently false information. Without subpoena power, Najjar and his investigators had little at their disposal to force any of these individuals' full cooperation.

Shapiro's attorney came to the rescue. In addition to the criminal case, Shapiro also was in the midst of bankruptcy proceedings initiated by investors in Shapiro's investment scam in an effort to recoup some of their money. Shapiro's attor-

ney in the criminal case, Maria Elena Perez, saw an opportunity in bankruptcy court. She suggested to Najjar and his
lead investigator that she could qualify for practice in bankruptcy court and use bankruptcy subpoenas to compel the
appearance and testimony of witnesses who were otherwise
reluctant to cooperate in the NCAA investigation. Najjar's
investigative team could draft questions designed to elicit
the information they sought from the witnesses and funnel
those questions to Perez. She then could ask the questions
of the witnesses during bankruptcy depositions, at which
the witnesses would be sworn under oath to tell the truth.
Enforcement staff members would have direct access to the
answers, because they would be permitted to sit in on the
public bankruptcy depositions.

Perez's assistance would come at a price, of course. On
October 4, 2011, she submitted a written proposal to Najjar,
suggesting depositions of nine persons, including Sanchez,
Allen, four coaches, and others. She estimated her "expenses
and legal fees" to be approximately $20,000—a hefty sum, but
the Miami case, because of its notoriety, was extraordinarily
important to the NCAA. Jim Isch, the NCAA's chief operating
officer at the time and the person who would have to okay
such a payment, later would say that he was prepared to provide the enforcement staff whatever financial resources they
needed to put together a strong Miami case.

Najjar followed up on October 10 with an email message to
his supervisors, vice president of enforcement Julie Roe Lach
and managing director of enforcement Tom Hosty:

Julie/Tom,

I have been exploring the possibility of having Nevin
Shapiro's criminal attorney, Maria Elena Perez, assist our
investigation by conducting depositions of the following key
witnesses who are outside the NCAA's jurisdiction:
1. Mario Sanchez [. . .]
2. Sean (Pee Wee) Allen [. . .]

3. Michael Huyghue, former sports agency partner with Shapiro.

4. David Leshner, friend of Shapiro's [...]

5. [Other individuals ...]

The depositions would be conducted by Perez and she has agreed to ask any questions we provide her. Additionally, members of the enforcement staff will be able to attend the depositions, as they are open to the public. Other than conducting these depositions, I do not believe we will be able to secure interviews with the witnesses or as in the case of Allen, will simply lie to us during an interview.

Additionally, Perez will also provide us documents, such as summaries of the FBI 302 reports, Shapiro's yacht records and bank and credit card records. I have attached Perez' proposal, which may be adjusted downward slightly because we do not want to depose the four listed coaches. However, we will be looking at roughly $20,000 in total costs. If we could discuss ... the viability of this in the near future, it will be helpful. Thanks,

Ameen R. Najjar

As full disclosure, I know Ameen Najjar, Julie Roe Lach, and Tom Hosty quite well. All three were directors of enforcement during my time on the infractions committee, and I consider them friends and professional colleagues. When David Price, who served as the NCAA's vice president of enforcement from 1998 to 2010, retired from his position, Lach and Hosty were both finalists for the job. Lach was promoted to vice president, and a new managing director position was created for Hosty.

Hosty found this "creative solution for bigger break-throughs on evidence" to be "most intriguing." Lach also was on board—the $20,000 price tag was a concern, but she quickly received the go-ahead from Isch on the financial end. Lach also wanted to ensure that the NCAA's in-house legal staff was alright with the plan, particularly since Perez effectively would be retained as outside counsel for the NCAA. Under internal NCAA guidelines, responsibility for making and monitoring such arrangements fell within the purview of the general counsel's office.

After reviewing the matter, an attorney in the general counsel's office informed Najjar by email that he should *not* engage Perez. In part, that advice reflected the concern of both the reviewing attorney and the general counsel himself that such an arrangement would improperly extend the enforcement staff's investigative reach beyond that contemplated by the NCAA membership: "Understanding that there are at least three individuals that will not speak with us, but would be compelled to do so under the bankruptcy proceeding, our advice would be to not use a source's criminal attorney in this manner."

Unwilling to accept no (or at least "our advice would be" not to do this) as an answer, Najjar requested a meeting with the two attorneys from the general counsel's office. Both Lach and Hosty also were invited to attend, but Lach was home sick on the day of the meeting and had to participate by phone. Later, perhaps because she had been "participating" under the effects of her illness, Lach could not recall that the meeting even took place. Hosty was busy preparing for a hearing in another infractions case and could not attend the meeting either. Because of these circumstances, neither Lach nor Hosty was present to hear the general counsel this time issue a *directive* to Najjar: the proposed arrangement with Perez is *improper*, and she should not be engaged to assist the enforcement staff (though if public depositions did occur, enforcement staff could attend).

Najjar was undeterred. Shortly after the meeting, he emailed Perez to say that he had run into "a problem with our legal dept concerning 'retaining' you but there is a way around it." He suggested that the NCAA could not officially "retain" Perez or pay her for "billable hours," but they could "reimburse" her for her "costs and expenses." Perez took Najjar's message as a green light and began preparing for depositions. In the meantime, Najjar assured both Lach and Hosty that while the general counsel's office initially had a concern about "retention" of Perez, that issue had been resolved and the general counsel had approved the plan. Of course, Najjar had obtained no such approval, but unfortunately, neither Lach nor Hosty confirmed the Perez arrangement with the general counsel's office—perhaps understandably, because they trusted the representations of their professional colleague, Najjar, with whom they had worked for years, all three on the same level as directors of enforcement prior to the 2010 promotions of Lach and Hosty.

Perez's work on behalf of the NCAA, then, began in late 2011. The depositions proceeded on schedule, and no one was the wiser, until September 2012, when a dispute arose about Perez's billings for her work. Lach had told Najjar he had a $15,000 budget for the Perez depositions, but Perez submitted an invoice for $57,115, reflecting over 150 hours spent preparing for and participating in depositions, at $350 per hour. Good work if you can get it.

Lach, surely a bit stunned, sought the advice of the general counsel's office on the legitimacy of some of Perez's charges. One might imagine the general counsel's own stunned reaction: *They're ALL illegitimate, because we told you last October that you could NOT enter into this arrangement!* However, by this time, the enforcement staff already had paid Perez about $10,500.

After an internal review, NCAA personnel concluded once again that it was improper to use Perez to gain information that otherwise would have been unavailable to the enforcement staff. Despite their conclusion that Najjar had entered into the relationship with Perez without authority, the legal and enforcement staffs agreed to a final payment to Perez of about $18,000. They also notified the University of Miami of their conclusions and agreed to remove from the investigative file any information derived, either directly or indirectly, from Perez's involvement in the bankruptcy proceedings. The latter move ensured that any forthcoming allegations against the university would not be based on information gained improperly through the Perez liaison.

Participants in the NCAA infractions world often talk about "rogues"—those individuals who commit violations despite rules education and clear guidance about the importance of rules compliance. Schools in trouble often are eager to shift blame to these individuals: *We have sound compliance programs and strongly reinforce a culture of compliance; we've done all we can and are as shocked as anyone to learn that Assistant Coach (or Booster) went* rogue *on us.* In the meantime, Assistant Coach, who's been fired, sits at the infractions hearing with a bewildered look, asking the committee, "Do you really think Head Coach or Athletics Director didn't know what I was doing?"

Najjar apparently went rogue—ignoring the advice of legal counsel, entering into the arrangement with Perez on his own, and then lying to his supervisors about whether he had permission to do so. Surely that behavior is unconscionable, particularly if Najjar wanted to keep his job. (He didn't keep his job.) But outside of internal management issues at the NCAA, how big of a deal was this?

Perez's proposal raised a couple of red flags with the general counsel's office, including the fact that the use of Perez in the bankruptcy proceedings would allow NCAA investigators to gain access to information they would not otherwise be able to obtain. One has to assume as well that the general counsel and his staff simply believed that the Perez arrangement did not pass the smell test. Since when does the NCAA pay the attorney of the principal culprit in a major infractions case to assist with the enforcement staff's investigation? Apparently left unspoken (unrecognized?) was a further potential concern—that the manipulation of the bankruptcy proceedings may have been a breach of professional ethics, if not an actual fraud on the bankruptcy court.

On the other hand, several mitigating factors were in play. Despite its questionable nature, the conduct of Najjar and

Perez apparently broke no laws, formal rules of professional conduct, or even NCAA bylaws. And from nearly the moment he took over as NCAA president Mark Emmert preached a get-tough attitude toward rule breakers. He viewed himself as a change agent who was going to crack the culture of wrongdoers making a "cost-benefit analysis" of rule breaking. He brought together a group of university presidents for an enforcement summit and led a series of "reforms" to address the problem, including a beefed-up enforcement staff, major changes to the composition of the Committee on Infractions, a multi-tiered violation structure, and a new set of penalty guidelines.

As soon as news of the Miami case became public in August 2011, in a report published by Yahoo! Sports, observers began calling the case a game changer, even speculating that it may be the case in which the NCAA revisits the death penalty for the first time in twenty-five years. One can imagine in this environment the pressure felt by the enforcement staff to build as strong a case as possible.

Enforcement staff members also reported that they had been encouraged to get creative in their efforts to gather information. When one considers the practicalities of conducting an investigation without subpoena power, it is little wonder that Najjar and his supervisors were intrigued by the possibilities presented by Perez's proposal. Indeed, the proposal was not dissimilar to means employed by NCAA investigators in past cases, particularly those that have involved related criminal investigations. When major players in an infractions case have been engaged in criminal conduct (for example, Ed Martin running an illegal gambling operation in Michigan's men's basketball case or Logan Young's racketeering conspiracy in the Alabama football case), it is not unusual for the enforcement staff to work cooperatively with prosecutors and to leverage the fact-gathering processes available to those prosecutors to garner important information for the infractions case.

Despite these mitigating factors, NCAA president Mark Emmert decided the enforcement staff's conduct in the Miami investigation was a *really big* deal. On January 23, 2013, Emmert participated in a telephone conference call with the media and announced that he was "deeply disappointed and frustrated and even angry" about the "stunning" and "grossly inappropriate" conduct of his enforcement staff. Characterizing the matter as "a shocking affair," Emmert went on to declare, "When you have something as candidly dramatic as this occur, you can't just offer words. You have to offer a demonstration that you are getting this right."

Emmert's response was as "candidly dramatic" as his performance in the Penn State case. His demonstration that he was getting things right included hiring an outside law firm to investigate his own investigators—not only to determine what happened in the Miami investigation but also to review more broadly the NCAA's entire enforcement operation. And similar to the NCAA's use of the Freeh report in Penn State, Emmert retained not just any outside counsel but the heavyweight international law firm of Cadwalader, Wickersham, and Taft, a highbrow firm based in New York City. The six-lawyer review team was headed by Ken Wainstein, who had formerly served as homeland security advisor to President George W. Bush and as general counsel of the FBI.

Wainstein delivered his report on February 17, 2013, and the NCAA immediately made the full report available online. This remarkable document provides a step-by-step account of the actors involved and the actions they took in the Miami investigation. Among the key findings was the following: "The facts do not establish that any NCAA employee knowingly violated a specific bylaw or law. While the Enforcement Staff may have disregarded the advice of the Legal Staff in proceeding with the proposal, that conduct does not appear to have violated any written NCAA rule. We have also found no apparent violation of the Bankruptcy Code, the Federal Rules of Bankruptcy Procedure, or Bankruptcy Court orders by NCAA staff."

The report did, of course, fault Najjar for "knowingly circumvent[ing] the legal advice against engaging Ms. Perez," characterizing his conduct as "simply not reasonable." It also took to task Najjar, as well as Lach and Hosty, for paying "insufficient attention" to concerns that the Perez proposal "could be—or at least could be seen as—an abuse of the bankruptcy process" and that it could have improperly extended the enforcement staff's investigative reach: "There are any number of techniques that, though permissible in the law enforcement context, are considered over the line for NCAA investigations. Mr. Najjar and his supervisors never considered whether the Perez proposal fell within that category."

Finally, the Wainstein report criticized Lach and Hosty for their "insufficient oversight" of Najjar's activities with Perez. Of course, they knew what Najjar was doing; they simply thought he had received the okay from the general counsel's office, because that's what he told them. On the other hand, they also knew of the general counsel's initial concern about the Perez proposal and certainly could have had further conversations with the legal staff to ensure that they were indeed on board. Interestingly, the report also makes clear that the University of Miami's attorneys, both internal and external, had knowledge from the outset of what Najjar and Perez were doing in the bankruptcy proceedings. In that light, university president Donna Shalala's public outrage at the "unprofessional and unethical" investigation rang a bit hollow.

As a result of the findings in the Wainstein report, vice president of enforcement Julie Roe Lach was fired. (Ameen Najjar had already left the NCAA months earlier.) Lach's termination was a huge deal. She had been on the job for barely two years and was one of President Emmert's first big hires. In announcing her appointment in 2010 to considerable public fanfare, Emmert described Lach as the perfect person to succeed longtime vice president David Price, who was retiring.

A former college basketball player, Lach had experienced a steady (some might say meteoric) rise within the NCAA, beginning as an intern and later working in the area of student-athlete reinstatement. She completed her law degree in 2004, became a director of enforcement that same year, and began working alongside a handful of experienced directors, including Hosty, who had joined the enforcement staff in 1993. Najjar came aboard the same year as Lach, in 2004. Emmert seemingly went out on a limb in selecting the thirty-five-year-old Lach as his chief rule enforcer, but his confidence in her abilities was reinforced by the recommendation of Price, who said in 2011 that it was "just obvious she was going to be a superstar from the outset." To lose such a promising young talent had to have been a real blow to Emmert and to the NCAA organization.

To replace Lach, Emmert brought in Jonathan Duncan as interim vice president. A first-rate Kansas City lawyer, Duncan had represented the NCAA as outside counsel in numerous matters over the prior fifteen years. One of those matters involved a long-running lawsuit by a former basketball coach at the University of Buffalo, arising from an infractions case decided in 2001. It was the first appellate case I argued for the Committee on Infractions, and Duncan represented me when I was deposed by the coach's attorneys in 2011. Duncan brought an experienced, steady hand to the NCAA enforcement team at a time when steadiness was desperately needed. Among his initial tasks was to work in coordination with the Wainstein group at the Cadwalader law firm on a thorough review of all enforcement processes and procedures. In short order, Duncan's "interim" label was removed, and he became permanent vice president of enforcement.

So what is one to make of the Miami investigation? Is the enforcement staff a bunch of bumbling fools, as they're often portrayed in the media? One ESPN writer, in my mind, got it mostly right in the aftermath of the Miami missteps: "The enforcement staff is well-intended but overmatched and ineffective. Not because they don't care. Not because they are out to get anyone. They are good people. Smart people. Hard-working people. But in a highly sophisticated sports world, they are armed with the investigative tools of Inspector Clouseau. How in the world are these people supposed to do their jobs? By monitoring Twitter, Facebook and message boards and hoping someone says something stupid? By insisting that the guilty admit their guilt because they were told to? My 8-year-old is savvy enough to circumvent that one on occasion."

I think the writer got it *mostly* right by highlighting the difficulty of building a case without subpoena power. I also agree with her characterization of the enforcement staff—they are good, smart, hardworking people who are well intentioned—and that includes Julie Roe Lach; Tom Hosty; and at least during the six years in which I observed his work, Ameen Najjar.

I do not agree, however, that the enforcement staff is ineffective, at least in the general run of cases. During my time on the infractions committee, I had the opportunity to review over one hundred cases (including summary dispositions that were resolved without a hearing). That included reading the enforcement staff's case summaries, along with supporting documentation, including transcripts of staff interviews with witnesses. I also observed the investigators' oral presentations at infractions hearings. My overall impression from those encounters was quite positive—I found the enforcement staff comprised generally of intelligent, capable, professional, and dedicated individuals who put together solid cases against rule breakers, particularly considering the investigative constraints under which they must work.

Sometimes the enforcement staff did seem overmatched; typically, schools and coaches are represented by high-powered, experienced attorneys who are knowledgeable about NCAA affairs. Indeed, many of those attorneys used to work *for* the NCAA, and they know much more about the process than newly hired investigators. And of course, the quality of work varies among the staff, but that is true in any organization. The committee quickly learned which of the enforcement staff members consistently did a thorough, professional job and which members were inclined to cut corners or were simply not quite as capable as their colleagues.

Could the enforcement staff be more effective? Certainly, but working for a membership-driven organization like the NCAA necessarily carries with it certain constraints, especially limitations on investigative powers. Some of those constraints are highlighted in the Wainstein report:

> In granting this mission to enforce the rules of the Association, the membership also defined the scope of the Enforcement Staff's investigative authorities. In particular, concerns over vesting too much power in the Enforcement Staff led the membership to carefully determine when and under what circumstances the staff or student-athletes of a member institution are obligated to cooperate with an NCAA investigation. For example, the members have established the "cooperative principle," imposing an affirmative obligation on each member institution and its representatives to cooperate with Enforcement Staff investigations and deeming a failure to cooperate to be a basis for sanctions or disassociation. The membership has not agreed, however, to provide any more far-reaching authority to compel cooperation.
>
> Beyond the specific investigative authorities that the membership has blessed, the Enforcement Staff operates under a set of expectations about the lengths to which they can go to investigate a case. Though unwritten, there is an understanding among the membership that they should forgo investigative techniques that might give the Enforcement Staff too much power, especially in the academic environment where they operate.

Thus, one must accept the fact that the enforcement staff's lack of subpoena power, for example, may pose difficult investigative problems in many cases, particularly when key witnesses are no longer students or employed staff members at an NCAA member institution. The NCAA took considerable heat for the length of the enforcement staff's investigation into the USC football program, but one can imagine that the investigation would have been furthered significantly had Reggie Bush, the *former* student athlete at the heart of the case, cooperated with investigators. Similarly, in the Ohio State football case, the attorney for Terrelle Pryor, the school's star quarterback who played a central role in that case, made it clear that investigators would get no cooperation from his client: "He doesn't need a reason. He's no longer a student-athlete." And we'll probably never know if NBA star Derrick Rose *really* had someone take the SAT for him, because neither he nor any of his associates cooperated in the University of Memphis investigation.

The enforcement staff faces other challenges as well, including relatively high staff turnover. Many staff members are hired away by schools or conferences seeking compliance expertise and willing to offer higher salaries. Nonetheless, in my experience, the enforcement staff typically has done a credible job of investigating and building cases. Occasionally, there are screwups, and even minor transgressions can cascade into a firestorm in a highly publicized case. One of the initial investigators in the Miami case was Abigail Grantstein, who was fired in 2012 after improprieties surfaced in another case on which she was working. Grantstein's transgression? Apparently poor judgment in picking boyfriends.

Unfortunately for Grantstein, a former student athlete at Ohio State and graduate of the University of Kansas law school, the case was nearly as high-profile as the Miami case. It involved the recruitment of basketball player Shabazz Muhammad, a McDonald's All-American ranked as the number-one high school recruit in the nation by some recruiting publications. Before eventually landing at UCLA, Muhammad apparently violated NCAA amateurism rules by accepting impermissible benefits during recruiting trips to Duke and North Carolina. The alleged violations came to the attention of the NCAA enforcement staff, which assigned Grantstein, an assistant director of enforcement, to investigate under the

supervision of one of the enforcement directors. A preliminary investigation provided evidence of rule violations, and
shortly before the start of the 2012–13 basketball season, the
NCAA declared Muhammad ineligible to compete.

About this same time, an attorney was seated on an airplane
listening to a loud conversation in the row of seats in front of
her. A man was telling another passenger about the Shabazz
Muhammad case. The attorney candidly admitted she had
never heard of Muhammad and didn't even know what sport
he played. But she was disturbed by "the cavalier discussion
of this young man's future being tossed about for everyone
to hear." Muhammad's future, according to the man in front
of her, was bleak, at least in terms of competing at the college
level: "My girlfriend is investigating him and he's dirty. . . . I
can guarantee you that he's not going to play." According to
the attorney, the man referred to taking money and kept saying, "Abby knows it," and, "They're dirty and they were taking money and she's going to get them."

"Abby" was described by her boyfriend as an NCAA investigator and former college athlete with ties to Kansas. So Grantstein was burned quickly when a report of this conversation
surfaced. The attorney who overheard the conversation was
"offended in the delight he seemed to take in something that
was very serious and could ruin this man's life." So she tracked
down the email address of Dennis Thomas, a former chair of
the Division I Committee on Infractions and commissioner of
the Mid-Eastern Athletic Conference, and reported the incident to him soon after the flight. Dr. Thomas referred the matter to NCAA officials, who knew immediately that the report,
from a disinterested witness who provided details that were
easy to corroborate, was credible.

Grantstein was fired, and Muhammad's eligibility was
quickly restored in an agreement between the NCAA and UCLA.
The university acknowledged that amateurism violations had
occurred, and it proposed a penalty essentially of "time served"
(a three-game suspension constituting 10 percent of the bas-

ketball season), in addition to requiring Muhammad to pay back about $1,600 in impermissible benefits. In its public statement on the matter, the NCAA press office stated, "The NCAA agreed the actions taken by the university were sufficient. Because Muhammad has already sat out three games, he is now eligible to compete."

Muhammad lived up to expectations, earning first-team Pac-12 honors and being named co–Freshman of the Year in the conference. He then became just the latest in a long string of "one-and-doners," declaring for the NBA draft and earning a first-round selection in 2013. He competed for the Minnesota Timberwolves for five years; as this book was going to press, he was competing in the Chinese Basketball Association.

Not surprisingly, the NCAA took a big hit in the Muhammad case, with many commentators suggesting that the enforcement staff caved on the investigation and reinstated Muhammad quickly because of the incident with Grantstein's boyfriend. Muhammad's attorneys, of course, suggested that the midair conversation was evidence that the NCAA had prejudged Muhammad's guilt before completing its investigation.

I don't know whether the NCAA caved. Certainly, the resolution was consistent with a lot of other student-athlete reinstatement matters—a modest suspension from competition and repayment of ill-gotten gains. And perhaps the reinstatement staff was inclined to go easier because the violations occurred during Muhammad's recruitment by *other* schools, not by UCLA. As one commentator pointed out, however, the NCAA's student-athlete reinstatement guidelines suggested a presumptive penalty that would have withheld Muhammad from *30 percent* of the season's competition because the improper benefits he received exceeded $1,000. The guidelines do invest the reinstatement staff with discretion to adjust the presumptive withholding penalty upward or downward based on aggravating or mitigating factors. In Muhammad's case, his parents insisted the benefits came from a close family friend, so there may still have been some question whether violations actually had occurred.

In any event, the incident on the plane does illustrate, much as the Miami investigation did, that the actions of one bad actor (and in this case, not even an actor within the NCAA organization) can taint the entire enforcement team. One of Muhammad's attorneys said that the matter "puts a far brighter light on the failings of the NCAA process." Well, not really . . . it shines a light on the foibles of human nature and the dangers of talking out of school. But in the world of NCAA enforcement, it also adds to a widely held perception that NCAA processes are fatally flawed.

I don't know Abby Grantstein, but I feel for her. She must have been a good investigator to have been assigned to work on the Muhammad and Miami cases. But her promising career came crashing down as a result of a "loud-mouthed boyfriend" (as one reporter aptly described him), and her name is now known by far too many sports fans.

Other enforcement staff screwups occur occasionally in cases that are not as high profile as the Shabazz Muhammad or Miami cases, so most people have never heard of them. One case I remember well, because I handled the appeal, involved the men's soccer program at the University of West Virginia. The case involved numerous major violations by the head coach, but a significant procedural issue arose at both the infractions hearing and on appeal before the Infractions Appeals Committee.

One important procedural safeguard for individuals involved in major infractions is the right to have an attorney or other representative present during questioning by the NCAA enforcement staff. The soccer coach in the West Virginia case was informed of that right, both in writing prior to the staff interview and orally at the outset of the interview. But when the coach asked if he could terminate the interview at any point to seek the advice of counsel, an NCAA investigator told him that such a termination could result in a further allegation by the enforcement staff of a "failure to cooperate."

This statement by the enforcement staff representative clearly was out of bounds. One either has a right to an attorney or not; that right cannot be conditioned on allowing the enforcement staff to conduct its interview without interruption. So when the issue arose at the infractions hearing, the Committee on Infractions expressed its deep concern. The committee upbraided the investigator for his conduct and included the following in its public infractions report:

> At the hearing, the enforcement staff representative offered as explanation his concern that interview termination "once its focus is known," offers an interviewee an opportunity to fabricate, alter, or destroy information, using the need to consult a lawyer as pretense. The committee does not dispute that an investigation might be impeded in the way suggested by the enforcement staff representative. The committee nonetheless strongly disapproves of a practice in which an individual is told that he may be subject to a failure-to-cooperate allegation should he terminate an interview to seek legal assistance. The committee inquired at the hearing as to the frequency of use of this practice by the enforcement staff; it appeared that this was the only time it had occurred. The committee expects that this case will continue to be the only occurrence.

So it is true that the NCAA enforcement staff blunders occasionally. By focusing on its missteps in this chapter, I do not mean to imply that those missteps are common. To the contrary, one reason these examples stick out is because they are rare. For the most part, the enforcement staff knows what it's doing and performs its work with integrity, diligence, and competence. That story just doesn't get much traction.

Enforcement staff positions are coveted, and competition for the positions is keen. The staff can be highly selective in adding new members to its team. Most of the staff members have law degrees, many have a background in intercollegiate athletics, and typically they have held positions of responsibility in other fields. Tom Hosty, for example, was a prosecutor in Kansas City prior to joining the NCAA. Ameen Najjar had served as a police officer and, after earning his law degree, as legal counsel for the Indianapolis Police Department.

Field investigators, known as assistant directors of enforcement, work under the guidance of one of several experienced directors of enforcement, most of whom have worked their way up through the ranks. Managing directors serve at a step above the directors, and overseeing the entire enforcement enterprise is a vice president of enforcement—the position formerly held by Julie Roe Lach and now held permanently by Jon Duncan.

After information of a potential violation comes to its attention, the enforcement staff conducts a preliminary investigation to determine if there is any substance to the report. Pursuant to NCAA bylaws, the staff must determine whether to proceed to a formal investigation "or whether the matter may be resolved without a formal investigation. If an investigation is warranted, the enforcement staff shall conduct an investigation on behalf of the entire membership to develop, to the extent reasonably possible, all relevant information."

Before beginning an investigation on campus, the enforcement staff will provide a notice of inquiry to the university's president or chancellor. That notice signals the start of a formal investigation, which is conducted on campus and wherever else the evidence leads. In recognition of the voluntary nature of the association and the cooperative principles that guide enforcement matters, the staff's investigation often is conducted jointly with representatives of the university and sometimes of the athletics conference.

The next step in the process is interesting, requiring a prediction by the enforcement staff. If it determines that sufficient evidence exists "to conclude that a hearing panel of the Committee on Infractions could conclude that a violation occurred," the staff issues a notice of allegations to the university president or chancellor, specifying the alleged violations, as well as "the details of the allegations." Based on years of experience, the directors of enforcement typically make pretty accurate predictions—they know the types of evidence that are likely to support a committee finding of a violation.

A similar notice of allegations is sent to any "involved individual"—any current or former institutional staff member who is believed to have been involved in the violations and who is asked to respond to allegations in writing and appear before the Committee on Infractions. Note that this definition does not include boosters. Even though their conduct may be at the heart of an infractions case and that conduct is addressed in NCAA bylaws, they cannot be compelled to cooperate, and they cannot be directly punished by the NCAA (although *schools* may be ordered to disassociate a booster).

Similarly, student athletes may be involved in violations, but their conduct is considered by a membership services and reinstatement staff of the NCAA, a group separate and apart from the enforcement staff that focuses on the reinstatement of student-athlete eligibility. In nearly ten years on the infractions committee, not once did I observe a student athlete testify at an infractions hearing. However, a recent report indicated that a student athlete did testify at the 2017 University of Mississippi football infractions hearing, "in what is believed to be a first in NCAA compliance history." The student athlete, a linebacker at Mississippi State, purportedly testified that an Ole Miss booster offered to pay him $10,000 to enroll at Mississippi. The case may signal something of a shift in procedure, but presumably the appearance of a student athlete at an infractions hearing will remain exceedingly rare.

University representatives and involved individuals (typically through their attorneys) submit written responses to the notice of allegations. Depending on the breadth of the allegations, the responses, especially from institutions, can comprise hundreds of pages, include dozens of exhibits, and fill multiple three-ring binders. The enforcement staff submits a written reply to the parties' responses and then prepares a case summary (recent legislation refers to it as "a statement of the case") that outlines its allegations and supporting evidence. Typically, it also includes a summary of any refuting evidence submitted by the school or involved individuals.

The NCAA bylaws permit cases to be resolved by summary disposition, without an infractions hearing, if all parties are in agreement with the facts and proposed penalties. The use of the summary disposition process has increased significantly over the years, for good reason. It saves the time and expense of a hearing (which may be unnecessary if no fact disputes exist) and allows a case to be decided more quickly. The use of the process, however, is subject to Committee on Infractions approval. The enforcement staff, institution, and any involved individuals submit a joint written report to the committee, outlining proposed findings of fact and penalties. The enforcement staff also must convince the committee that a "complete and thorough" investigation of the violations occurred and that the institution "cooperated fully" in the process. The committee then can either accept or reject the report.

If the summary disposition process is not used or if the Committee on Infractions rejects a proposed summary disposition, the committee schedules an infractions hearing. Shortly before the hearing, the enforcement staff conducts a prehearing conference with institutional representatives and, separately, with any involved individuals and their representatives (again, typically attorneys). This conference allows the parties to hash out disagreements and make any necessary modifications to the case summary prior to the hearing.

The Committee on Infractions (now a five- to seven-member panel drawn from the full committee) conducts a closed hearing (that is, not open to the media or other members of the public) at which all parties are provided an opportunity to present relevant evidence. Following the hearing, the committee deliberates and issues a public infractions report (recently

renamed a public infractions "decision"), outlining all findings of violations and penalties. A school or involved individual that is found in violation of NCAA rules has a right to
appeal the decision (or some aspect of it) of the Committee
on Infractions. All appeals are considered by a separate, independent body—the Infractions Appeals Committee, whose
decisions are final.

So the process itself is relatively straightforward, and one
can see that institutions and involved individuals have ample
opportunity throughout the process to have their say. Much
has been written and discussed over the years about whether
the NCAA infractions process implicates the constitutional
rights of individuals punished in the process—most commonly, whether one's property rights (continued employment,
for example) can be denied without due process of law.

Federal and state constitutions, however, constrain only
governmental power, so constitutional rights, including due
process rights, are not implicated unless the entity allegedly
depriving one of such rights is a governmental actor (also
known as a "state actor"). Thus, the NCAA cannot violate one's
constitutional rights unless it is a state actor. In a controversial 1988 decision, the U.S. Supreme Court held that actions
taken in the NCAA enforcement process did *not* constitute
state action.

The case involved Jerry Tarkanian, the colorful men's basketball coach at UNLV. As noted in chapter 6, Tarkanian had
a way of stepping into hot water and drawing the attention
of the NCAA enforcement staff. When UNLV suspended him
as a result of a Committee on Infractions determination that
he had committed ten rule violations, Tarkanian sued both
UNLV and the NCAA, alleging a violation of his due process
rights. Despite the fact that the NCAA exercises its authority
through a delegation of powers by NCAA member institutions,
including many, like UNLV, that are state institutions, the U.S.
Supreme Court held in a 5–4 decision that the NCAA was not a
state actor and thus could not commit due process violations.

Although the NCAA v. *Tarkanian* decision has now been on the books for thirty years, many critics of the NCAA continue to press the notion that the enforcement process deprives individuals of their due process rights. But even without the *Tarkanian* decision, the argument is "much ado about nothing," as one of my former colleagues on the Committee on Infractions put it in a recent publication. Josephine (Jo) Potuto is a distinguished law professor at the University of Nebraska, a former chair of the infractions committee, and an expert on both constitutional law and NCAA powers. She testified at special congressional hearings in 2004 on matters related to due process and the NCAA. Professor Potuto debunks the notion that NCAA enforcement practices would change significantly if the NCAA were to be found to be a state actor—that is because the current enforcement system provides ample process to both individuals and institutions in infractions cases. The essence of *due* process is notice of allegations and an opportunity to be heard—both of which are provided in spades by the current enforcement and infractions procedures.

That said, basic *fairness* should govern NCAA processes, whether constitutional claims are pertinent or not. Ultimately, that is the goal—to ensure the fair administration of intercollegiate athletics. And NCAA critics play a vital role in promoting basic fairness, particularly if their criticism is informed and constructive. Tarkanian played that role effectively, and even he acknowledged later in life that enforcement procedures had become much fairer over time: "They were the worst organization that I ever encountered in the 1970s. Now they give you a pretty good form of due process. They tape your interviews, they let you read your interviews, and you can have someone present while they interview. In 1977, you could have none of that. It would be their recollection of what was said."

9

The Committee

The NCAA must be disbanded. Destroyed.
They are criminals.

COMMENT ON CBSSPORTS.COM, FEBRUARY 28, 2014

The above comment came in response to an article by CBS Sports' Dennis Dodd reporting on litigation between the NCAA and Todd McNair, a former assistant football coach at USC. McNair had been sanctioned in a high-profile infractions case a few years earlier, and he was suing the NCAA for defamation based on statements made about him in the public infractions report. Dodd's article focused on a legal dispute relating to whether all NCAA documents in the infractions case would be unsealed by the court and made public.

A year later, after the court unsealed many of the documents, USC issued the following statement: "After an initial review of this first set of documents unsealed by the court in the *McNair v. NCAA* lawsuit, it is evident that the content confirms bias against McNair and USC by and on behalf of the NCAA and its Committee on Infractions. We are extremely disappointed and dismayed at the way the NCAA investigated, judged and penalized our university throughout this process. USC hopes that the transparency in this case will ultimately lead to review and changes so that all member institutions receive the fair and impartial treatment they deserve."

Lawsuits have a way of forcing transparency. A party to a lawsuit essentially can request that the other side disclose any and all documents that are relevant to the suit. And if they are relevant, and not protected from disclosure by some other legal principle (such as trade secret protection or privileged attorney-client communications), a judge will order disclosure, even if a party wants to keep the information hidden. The Division I Committee on Infractions has learned this lesson the hard way; for the first time, in the aftermath of the USC infractions case, the committee's *deliberations* were on display for all to see. Coach Todd McNair's defamation suit against the NCAA provided an extraordinary look inside the workings of the committee. In the process, the suit shined a light once again on the basic fairness of NCAA processes, just as the Wainstein report did in examining enforcement staff conduct in the Miami investigation.

We'll return to the USC case later in this chapter, so hold tight. In the meantime, I want to provide an overview to be sure the reader fully understands the roles of the various actors in the rules-enforcement process. This book, for example, has discussed numerous decisions of the Committee on Infractions. But who *is* this committee, and how does it fit into the enforcement scheme?

One critical element—the separation and independence of the enforcement staff and the Committee on Infractions— bears repeating, because it is commonly misunderstood. Commentators and sports fans often speak about the NCAA without making this important distinction. Enforcement staff members are salaried employees of the NCAA and are headquartered at the NCAA national office in Indianapolis. They are investigators and "prosecutors" whose job is to investigate allegations of NCAA violations and to present evidence of violations to the Committee on Infractions, typically at an infractions hearing (though sometimes by way of a summary disposition report).

Members of the committee, on the other hand, are unpaid *volunteers* from around the country whose job is to hear and evaluate evidence presented by all parties at an infractions hearing. They typically are nominated to serve—by the leadership of an athletics conference, for example, or by some other source, including current members of the committee—and their selection is subject to approval by the NCAA Board of Directors. The committee collectively acts as the "trial judge" in an infractions case, determining whether or not violations have occurred and imposing penalties on rule breakers.

The enforcement staff conducts its investigations without involvement of the Committee on Infractions. Indeed, the members of the committee typically know nothing about a case until the enforcement staff has completed its investigation and has sent the committee its allegations, supporting evidence, and the responses of the school and involved individuals. Usually that occurs a few weeks before the hearing. The enforcement staff, then, has free rein in its investigation and follows the evidence wherever it may lead.

At the hearing, the enforcement staff presents its case before the committee, as do the school and any involved individuals. The burden of proof is on the enforcement staff to prove that violations occurred. If the Committee on Infractions is persuaded by the enforcement staff's case, it will make findings of violations. But if the staff does not make a persuasive case, the committee will not make findings, and plenty of examples exist in which the committee has determined that the enforcement staff did not meet its burden of proof.

The committee also may disagree with the staff on the seriousness of violations. In 2011, for example, the committee determined that violations committed in the University of Tennessee football program were all secondary, contrary to the enforcement staff's presentation of a case of major violations. In earlier days, the enforcement staff made penalty recommendations (it no longer does), and the committee sometimes disagreed with those recommendations. The best example came in the SMU death penalty case, discussed in chapter 2. The infractions committee rejected the enforcement staff's argument for leniency and imposed the death penalty.

Thus, when observers direct their anger or frustration at

the NCAA for what occurred in an infractions case, they should take care to aim their arrows at the body or group that is responsible. Often that body is the NCAA membership as a whole. As a voluntary association, the NCAA member institutions ultimately are responsible for establishing the rules and overseeing the infractions and enforcement processes. The NCAA Division I membership is represented by a twenty-four-member board of directors composed primarily of university presidents and chancellors. The duties and responsibilities of the board of directors include establishing general policy, enacting legislation (bylaws), and reviewing and approving "policies and procedures governing the infractions program."

So if someone objects to a "petty" rule, that objection is more appropriately directed toward the membership as a whole (or at least the board of directors) rather than toward the enforcement staff or the Committee on Infractions, both of whom are doing their jobs by enforcing the rules set forth in the bylaws. Similarly, if one is frustrated by delay in a seemingly endless investigation or by the failure to put together a strong case, the NCAA enforcement staff may well deserve some heat, but not the Committee on Infractions. And if one is offended by the severity (or leniency) of a penalty imposed in an infractions case, the infractions committee is the reasonable target, but not the enforcement staff, which plays no role (anymore) in recommending sanctions, let alone in the imposition of penalties.

I was appointed to the Division I Committee on Infractions in April 2000. I was humbled to join a group chaired by Jack Friedenthal, a nationally recognized legal scholar who had served on the faculty of the Stanford Law School and later as dean and professor at George Washington University. He was joined by Gene Marsh and Jo Potuto, who held endowed positions on the law school faculties at the University of Alabama and the University of Nebraska, respectively; Dick Dunn, an English professor at the University of Washington; Andrea Myers, athletics director at Indiana State University and one of only a handful of female athletics directors in the country; Tom Yeager, commissioner of the Colonial Athletic Association and a former NCAA enforcement director; Fred Lacey, an esteemed attorney and former federal district judge from New Jersey; and Jim Park, another prominent attorney from Lexington, Kentucky, who had represented the University of Kentucky in a major infractions case earlier in his career.

Dunn, Friedenthal, Marsh, and Potuto all had served as their universities' faculty athletics representatives. In that capacity, they had represented their universities and faculties in NCAA and conference governance matters and had overseen a wide range of athletics-related duties on their campuses.

Over the next several years, I had the privilege of working with several other athletics directors or deputy athletics directors, including Melissa Conboy of Notre Dame, Paul Dee of Miami, Ted Leland of Stanford, Craig Littlepage of Virginia, and Gene Smith of Arizona State (and later Ohio State); conference commissioners Britton Banowsky of Conference USA and Dennis Thomas of the Mid-Eastern Athletic Conference; Eileen Jennings, general counsel at the University of Central Michigan; Bonnie Slatton, professor of health and sport studies (and faculty athletics representative for twenty years) at the University of Iowa; and highly regarded public members of the committee, all lawyers, including John Black of Kansas City, Brian Halloran of Malibu, Jim Lechner of New Jersey (a former federal district judge), and Tom Phillips of Austin (a former chief justice of the Texas Supreme Court). Greg Sankey, the commissioner of the Southeastern Conference, recently served for several years as chair of the committee. Greg Christopher, director of athletics at Xavier, was chair as of this writing, with his term as chair expiring in 2020.

I include these names and titles to let the reader know that the members of the Committee on Infractions are individuals who command respect individually as a result of their professional accomplishments. As a collective body, they comprise a formidable group indeed. I readily acknowledge my bias, but I have never worked with a more professional, hard-working group of colleagues. Like the enforcement staff, the infractions committee occasionally has a misstep, but for the most part, the committee members' integrity and competence shine brightly—at least to those who have observed the committee up close. With rare exceptions, even those individuals who endure the painful process of appearing before the committee have praise for the members' level of preparation and dedication to fairness in the proceedings.

The time demands on committee members are truly extraordinary. Typically, preparation for infractions hearings means poring over literally boxes of materials. Following hearings, committee members spend many hours deliberating and reviewing drafts of public infractions reports. Between meetings, members participate in training sessions, review summary disposition reports, discuss policies and procedures, and engage in other committee-related tasks. It is a job only for the committed—both to doing the work and to policing college athletics—and numerous committee members over the years have resigned before their terms expired, because they came to realize that the commitment was too much.

Because of the importance and high-profile nature of the committee's work, NCAA leaders seek to populate the committee with persons of stature and gravitas, so their decisions will be respected. But that creates a dilemma, because almost to a person, these individuals have been tasked with an immense array of responsibilities back home in their day jobs. Occasionally, a committee member will be retired or semiretired, but that is a rarity. Somehow the work got done, but it was never easy. My own day job was as a law school dean and professor, and I can honestly say that never before in my career, or in my educational studies, did I pull all-nighters until I had NCAA deadlines.

Because the Committee on Infractions consists of volunteers, it is assisted by a handful of NCAA staff members who reside in the Indianapolis area and work out of NCAA headquarters there. Shepard (Shep) Cooper has been a director of the infractions committee since 1999, and he has an immense knowledge of infractions cases that have come before the committee during his tenure. He does not have a vote in the deliberative process, but he always has been a valuable resource to the committee because of his institutional memory. Committee members wisely tap into his knowledge in their efforts to strive for consistency.

In my early years on the committee, Shep and his trusted assistant, Cheryl DeWees, handled all matters related to the committee by themselves. Division II has its own infractions committee, and the office of the *Committees* on Infractions handles those matters as well. While the Division II caseload is not as heavy as in Division I—and certainly doesn't generate the same level of publicity—it still provides substantial work for the office, so Shep and Cheryl had a daunting set of responsibilities. Jim Elworth, a former prosecutor and member of the NCAA enforcement staff, joined the staff in the early 2000s to provide assistance to Shep. More recently, a revamping of the office added a managing director, Joel McGormley, and more personnel. The office staff now numbers seven.

The directors of the committee sit in on infractions hearings and committee deliberations, taking notes of the proceedings and providing assistance where necessary. Typically, one of the directors will take the lead in writing initial drafts of the public infractions reports, for later review and editing by committee members.

In addition to assisting the committee with particular infractions cases, the staff coordinates committee travel, hotel arrangements, and logistics for infractions hearings. During my years on the committee, members typically flew into Indianapolis (or wherever else the hearing may be held) on Thursday night, in time for an infractions hearing that began bright and early Friday morning. Most cases could be heard within six to eight hours, but it was not unusual for a hearing that involved a large number of alleged violations to extend well into the evening hours. Occasionally, a case was limited enough that it could be heard in a half day, in which case the committee would take up other matters (for example, summary disposition cases or appeals from penalties in cases involving only secondary violations) during the afternoon.

A similar schedule occurred on Saturday, with a separate infractions hearing involving another school. Then on Sunday, the committee began early in the morning again and spent several hours to deliberate on the cases and reach tentative decisions on findings and penalties. Typically, the committee finished its work in the early afternoon, and committee members flew home in time to return to their real jobs on Monday morning. Committee panels now typically meet during the week rather than on weekends.

Hearing weekends could be exhausting, but we enjoyed both the camaraderie of the committee and the shared sense of purpose in trying to keep college athletics as clean as possible. We also were fed well; many of us counted on gaining five pounds during a hearing weekend.

Accommodations also were good, though by no means extravagant. During my time on the committee, the NCAA had a policy of not paying over $170 per night for a hotel room. Cheryl did her best to negotiate favorable rates with upscale hotels, but some venues simply remained off-limits. The committee met a few times in Colorado, for example, but we were never able to darken the doorways of the Broadmoor in Colorado Springs.

Why Colorado? An attitude existed in my early days on the committee that committee members who gave so much time and energy to the process should not have to hold all their meetings in Indianapolis, where the NCAA is headquartered. And because most of the hearing participants (committee members, school representatives, involved individuals and their attorneys, court reporter) would be flying in from elsewhere, it would not be significantly more expensive to meet in someplace nice—Beaver Creek, Jackson Hole, Lake Tahoe, Monterrey, New York City, Tampa, Tucson in February. The cost of hotels would remain roughly the same (no more than $170 per night), and airline tickets into another city often would be less expensive and more convenient than flying into Indy.

NCAA staff members did have to fly away from their homes to attend hearings outside Indianapolis, and that did add some marginal cost to the proceedings. Staff members, however, also worked very hard and were expected to work weekends when the committee met for hearings. Most of the staff members appreciated the opportunity to get away, particularly to an attractive destination where they might be able to tack an extra day of vacation onto their trip.

Why not meet in the general area of the school on the hot seat? To negotiate hotel reservations and hearing rooms, Cheryl typically was working a year in advance, and it was impossible to predict which schools would be appearing before the committee a year later. I sometimes felt badly for school officials, particularly from less-endowed institutions, who ended up traveling across the country for a hearing, but I didn't see a feasible way of avoiding that. Besides, the committee typically had two schools in front of it during each hearing weekend, so even if one school were to be accommodated, it was unlikely that the other school would be in the same area.

So it was nice on occasion to travel to a city one would otherwise not be able to enjoy . . . but it was not as enjoyable as it might sound. Hearing weekends typically were *packed* with committee obligations. If all went according to schedule, a hearing might end by 5:00 p.m. or so, and the committee at least would have the opportunity to walk to a restaurant for a leisurely dinner together. But sometimes the hearings ran late, we canceled dinner reservations, and convened at 9:00 p.m. in a hotel room to eat room service hamburgers. Spouses or partners sometimes accompanied committee members (at their own expense), but not very often; my wife swore off infractions-hearing trips after she accompanied me to Savannah for hearings that went well into the evening and she spent virtually her entire time, including meals, alone. I was not the only member who felt at times that we would be better off to schedule all infractions hearings at hub airport hotels (Atlanta, Chicago O'Hare, Dallas–Ft. Worth) since we rarely had time to play anyway.

Toward the end of my tenure in 2010, things changed. Ostensibly for cost consciousness, though probably more for perception purposes, NCAA officials decreed that infractions hearings would be held in Indianapolis, at least most of the time. I happen to love Indy, particularly when staying downtown in what is now a lively, bustling city. But it was nice to shake up the routine, particularly for those of us from the West who traveled through two or three time zones to attend hearings in Indianapolis. Perception matters, though, so conducting hearings at less glamorous locations probably sent a positive message—hearing weekends are for business, not pleasure.

Speaking of perception, my very first infractions hearing stands out as a head-scratcher. Readers may have noticed Lake Tahoe mentioned earlier as a hearing venue. The lake straddles the California-Nevada state line, and we were careful to meet at a hotel in South Lake Tahoe, *California* . . . about fifty yards west of the state line. The NCAA does not like Nevada's sports wagering, so we would *not* meet in Nevada. No, we (and all other hearing participants) would just fly into Reno (the closest major airport to Lake Tahoe), rent our cars and pay for our gas in Nevada, and walk fifty yards from Hotel California to experience the joys that Nevada has to offer.

As noted in chapter 6, the *Tarkanian* case in the late 1980s led to substantial revisions in NCAA enforcement and infractions processes, primarily on the recommendations of the special review committee headed by Rex Lee, which submitted its report in 1991. As a result of the Lee report, the Committee on Infractions in the 1990s was comprised of eight members, with a separate, independent, five-member Infractions Appeals Committee to review decisions of the infractions committee.

NCAA bylaws enacted to address membership requirements for the infractions committee included provisions for at least two members of each sex and two public members who were not associated with an NCAA member institution or athletics conference. Under bylaws that still hold today, each member can serve for a three-year term, renewable twice, so a true full term on the committee is considered to be nine years.

A ninth member of the committee, a coordinator of appeals, was added in 2000. This is the role I assumed. Prior to that time, the chair of the committee typically handled appeals, but in light of the chair's workload, including substantial administrative responsibilities not shared by other committee members, that approach simply became untenable. Indeed, a spate of appeals in my early years as appeals coordinator made even the new structure unmanageable, so the bylaws again were amended in 2004 to add a second appeals coordinator—the tenth member of the committee.

That structure remained until 2013, when, with the encouragement of President Mark Emmert, the NCAA Board of Directors expanded the committee to as many as twenty-four members, from which smaller hearing panels (five to seven members) could be drawn. The rationale for the expansion was "to review cases more quickly and efficiently." Announcing the change, Oregon State University president Ed Ray, who served as chair of Emmert's enforcement working group, said, "A primary complaint we heard from the membership was that processing major cases took too long, not only from the investigative stage but also once it was agreed that there was a major infraction—it took too long to get on the Committee on Infractions hearing docket."

An accompanying NCAA press release stated that with the newly expanded committee structure, "the time to process the less-complicated cases could be cut in half. . . . Hearings for Level I cases will be scheduled about 10 times annually (compared with the five meetings the current Committee on Infractions schedules). Level II cases can be scheduled monthly if necessary."

I don't know where that nonsense came from, but I have my suspicions. The presidents on the working group (and at a presidents' retreat in August 2011) heard from a few of their fellow presidents whose institutions had been involved in major infractions cases; those vocal presidents had a notion that their cases dragged on too long. And maybe they did ... but not because of any backlog at the Committee on Infractions level.

The working group clearly was misguided. At least from the time I joined the infractions committee in 2000, the committee met in every even month, six times per year, like clockwork. At each meeting, the committee typically held two hearings, involving alleged major infractions committed by representatives of two different schools. If a case (like Howard University or Southern Cal) involved numerous violations or was complicated in some other way, the committee might hear only one case during a meeting, but such complications were rare. It was not so rare, however, for the committee to hear only one case during a meeting—or even to cancel the bimonthly meeting altogether—*because there were not two cases in the pipeline, ready for a hearing.*

In other words, seldom was there a backlog due to the infractions committee's full plate. I recall only two instances in ten years in which the committee had to address a minor backlog of cases that were ready for a hearing. In one instance, the committee squeezed three hearings into one meeting to catch up. In the other, the committee scheduled a special meeting in an odd-numbered month to hear an additional case.

The proof is in the numbers. One would expect the regular schedule of the infractions committee, hearing two cases per bimonthly meeting, to yield 12 hearings per year, or 120 hearings over a ten-year period. In the ten years from January 2000 to December 2009, there were 109 cases in which the committee found major violations. Of those 109 cases, the committee conducted 90 hearings (counting Howard's double hearing as one) and decided 19 cases by summary disposition. In essence, then, the committee did not even have a full plate of cases. So it is difficult to see what problem the board of directors was addressing in expanding the size of the committee "to review cases more quickly."

That is not to say that the infractions committee did not have a heavy workload. Even ninety hearings in a ten-year period (nine per year) was a lot, particularly for a group of volunteers with full-time jobs. Moreover, a strong uptick has occurred in the number of cases determined by summary disposition, without a hearing. A substantial percentage of cases in recent years have been decided by summary disposition. While not as time consuming as cases that go to a hearing, summary disposition cases still must be reviewed by the committee, and they add significantly to the committee's workload. In addition, the committee reviews appeals from secondary (now Level III and IV) cases and attends to other matters, such as reviewing annual compliance reports from schools on probation.

So if the expanded committee structure is meant in part to reduce the workload on the committee, that goal is commendable. The notion that cases took too long to work through a committee bottleneck, though, is simply not grounded in reality. And unless we expect a surge in wrongdoing (the opposite of what the board of directors hopes to achieve with its new "reforms"), it is particularly unrealistic to think that Level I cases will be heard ten times per year or that there will be a need to schedule Level II cases on a *monthly* basis. There simply are not that many cases. Indeed, it is ironic that the committee faced a drought of cases shortly after the committee expanded in size. Bob Bowlsby, the Big 12 commissioner, took note in an infamous statement during the conference's football media days in July 2014: "Enforcement is broken. The infractions committee hasn't had a hearing in almost a year, and

I think it's not an understatement to say that cheating pays presently." Since 2014, the pace of major cases has picked up.

A potential benefit to the Committee on Infractions' expanded membership is the addition of individuals with experience that has not been represented previously on the committee. For example, during the ten years I served on the committee, it did not have a member with Division I coaching experience. Committee members were expected to attend all meetings, and active coaches were unlikely to be able to attend meetings scheduled during their competitive seasons. In addition, NCAA officials felt that active coaches would be reluctant to sit in judgment of their peers. With the committee expansion, however, membership was extended to two *former* head coaches—Lloyd Carr of Michigan (football) and Bobby Cremins of Georgia Tech (men's basketball)—who could bring their unique perspectives to the process. (Cremins remains on the committee as of this writing, but Carr no longer is a member. Joe Novak, former head football coach at Northern Illinois, replaced Carr. Jody Conradt, a legend in women's basketball at the University of Texas, joined the committee in 2017.)

The expansion of the infractions committee has raised an important issue regarding *consistency* of findings and penalties. Over time (particularly over a full nine-year term), members of the ten-person committee developed a strong sense of how a particular infractions case compared to other major cases in the past. While it may not have always succeeded, the committee made every effort to ensure that its findings and penalties fit within the general universe of cases. Even though each case has different facts and circumstances, patterns do develop, and a high level of consistency was attainable from committee members who attended nearly all major infractions hearings. An expanded committee, from which five- to seven-member panels are drawn from a larger pool of committee members, is more susceptible to inconsistent results.

In announcing the new membership structure, NCAA officials acknowledged the concern about consistency but suggested three ameliorating factors: (1) each hearing panel would include several members, including the chair, with experience in handling infractions cases; (2) the entire Committee on Infractions would meet "at least twice annually (at least once in person) to review cases across panels and check for consistency"; and (3) new penalty guidelines would provide some level of consistency, at least in terms of the penalties imposed on rule breakers.

The new structure is still playing out, so any meaningful assessments of its effectiveness would be premature. Reducing the workload, by spreading the work around to as many as twenty-four members, seems likely to increase some committee members' level of attention to particular cases. In my experience, members of the committee typically have been very conscientious, but ten to twelve hearings per year can be taxing on anyone, let alone individuals with high levels of responsibility in their real jobs. Reducing that level of commitment to two to three hearings per year reduces the burden significantly, which in turn may result in greater engagement and more thoughtful results.

My personal doubts remain, however, on the consistency issue. The new panels simply will not have the same collective level of experience as the former ten-member committee, and from a practical standpoint, a requirement of twice-yearly meetings of the full committee (up to twenty-four members who maintain heavy schedules and responsibilities in their day jobs) seems like wishful thinking, even if one is by conference call. Penalty guidelines may help with consistency in penalties, but the guidelines still allow for substantial flexibility, and the processing of an infractions case involves much more than the imposition of penalties.

With that overview, let's return to the USC case. Because of its high profile, many readers are familiar with the basics. In 2004 running back Reggie Bush and his family and friends began receiving improper benefits from "professional sports agents and/or persons who acted on behalf of these agents," in the words of the NCAA's eventual infractions report. At the time, Bush was a *beast*—a Heisman Trophy candidate as one of the top collegiate football players in the country. The benefits Bush and his parents received—"cash, merchandise, an automobile, housing, hotel lodging, and transportation"— were "valued at many thousands of dollars."

In 2001 the NCAA infractions committee had sanctioned USC for major violations involving academic fraud in its football and women's swimming and diving programs. The Bush violations beginning in 2004, then, put USC squarely within the repeat-violator window.

On April 21, 2006, an unnamed source contacted NCAA staff members with information that Bush may have received improper benefits while competing at USC. The tip came eight days before the New Orleans Saints selected Bush number two overall in the 2006 NFL draft and four months after Bush won the 2005 Heisman Trophy. The enforcement staff conducted a lengthy investigation, extended by the failure of key witnesses, including Bush and his family members, to cooperate with investigators. The investigation also became drawn out when the enforcement staff turned up major violations in the men's basketball and women's tennis programs—including agent, or amateurism, violations involving O. J. Mayo, a star one-and-done basketball player for the Trojans.

The Committee on Infractions finally heard the case during an unusually long hearing (lasting nearly three days) on February 18–20, 2010. Four months later, in June 2010, the committee released its public report. In a tone similar to what it had used in the 2002 Alabama football case (lecturing on the evils of boosters), the committee had harsh words for agents and handlers, whose actions strike "at the heart of the NCAA's Principle of Amateurism." The committee also tagged USC with the dreaded "lack of institutional control" finding, emphasizing the university's failure to commit adequate resources to rules-compliance programs or to engage in the kind of heightened scrutiny necessary to monitor the activities of elite athletes.

Harsh penalties should have been no surprise, considering USC's repeat-violator status, lack of institutional control, and serious violations in three different sports. Another significant factor the infractions committee takes into account in imposing sanctions is the level of recruiting or competitive *advantage* a school obtains from the violations. It stands to reason that a Heisman Trophy winner (or a one-and-doner drafted number three overall in the NBA draft, as Mayo was in 2008) provides a team a substantial competitive advantage. Nonetheless, the penalties were harsher than many expected, particularly in the football program—a two-year ban on postseason competition, a vacation of records in contests in which Bush had competed (which led the BCS to strip USC of its 2004 national championship), severe scholarship restrictions, and more.

I did not participate in the USC infractions case. I completed my service on the infractions committee in late January 2010, just three weeks before the USC infractions hearing. So I leave it to others to debate the fairness of the USC sanctions. I can say, though, that in light of the serious aggravating factors noted above, including USC's infractions history—not only its repeat-violator status but also the fact that this case was its sixth major infractions case, all involving the football program—the intensity of some of the criticism seems over the top. Take one ESPN writer's comments, for example: "It's become an accepted fact among informed college football observers that the NCAA sanctions against USC were a travesty of justice, and the NCAA's refusal to revisit that travesty are [sic] a massive act of cowardice on the part of the organization. That's the take of all clear-thinking people. (NCAA folks, just admit you blew it. The NCAA would take a huge step toward wiping away dumbfounding hypocrisy with a moment of honest self-reflection.)"

The writer's comment about hypocrisy was directed squarely at the chairman of the Committee on Infractions when the

USC penalties were announced—Paul Dee. Dee, who is now deceased, was at the time the athletics director and general counsel at the University of Miami. Dee served with distinction for nine years on the Division I infractions committee, but it may have been a cruel twist of fate that made him chair of the committee during the USC proceedings. Within months after the USC report was announced, at a Dee-led press conference in which he made such comments as "high-profile players demand high-profile compliance," the Nevin Shapiro allegations discussed in the last chapter came to light at Dee's own school. So he became instant fodder for critics of the USC sanctions, who found it hypocritical for Dee to admonish USC at the same time serious infractions, on a wider scale, were occurring on his own ship. (Despite enforcement staff improprieties in the Miami investigation, that university ended up with severe sanctions of its own, including a self-imposed two-year postseason ban.)

It has happened before, and it will happen again: infractions committee members' own schools (or schools from a member's conference, in the case of a conference commissioner member) sometimes come under scrutiny for major violations during the members' service on the committee. "Clear thinkers," though, will judge infractions cases on their own merits, assessing penalties in relation to the nature and seriousness of the infractions and the aggravating and mitigating circumstances in the case. If one does that in the USC matter and still concludes that the penalties were too harsh, so be it. But it is disingenuous to charge unfairness on the basis that one member (out of ten committee members, plus a five-member appeals committee that affirmed the penalties) also had difficulties at his or her school. Committee member Gene Marsh, for example, was faculty athletics representative at Alabama when that school's football program was sanctioned severely in 2002, but no one accused him of being a hypocrite because he also served on the committee at the time.

Issues of fairness go deeper in the USC case, though. Another part of the infractions committee's decision found assistant coach Todd McNair in violation of ethical-conduct legislation. After the three-day infractions hearing, the committee deliberated and ultimately found that McNair "knew or should have known" that Bush had received improper benefits and that McNair "provided false and misleading information to the enforcement staff" during its investigation. At the hearing, McNair continued to maintain that he did not recall *ever* talking to an involved agent (or wannabe agent)—despite phone records indicating conversations between McNair and the agent and the agent's own statements regarding the substance of the conversations, including payment of benefits to Bush and his family.

Admittedly, the agent, Lloyd Lake, was an unsavory character with a criminal conviction on his record. As one of the committee members later stated, just being a criminal doesn't make him a liar. But certainly his credibility (and that of other witnesses, including McNair) must be assessed damn carefully. This the committee members tried to do in deliberations after the infractions hearing, both in person and in email exchanges between the time the committee members left the hearing site and when they released their public infractions report. The committee's ultimate resolution, after considerable back-and-forth exchanges, was that they found Lake more credible than McNair. That, in turn, led to the committee's finding that McNair engaged in unethical conduct.

Nothing seemed amiss. The committee regularly is called on to assess the credibility of witnesses. It is an extraordinarily difficult task, of course, when the witness is not present at the hearing; it is less so when the committee can observe the witness's demeanor and ask questions at the hearing, which the committee did with McNair. And despite reservations about Lake's own character (one committee member wryly noted that "Lake is not the guy you want living next door to you"), the committee simply didn't believe McNair.

How do we know all of this? Because after the infractions

report was released, McNair sued the NCAA for defamation of character. As noted at the beginning of this chapter, he was able to use the discovery process in his lawsuit to compel the NCAA to turn over all email messages relating to the case from NCAA personnel, including the emails of committee members and committee director Shep Cooper. The NCAA attorneys, not surprisingly, fought to keep the emails under wraps. In particular, disclosure of the committee's *deliberations* would be extraordinary. Just like a jury, the committee members must have confidence that they can be completely candid in discussing the evidence presented at an infractions hearing and engage in a vigorous give-and-take process that weighs the strengths and weaknesses of the parties' cases.

Unlike a jury, which sits in a jury room and discusses the case in confidence until a final verdict is hammered out, the Committee on Infractions deliberates over an extended period of time. By the time the infractions hearing ends, the committee members already have spent an enormous amount of time and energy traveling and listening to the evidence (over three to four days, in the USC case). Typically, they discuss the matter in person for several hours and reach *tentative* decisions on findings and penalties before leaving town. A committee staff director begins drafting a report, under the direction of a committee member who is assigned lead responsibility on the case. The report, which may go through several drafts, incorporates the committee's tentative decisions reached during on-site deliberations, but everyone understands that the process—and the deliberations—will continue until the report is finalized. That occurs after the committee reconvenes on at least one conference call (sometimes it takes more than one phone call) to approve, line by line, the infractions report.

The committee operates by consensus, not unanimity. Members often disagree on findings and penalties, and after full consideration of differing views, votes have to be taken to resolve those disagreements. The discussions are thorough and candid; each member has full opportunity to say his or her piece. But in the end, the committee speaks with one voice. Some people, including at least one former committee member, have called for dissenting opinions in infractions reports, but the committee as a whole always has taken the position that consensus opinions are likely to engender more respect for the decision-making process than fragmented opinions that explicitly highlight divisions on the committee.

The USC case seems to bear this out. After committee members' email messages were disclosed (following an appellate court decision in February 2015 unsealing documents filed by the NCAA in the McNair suit), many commentators seized on one member's comment in deliberations that an enforcement staff interview of McNair was "botched." The investigator had questioned McNair about a phone call he had with the agent but misidentified the year of the call as 2005 rather than 2006. The implication is that the case against McNair, and potentially USC, was weak. But that is a small part of the overall case, and the comment shows that the committee was doing what it's supposed to do: engage in a thorough assessment of all strengths and weaknesses of the parties' cases. This particular weakness in the enforcement staff's case was one factor to take into account in assessing the evidence as a whole.

Criticism also has been directed at emails sent by two non-voting members of the infractions committee. One member, Roscoe Howard, had recently been appointed to the committee and participated in the USC hearing as an observer. The other member, Rod Uphoff, was my successor as one of two coordinators of appeals for the committee. Neither Howard nor Uphoff was a voting member of the committee in the USC case—newbies acting as observers do not vote, and the bylaw that created the position of appeals coordinator (my position, first created in 2000) provided that the coordinators of appeals, while members of the infractions committee, did not vote either. Nonetheless, both Howard and Uphoff shared lengthy emails, analyzing the evidence against McNair and USC, with the rest of the committee during posthearing deliberations on the case (just prior to the committee's first conference call to discuss the draft report).

The Howard and Uphoff emails reflect thorough and thoughtful analyses of the evidence by two seasoned attorneys. Howard is a former U.S. attorney, and Uphoff, a distinguished law professor, served on the Terry Nichols defense team in the Oklahoma City bombing case. Critics have characterized the emails as an attempt to improperly influence the voting members of the committee. Surely they were attempting to influence their fellow committee members. Why else would they have written their memos? But were their efforts *improper* because they were nonvoting members?

My own participation in deliberations (likewise, as a nonvoting appeals coordinator) evolved during the course of my tenure as a committee member. I was more of a listener when I began my service on the committee. Over time, however, as I gained more experience and developed a body of knowledge, based primarily on the numerous appeals I handled for the committee, my participation certainly increased. My fellow committee members viewed me as a valuable resource, and they sought my opinion regularly—particularly during the deliberations phase—in order to inform their own positions in a case. They knew my opinion was just that, however, and ultimately *their votes* would decide the case. Again, I did not participate in the USC case, but I suspect the committee similarly valued, and welcomed, the insights of both Howard and Uphoff—not as experienced committee members (because they were new) but as knowledgeable trial attorneys with decades of experience in evaluating evidence in a wide variety of cases.

In light of the emails, critics claimed that the committee was biased, but those claims miss the mark. It's one thing to have bias against a party before hearing the evidence; it's quite another to take a strong position after hearing all the evidence. Jurors, for example, may take a dim view of a criminal defendant they have just convicted on the basis of the evidence, but that hardly opens them to charges of bias. In the USC case, the emails in question all occurred during *posthearing* deliberations among committee members (or committee staff); they do not reflect the committee's *prejudgment* of the case before the presentation of evidence. The evidence was all in, the hearing was over, and the committee members were assessing the case based on that evidence.

The emails do include strident language about the various parties—perhaps to be expected when the group is deciding, for example, whether McNair was lying, USC failed to commit adequate resources to rules compliance, or the enforcement staff botched an interview. Deliberations can be contentious, and positions taken forcefully. But complete candor is encouraged by the confidential nature of the discussions.

Once the confidentiality of deliberations is breached, however, statements take on an entirely new light. A statement, for example, that McNair is "a lying, morally bankrupt criminal, in my view, and a hypocrite of the highest order" might stick in the craw of many observers. That statement, from committee director Shep Cooper in an email to appeals coordinator Uphoff, likewise came under heavy fire. Harsh? Undoubtedly. But it was a private communication between two nonvoting individuals, apparently not shared with others, expressing Cooper's personal opinion of McNair based on Cooper's own view of the record and observation of McNair's demeanor at the hearing. Certainly, the comments reflect Cooper's disdain for McNair, but how they reflect on the *voting committee's* decision in the case is far less apparent. Cooper, by the way, is the son of a longtime Division I football coach, and he has devoted his career to NCAA rules enforcement, so the stridency of his comments should not be particularly shocking. I can also say that based on my experience working extensively with Cooper over nearly a decade, he is a person of the highest character and integrity.

In the end, McNair's defamation claim failed. After seven

years of litigation, a jury found that McNair could not clear even the first hurdle of a defamation claim—that the statements made about McNair in the public infractions reports (both from the infractions committee and the appeals committee) were false. The litigation had taken many twists and turns along the way, but one of the most significant rulings was an appellate court order publicly disclosing all relevant NCAA documents, including those mentioned previously. That is why we now have an open window, for the first time, into the committee's deliberative process.

On one occasion in 2003, the Committee on Infractions nearly imploded over directions from the NCAA general counsel to disclose what occurred during committee deliberations. Committee members were extremely reluctant to comply, contending that even such *internal* disclosure, to the NCAA's own counsel, would constitute a serious breach of the absolute confidentiality essential to full and fair deliberation of infractions cases. Committee members should not be chilled in their discussions by the prospect that their conversations will be exposed for others to see.

Once the USC documents were exposed, for the world to see, examination of the committee's deliberative process in that case was fair game. And perhaps that transparency will, as USC suggests, "lead to review and changes" that focus on fairness in the enforcement process. One change surely has occurred; it seems unlikely that the Committee on Infractions will continue to *deliberate* by email. One of the most telling remarks from the USC file is an email comment by one committee member to her colleagues during the heat of deliberations: "I am becoming increasingly uneasy with conducting our deliberations by email. I am concerned about confidentiality . . ." Lesson learned.

10

Student Athletes?

I want to let you know that I passed all your football
players. Most of them actually passed on their own.

UNIVERSITY OF NORTH CAROLINA AT CHAPEL HILL

TEACHING ASSISTANT

When North Carolina and Syracuse squared off in the semifinal game of the Final Four the first weekend of April 2016, it
should have been a dream matchup—two storied programs
in men's basketball's greatest event. Many in the know, however, cringed and came up with colorful labels for the game:
the Corruption Classic, the Scandal Semifinal, the Academic
Fraud Bowl . . . in other words, a showcase of what's wrong
in big-time collegiate athletics.

Syracuse wasn't even eligible to compete in the Big Dance
the year before; it had self-imposed a postseason ban in 2015
following an infractions committee hearing to consider violations dating back to 2001. The violations included academic
fraud; cash payments and other impermissible benefits from
boosters; and failure to follow the university's own drug-
testing policy, which led to men's basketball players practicing and competing despite multiple positive drug tests. At the
time of the 2016 Final Four semifinal, Syracuse had barely
served one year of a five-year probation, the longest probationary period imposed by the NCAA to date. North Carolina,
in the meantime, was the subject of long-running investigations into what many knowledgeable observers consider to

be the worst case of academic fraud in NCAA history, with violations spanning nearly twenty years.

Another storyline dominated news accounts of Syracuse's unexpected march to the Final Four in 2016. A number-ten seed, the Orange overcame not only its underdog status but also major sanctions imposed by the infractions committee in March 2015—in addition to the postseason ban (self-imposed by Syracuse but adopted by the committee) and five-year probation, Syracuse received substantial scholarship cuts, recruiting restrictions, a financial penalty, a vacation of wins in which ineligible student athletes had competed, and an unprecedented nine-game suspension imposed on legendary coach Jim Boeheim. As noted in chapter 4, the case provided the first major test of new NCAA legislation holding head coaches responsible for the misconduct of their subordinates. To reach the Final Four after all that calamity showed just how extraordinary a coach Boeheim was. Boeheim characterized his team's response to a fourteen-point first-half deficit against number-one-seeded Virginia in the Elite Eight as "the best comeback I've seen at Syracuse. I haven't been there forever, but 56 years. It's the best comeback we've ever had." He just as easily could have been referring to the team's comeback from major sanctions.

A glance at the infractions committee report, however, may give observers a more jaundiced perspective on the heroic-coaching-effort narrative. The public report found that "for approximately 10 years, [Boeheim] failed . . . to promote an atmosphere of compliance within his program." Many of the academic violations were committed by Boeheim's director of basketball operations, whom Boeheim "specifically hired to handle academics" and whose conduct Boeheim "failed to monitor." Without such monitoring, Boeheim's "student-athletes and staff felt comfortable committing academic extra benefit and academic fraud violations." The infractions committee concluded, "The behavior in this case, which placed the desire to achieve success on the basketball court over academic integrity, demonstrated clearly misplaced institutional priorities."

One episode in particular demonstrated an even broader institutional failing. In January 2012 an undefeated and number-one-ranked Orange team found itself with a major problem—star seven-foot center Fab Melo, whom Boeheim characterized as "the best defensive player in the country," was not cutting the mustard academically. Because he failed to meet the NCAA's progress-toward-degree requirements, Syracuse was forced to declare him academically ineligible. But the powers that be were not done. They requested a waiver of the requirements due to "medical and personal difficulties" Melo had experienced at the institution. The appropriate NCAA staff members reviewed and denied the waiver request. Syracuse appealed, but the appeal was denied on January 24. The matter was now desperate, and as reported later by the infractions committee, "in order to keep one of their best players eligible the institution simply did not take 'no' from the NCAA for an answer." The Orange had started the season on a 20-0 run and had held the number-one national ranking since mid-December. The team lost its first game at Notre Dame just three days earlier, on January 21, and dropped to a number-three ranking.

As a longtime academic, I still shake my head in disbelief at the university's next move. On January 25, a day after the waiver appeal was denied, the athletics director convened a high-powered group to discuss Fab Melo's situation and potential options for a path toward eligibility. Astonishingly, in addition to the athletics director, the group included an associate provost, the faculty athletics representative, two deputy directors of athletics, the director of compliance, the director of student-athlete support services, and the director of basketball operations. Even convening such a group would be extraordinary; doubly extraordinary was the solution this gang of eight came up with: identify a course Melo had completed earlier and see the professor about a possible grade change, with the director of basketball operations left to oversee the details. As the infractions committee noted in its report, "a sense of urgency" existed—key games were coming soon: West Virginia three days later, on January 28; St. John's in Madison Square Garden on February 4; and eleventh-ranked Georgetown on February 8.

Melo and the director of basketball operations found an accommodating professor the day after the meeting, Thursday, January 26. Despite the fact that Melo had completed the course *over a year earlier*, the professor agreed that if Melo would submit a four- to five-page paper, with citations, she would consider raising his grade retroactively. The paper arrived, via Melo's student email account, twenty-seven hours later, on Friday afternoon. Unfortunately, despite intervention with the registrar by the professor, a deputy athletics director, the director of student-athlete support services, and the director of compliance, the grade change could not be processed by the close of business Friday, because the grade change form lacked the proper signatures. Melo did not play against West Virginia on Saturday, but thank God, the Orange squeaked out a 63–61 victory. But folks were not happy; over the weekend, the director of compliance emailed Syracuse's executive vice president/chief financial officer to tell him that the vice chancellor/provost would be "very disappointed" if the grade change were not approved.

On Tuesday, February 1, the grade change became effective, raising Melo's grade a full grade point, just enough to regain his academic eligibility. Melo was pumped and played a key role on Friday night in the Garden as Syracuse shellacked St. John's 95–70. The *New York Times* published this report:

> St. John's . . . was outrebounded by 42–31 and outscored by 52–20 in the lane as Melo returned to the Orange lineup after missing three games while resolving an academic matter. He changes Syracuse's makeup on both ends of the floor, and

he made his presence felt with 14 points, a career high, and 2 blocked shots.

"I intimidate other teams when they try to get layups," Melo said of his role at the base of the 2-3 zone. "That's what I do."

. . . With March approaching, Syracuse seems to have all the pieces to make a run in the N.C.A.A. tournament. The return of Melo, who was 5 of 6 from the field, has made the Orange one of the most complete teams in the country.

Alas, Syracuse was not meant to achieve the success of another Melo-led team nine years earlier, when freshman Carmelo Anthony earned Most Outstanding Player honors at the 2003 Final Four after leading Syracuse to its first national title. In late February 2012 the NCAA enforcement staff came calling, asking Syracuse officials to explain how Fab Melo could have created a paper, and earned his eligibility, in a day. Turns out, not surprisingly, that he didn't. The university engaged in a little forensic investigation and determined that the director of basketball operations, with the help of a basketball facility receptionist, did the work. Metadata and email exchanges revealed that the paper submitted on January 27 had been prepared and submitted by the two staff members. Staff members had made it a practice to gather usernames and passwords from men's basketball players so that the staffers could submit coursework and communicate with professors directly through the players' email accounts, essentially posing as the student athletes themselves. The metadata, however, revealed the *real* source of the academic work that was submitted.

Two days before the start of the NCAA tournament—with Syracuse holding a number-one seed, ranked number two nationally with a 31-2 record, and Melo having finished the regular season as one of the nation's top shot blockers and earning Big East honors as Defensive Player of the Year— the university issued a statement that Melo would not participate in the tournament due to an "eligibility issue." The details would come much later, in the March 2015 public infractions report.

At the time of that report, sports columns were awash in details of an even bigger academic fraud scandal, this time at the University of North Carolina at Chapel Hill.

What was part of the solution in the past?

• We put them in classes that met degree requirements in which
  —They didn't go to class
  —They didn't take notes, have to stay awake
  —They didn't have to meet with professors
  —They didn't have to pay attention or necessarily engage
  with the material

• AFAM/AFRI SEMINAR COURSES
  —20–25 page papers on course topic
  —**THESE NO LONGER EXIST!**

A PowerPoint presentation given by counselors from the Academic Support Program for Student Athletes (ASPSA) at the University of North Carolina at Chapel Hill (UNC) to the UNC football coaches and staff in 2009 sounded the alarm that sham classes they had relied on to keep athletes eligible would no longer be available due to the retirement of Debby Crowder. Crowder was the student services manager in the African and Afro-American Studies (AFAM) department at UNC. The AFAM courses referenced on the slide were "paper classes," requiring that the students enrolled in such courses just write a paper by the end of the semester—no class attendance or other coursework required. And even the paper requirement was dubious at best.

Another slide from the same presentation compared the GPAs of eight football players in AFAM courses to their other courses, reinforcing how important these particular AFAM courses were to the academic eligibility of the players.

	AFAM paper class GPA	Other GPA
Player 1	3.7	1.86
Player 2	3.2	1.9
Player 3	3.7	1.98
Player 4	3.63	2.036
Player 5	3.5	2
Player 6	3.85	1.99
Player 7	3.6	1.77
Player 8	3.7	1.8
Average	3.61	1.917

Prior to the PowerPoint presentation, Cynthia Reynolds, the associate director of the ASPSA and head football counselor, had written in an email to the football department that "Ms. Crowder is retiring at the end of July . . . if the guys papers are not in . . . I would expect D's or C's at best. Most need better than that . . . ALL WORK FROM THE AFAM DEPT. MUST BE DONE AND TURNED IN ON THE LAST DAY OF CLASS." The implication was that if Crowder could grade the papers before she retired, the student athletes would be guaranteed an A or B; if someone else graded them—on the basis of academic quality, for example—the grades likely would tank.

But wait . . . if *Crowder* could grade the papers? Crowder was not a faculty member; as student services manager, she had a strictly administrative support role within the department. Yet when Dr. Julius Nyang'oro took over as department chair in 1992, he gave Crowder free rein to "administer" the AFAM program as she saw fit. And she ran with her new-found freedom, in part because of her empathy for struggling students, particularly struggling student *athletes*. Before long she was manufacturing paper courses and managing them from beginning to end. A later investigative report clarified:

She created the classes in the . . . student and course records database;

She typically listed Nyang'oro as the instructor of record for these irregular courses, even though she knew that Nyang'oro would play no role in their instruction;

She registered the individual students who asked—or were proposed by ASPSA counselors—to be enrolled;

She sent the paper topics out to the students (or through the ASPSA counselors for student-athletes);

She received the completed papers from the students and graded them herself, cursorily skimming them over and awarding As or Bs so long as they satisfied the page-length requirement;

She typically filled out and signed the grade sheet with Nyang'oro's name;

And, she handled any grade changes from an incomplete to a letter grade in those instances when a student submitted his paper after the end of the semester.

The paper courses were "taught" on an independent study basis, which entailed no class attendance and required the submission of a single research paper. That was not unusual—independent study classes traditionally are taught in the same manner at most American universities. However, unlike courses in a traditional independent studies program, UNC's AFAM department did not involve any faculty member at any level. The students' only interaction was with Crowder, and because she was *not an educator*, she provided the students with no actual instruction, including any oversight of the students' research and writing process.

When curricular changes added a perspectives requirement for undergraduate degrees, which could be satisfied only through traditional lecture courses and thus limited the number of independent study courses in which a particular student could enroll, Crowder simply made some adjustments. She manufactured new AFAM lecture courses. The designation was in name only. Her AFAM lecture courses continued to operate in exactly the same manner as the paper courses always had—students could enroll in the course; attend no classes; turn in something, without regard to quality or relevance, at the end of the semester; and almost invariably receive an A or B.

I taught in higher education for thirty years. On top of my regular course load, I often would agree to supervise a couple of independent study papers each semester for students seeking the flexibility to earn an academic credit or two by exploring a topic in which they had a special interest. I also taught seminar courses, in which a substantial paper was the principal basis for the student's grade, as part of my regular course load. But enrollment in those paper courses was limited to ten students, because supervision of students' writing is an intensive, time-consuming process. In 2005 or 2006 a UNC administrator noticed that Professor Nyang'oro routinely was listed as "instructor of record" on roughly *three hundred* independent studies per year. Despite the fact that there was no way in hell that a single professor could do justice to that many papers, the administrator simply admonished Nyang'oro to reduce the number of his independent studies, without making further inquiry into whether any academic rigor existed in the coursework.

So red flags existed, but it was not until 2011, when two media reports emerged, that university officials began to take a serious look at the AFAM department. One report questioned how an incoming freshman football player slated for remedial writing could have earned a B+ in a summer, 400-level (senior level) AFAM bioethics course. The other report described plagiarism by a football player in a 400-level Swahili course, also offered by the AFAM department. As it turned out, Swahili courses were quite popular, in part because students were allowed to meet their foreign language requirement by writing a paper in English rather than in Swahili.

The media accounts spurred a senior associate dean in UNC's College of Arts and Sciences to begin an investigation. When he questioned Nyang'oro about the two incidents reported in the media, Nyang'oro said he did not recall teaching either of the students in question; *perhaps they were in Debby Crowder's classes.*

The cat was out of the bag, and once it was loose, things started to look really bad. A later independent investigation uncovered startling numbers: the corruption of the AFAM program had occurred for nearly twenty years (Nyang'oro carried on the fraudulent courses, at the urging of ASPSA football counselors, even after Crowder retired in 2009); Crowder and Nyang'oro had offered well over a thousand bogus independent studies in the paper-course format and 188 different "lecture courses" that operated in the same fashion, without student class attendance or faculty oversight; and over 3,100 students, nearly half of whom were student athletes, had enrolled in the sham courses.

Student-athlete involvement went well beyond football, crossing virtually all UNC sports. Representation in AFAM courses by men's basketball players was particularly high. The investigative report noted that 50.9 percent of student-athlete enrollments in AFAM paper courses were football players, while 12.2 percent were men's basketball players. But there were about nine times more football players on UNC's roster than men's basketball players. Ten of the fifteen players on the national champion men's basketball team of 2005 were AFAM *majors*, and during the 2004–5 academic year, members of the men's basketball team accounted for thirty-five enrollments in the sham courses.

Dr. Jan Boxill, a women's basketball academic counselor (in addition to being a philosophy professor and director of UNC's ethics center), also was a strong proponent of AFAM courses for the women's basketball players. An email exchange between Boxill and Debby Crowder is indicative of the nitty-gritty. Crowder wrote to Boxill, "Did you say a D will do for [the basketball player]? I'm only asking because 1. no sources, 2, it has absolutely nothing to do with the assignments for that class and 3. it seems to me to be a recycled paper. She took [another class] in spring of 2007 and that was likely for that class." Boxill replied, "Yes, a D will be fine; that's all she needs. I didn't look at the paper but figured it was a recycled one as well, but I couldn't figure out from where." Boxill and Crowder later reported that the exchange had nothing to do with academic eligibility for competition. The student athlete had used up her eligibility; the passing grade was needed for the student to graduate with a UNC degree. No worries, though, about the "recycled" paper and fraudulent credit.

These documents (including the teaching assistant's message at the beginning of the chapter, which was sent to the associate director of ASPSA) represent just the tip of the iceberg. To its credit, UNC investigated the matter to death—within a three-year period from 2011 to 2014, the school conducted four internal reviews and four external reviews, including one by a former North Carolina governor. In addition, UNC's accrediting agency, the Southern Association of Colleges and Schools Committee on Colleges (SACSCOC), conducted two of its own reviews, and the local district attorney worked with the North Carolina Bureau of Investigation in a joint criminal investigation. Nyang'oro was indicted in December 2013 for obtaining property by false pretenses—receiving payment for a course he never taught—but in July 2014 the district attorney dropped all criminal charges.

The review that has received the most attention is known as either the Cadwalader report or the Wainstein report. In February 2014 the university retained the high-brow Wall Street law firm of Cadwalader, Wickersham, and Taft to conduct an independent investigation. Kenneth Wainstein led the investigation, with a team of Cadwalader attorneys and paralegals. Wainstein brought superb credentials—and the massive resources of Cadwalader—to the task. Prior to joining Cadwalader, Wainstein served as general counsel of the FBI, the U.S. attorney for the District of Columbia, the Department of Justice's first assistant attorney general for national security, and Homeland Security advisor to President George W. Bush. Yes, this is the same Ken Wainstein hired by the NCAA to conduct an investigation of the enforcement staff after the Miami fiasco discussed in chapter 8. His report, released by UNC in October 2014, would garner instant credibility, in part because the Cadwalader team interviewed 120 witnesses and reviewed "1.6 million emails and other electronic documents."

Earlier reviews, before the Wainstein investigation, had been relatively benign. The NCAA enforcement staff, for example, had closed its own investigation back in 2011; a UNC Board of Governors report in February 2013 found no evidence of collusion between the athletics and AFAM departments; and accreditors in June 2013 decided not to sanction UNC. Time to move on. The pesky media, however, would not let sleeping dogs lie. A dogged investigative reporter for Raleigh's *News and Observer*, Dan Kane, kept seeking information from the university to determine if the AFAM scandal was primarily an *athletics* matter or a broader university academic matter. Sarah Lyall of the *New York Times* followed up on Kane's reporting to bring national coverage to the scandal. For example, the *Times* published a front-page story focused on the course that got Nyang'oro indicted—AFAM 280: Blacks in North Carolina, with an enrollment of nineteen, including eighteen current football players and one former football player, all reportedly steered to the course by the academic advisors in ASPSA.

The national coverage forced the hands of both UNC and the NCAA. UNC hired Wainstein in February 2014 "to ask the tough questions, follow the facts wherever they lead, and . . . take any further steps necessary to address any questions left unanswered during previous reviews." The NCAA enforcement staff reopened its investigation in June 2014.

The Wainstein report hit like a bombshell when UNC released it publicly in October 2014. Yes, the broad parameters of the AFAM scandal were already known—a 2012 report by former North Carolina governor James Martin, for example, had revealed many "anomalous courses" within the AFAM department over the years. But Wainstein's 136-page report was filled with tantalizing details . . . and painted a much uglier picture. *Really?!* At the nation's first public university, an institution that rightfully prides itself on its academic reputation, over *three thousand* students received sham credit in a fraudulent scheme that spanned nearly two decades? Over a *thousand* bogus independent studies and *scores* of make-believe lecture courses?

Understand that North Carolina hardly represents the NCAA's first major academic fraud case; the school has plenty of company. Most observers would have to agree, though— UNC sets the bar at a new low. Unfortunately, the UNC case also has highlighted vulnerabilities in the NCAA's ability to address even blatant academic fraud.

After reopening its investigation in 2014, the NCAA enforcement staff sent a notice of allegations to UNC in May 2015. An amended notice followed in April 2016, after the university discovered other potential violations following receipt of the initial notice. Not surprisingly, in light of UNC's public release of the Wainstein report, the enforcement staff alleged several major violations, including a lack of institutional control over the AFAM department; an institutional failure to monitor ASPSA, AFAM, and Jan Boxill, the women's basketball academic counselor; eighteen counts alleging Boxill's provision of academic extra benefits to student athletes; and unethical conduct (for failure to cooperate in the investigation) by Debby Crowder and Julius Nyang'oro. Interestingly, the amended notice did not directly allege academic fraud or misconduct; Boxill's provision of extra benefits is a different type of allegation, as will be explained later.

In August 2016, UNC responded to the amended notice of allegations with a full-frontal attack on the NCAA's jurisdiction to address academic matters on campus: "The Amended Notice of Allegations refer[s] to core academic issues of course structure, content, and administrative oversight that are beyond the scope of authority granted to the NCAA by its members. Such matters concern fundamental issues of institutional and academic integrity, not athletics compliance, and the University has addressed them with its accreditor. They are not the proper subject of an NCAA enforcement action."

When one considers past NCAA practice, UNC's response appeared extraordinary. The NCAA enforcement staff often has alleged—and the infractions committee has found—violations involving "core academic issues." When student athletes or institutional staff members have engaged in academic improprieties (typically for the express purposes of boosting student athletes' academic standing and thereby preserving their eligibility to compete), allegations and findings of academic fraud have been fair game.

But UNC found itself in trouble at the very time the NCAA membership was reevaluating academic misconduct, including a reexamination of when on-campus academic misconduct implicates the NCAA's rules-enforcement process. Tensions have long existed between university officials, who often believe that matters of academic integrity are for them to resolve, and NCAA officials focused on ensuring that competitors are truly *student* athletes. And the UNC response accurately pointed out that as a membership organization, the NCAA has only the authority "granted to [it] by its members."

In 2013 the vice president of enforcement had created an academic integrity unit to focus specifically on cases involving academic misconduct. Around the same time, NCAA president Mark Emmert had charged a new Division I Committee on Academics (comprised of twenty members, "including a minimum of two chancellors or presidents, one provost, four faculty athletics representatives, one director of athletics, one senior woman administrator, one conference administrator and one student-athlete") with gathering membership input and proposing new legislation dealing with academic integrity.

The work of those groups led to a significant policy shift in the NCAA's approach to academic misconduct—a shift toward greater *institutional* responsibility and away from NCAA authority. An NCAA media release in April 2014, for example, reported the following:

> The Division I Legislative Council reinforced Tuesday the membership's belief that academic standards and policies governing misconduct are the responsibility of individual schools and their accreditation body. . . .
>
> The Council approved an interpretation that clarifies the membership's position that it is a school's responsibility to decide whether or not misconduct involving current or future student-athletes or school staff has occurred and, if it has, to make sure the case is handled according to policies applicable to all students.
>
> "This clarification of the current rules is a first step toward a broader membership discussion of academic misconduct that will occur in the new governance structure," said Kevin Lennon, vice president of academic and membership affairs.

In mid-November 2015, *USA Today* reported on a speech NCAA president Mark Emmert made at the annual meeting of the Association of Public and Land-Grant Universities. The reporter accurately described Emmert's comments as a "plain-sounding statement that doesn't take long to have complex implications":

> We have to make sure that, as we think about academic integrity, we recognize everyone's role in this. The NCAA, as a self-governing organization, may set some minimum standard for admission and set some minimum expectations with progress toward degree and some standards and expectations towards graduation rates.
>
> But it's not the role of a national athletic association to go on to your campus and tell you what an English course has to be in order to have integrity. That's the domain of the faculty. . . . Some people somehow think that the NCAA ought to walk on to campus and say, "Look, let me tell you what this

class ought to look like in order to have integrity." That's not our job. But we've got to make sure you're doing it. We've got to make sure that we are not cheating young men and young women by not providing them academic programs of high quality that would serve them well over the long run.

Complex implications indeed. Academic integrity is the responsibility of the member institutions themselves, but the NCAA has to *make sure they're doing it*? How does that work?

Syracuse again provides an interesting example. The same two individuals most directly involved in the Fab Melo academic fraud (the director of men's basketball operations and the basketball facility receptionist, who also spent some time as a support services mentor) provided improper academic assistance to two other men's basketball players (identified in the report as student athletes 8 and 9). Due to the shifting sands—and the NCAA Legislative Council's official interpretation in April 2014 granting *institutions* the authority to determine whether academic fraud occurred—the NCAA enforcement staff "deferred to the institution to determine whether its academic integrity policy had been violated." Syracuse officials reviewed the matter pursuant to the university's internal policies and procedures and ultimately determined that there had been no violation of its academic integrity policy. Case closed? As it turns out, the university's determination was based solely on its *inability to locate pertinent records*. Syracuse's associate provost testified at the infractions hearing that the university could not locate the academic work submitted on the student athletes' behalf "because the institution typically operates under a one-year shred cycle."

Are you kidding me? The NCAA should *defer* to the institutions on whether academic fraud occurred and step aside in the face of a "determination" resting on a one-year paper-shredding policy? The Syracuse example—one of the first tests of an emerging institutional-responsibility model—clearly shows that the NCAA must retain some oversight role.

In the Syracuse case, NCAA officials thought so too. After a drawn-out procedural battle, a variety of NCAA decision-makers, including the enforcement staff and the infractions committee, determined that academic *extra-benefits* violations could occur even if a school finds no violation of its internal academic integrity policy. (Syracuse initially appealed that finding but abandoned its argument at the appellate hearing.) What does *that* mean? The bylaws always have provided two avenues for attacking academic fraud—straightforward academic misconduct (typically charged in the past as unethical conduct) and extra benefits. Extra benefits are defined as a student athlete receiving academic assistance (or any other benefit) not "generally available" to the overall student body, a violation that renders the student athlete ineligible in all sports. Most nonathletes, for example, don't have tutors writing (or even heavily editing) their papers and other assignments for them, so if that occurs for student athletes, an extra-benefit violation is in play.

Some of this is just nonsense. We all know that student athletes, particularly in big-time programs, receive all kinds of extra academic benefits that are unavailable to the general student population. How many nonathletes, for example, get the benefit of multimillion-dollar academic support centers or tutors who regularly hold their hands? In some ways, academic assistance to student athletes epitomizes the separation of athletes from their student peers. So one legitimately can ask why that assistance in itself does not constitute an extra benefit. The answer, of course, is that we recognize the excessive demands of time and energy imposed on student athletes, and we want to ensure that they have the same opportunity to succeed academically that their nonathlete peers have. Moreover, we often admit academically marginal students if they exhibit athletic prowess. So we have to help them. Not surprisingly, the NCAA bylaws add a second dimension to the definition of extra benefits. A benefit is impermissible if it is not "generally available" to the rest of the student body . . .

unless it's *"authorized by* NCAA *legislation."* Academic support programs available exclusively to student athletes are authorized. Indeed, academic support services for student athletes are *required*, and they "may be provided by the department of athletics."

The distinction between academic fraud and extra benefits regularly has been a source of confusion. Another example may help. One of the most interesting appellate cases I handled for the infractions committee involved the University of Georgia men's basketball program. In addition to his coaching duties, assistant coach Jim Harrick Jr. taught a two-credit-hour course on coaching basketball, which later became the subject of considerable ridicule, in part because the final-exam questions in the course included such gems as "How many halves are in a college basketball game?"; "How many points does a 3-point field goal account for in a Basketball Game?"; and "What is the name of the exam which all high school seniors in the State of Georgia must pass?" (multiple choice answers for this last question consisted of "Eye Exam," "How Do The Grits Taste Exam," "Bug Control Exam," and "Georgia Exit Exam"). The exam was indicative of the lack of rigor in the course, but even more problematic was the fact that as the semester progressed, Harrick discarded the syllabus, required no class attendance, and made the final exam optional. In other words, it turned into a sham course in which the students (all thirty-nine of whom "earned" an A) just had to attend some games and practices, which, of course, the three basketball players in the class already had to do as part of their regular routine.

The NCAA enforcement staff alleged, and the infractions committee found, both academic fraud (the three student athletes received academic credit and A grades for essentially doing no work) and extra benefits (the other thirty-six students at least had to do *something* outside their normal routine—attend games and practices—that the athletes did not have to do). Harrick's attorneys conflated the two issues, contending that *differential treatment* was required for any finding of academic fraud—so even if the course was a sham, the fact that thirty-six nonathletes *also* got an A and two hours of credit precluded a finding of academic fraud for the three athletes. The infractions committee (and the University of Georgia) rejected that argument. The committee had long recognized that while academic fraud can take many forms, one of its clearest manifestations arises when student athletes receive academic credit—and typically good grades—in courses in which they have done essentially no work. The extra-benefits violation was *in addition to* the academic fraud.

The essence of Harrick's argument raised its head again in the North Carolina case . . . and part of that was due to the lack of clarity from the NCAA on what exactly its jurisdictional reach was in academic matters. After the 2014 Legislative Council interpretation (and the Syracuse case), did *institutions* have exclusive authority to determine if academic misconduct had occurred, while the NCAA retained authority only to determine whether academic extra benefits had been given? If so, what happens when student athletes and nonathletes get essentially the same fraudulent credit?

In the UNC case, the Wainstein report noted that nearly half the enrollments in sham AFAM courses (or as UNC would put it, *only* half the enrollments) were of student athletes—47.4 percent of the enrollments in the sham lecture courses, for example—"even though student-athletes make up just over 4 percent of the Chapel Hill undergraduate student body." Despite this tenfold disproportionality in favor of student athletes, UNC's August 2016 response to the enforcement staff's amended notice of allegations focused on the "operation of an academic unit of the University that offered courses to the entire student body—not just student-athletes. . . . The anomalous courses were offered to the student body in general and therefore did not violate any NCAA rules." The response went on to describe the case as "an institutional matter beyond the scope of the NCAA's constitution and bylaws. The NCAA has neither the jurisdiction nor the expertise to regulate academic matters that affect a university at large. . . . The involvement of student-athletes does not give the NCAA the authority to intrude into matters of purely academic concern."

The UNC response echoed comments from prominent athletics personnel. Early on in the investigation, Bubba Cunningham, the UNC athletics director, said, "Since it's both students and student-athletes, we feel pretty confident that it's not an [NCAA] issue." Roy Williams, the men's basketball coach, told ESPN in 2012, "I'm telling you, it is not an issue for basketball. It is a university issue; it is an academic issue."

So let's get this straight—even though (according to the Wainstein report) there were 1,871 *student-athlete enrollments* in sham paper courses offered by the AFAM department between 1999 and 2011, it is not an NCAA or athletics problem because an equally large number of enrollments (2,062) came from nonathletes? (Never mind, for the moment, that the student-athlete enrollments represented 21 percent of all student athletes, while the nonathlete enrollments represented only 2 percent of all nonathletes.) In other words, the wider the fraud, the more insulated the athletics department?

Should it matter, for example, that UNC's frat men also discovered the slack AFAM department? The Wainstein report noted that the largest group of nonathletes to take the AFAM paper courses was "the fraternity network on campus." Fraternity members "looking for an easy high grade" also flocked to AFAM, to the point that some "took so many AFAM classes that they inadvertently ended up with AFAM minors by the time they graduated." As the Wainstein report put it, "the word got out among the fraternities and the brothers came in large numbers. Over the course of ten years, there were 729 enrollments in the paper courses by members of fraternities (and some sorority sisters)."

Not surprisingly, the shift toward focusing on extra benefits has elicited some colorful responses from commentators. In her observations of the UNC case, one of my favorite sportswriters, Dana O'Neil, put it this way: "The athletes did the baloney work in the baloney courses, and so long as the baloney courses weren't balonified solely for the benefit of athletes—in other words, they were equal-opportunity baloney classes made available to everyone at North Carolina—it's not an NCAA problem. In NCAA parlance, they call it involving the athletic nexus. In layman's terms, it's baloney."

I tend to agree. I don't believe that failing an extra-benefits test should negate clear academic fraud. Consider again the Georgia case, in which NCAA decision-makers didn't give a hoot that thirty-six of the thirty-nine members of Harrick's basketball coaching class were nonathletes. The three basketball players got two credit hours and A grades for doing virtually nothing, and *that* is academic fraud.

Until recently, academic fraud typically was alleged—and found—under NCAA bylaw 10.1, which addresses unethical conduct. The bylaw defined unethical conduct "by a prospective or enrolled student-athlete or a current or former institutional staff member" to include "knowing involvement in arranging for fraudulent academic credit." While the "arranging for" language perhaps could be interpreted in different ways, historically the bylaw left the Committee on Infractions unconstrained in addressing academic fraud head-on, as it did in the Georgia basketball case and many others. And the committee traditionally included several faculty members, who knew academic fraud when they saw it.

In the wake of the NCAA's reexamination of academic fraud, however, its Division I Board of Directors in 2016 approved the first changes to the academic fraud bylaws in over thirty years. In its press release announcing the changes, the NCAA media office stated that the goal of the new legislation was "to strike an appropriate balance between a school administration's role in deciding academic integrity issues on campus and the NCAA's collective role in reinforcing and upholding the NCAA's core academic principles." Effectively, the legislation, like the 2014 interpretation before it, shifted the balance toward academic administrators and faculty, who long have adhered to the belief that *they* should be the ones addressing academic misconduct.

The legislative changes took effect on August 1, 2016, just in time for UNC to use them in its response in the infractions case. Indeed, it surely is no coincidence that the university's attorneys waited until exactly August 1 to submit the UNC response to allegations the NCAA delivered in April. The response suggested that "rules effective on the date of this Response" undermined many of the enforcement staff's allegations, particularly those involving women's basketball academic counselor Jan Boxill and UNC's failure to monitor her activities.

The bylaw changes are substantial. First, they remove all mention of academic fraud from Article 10 (addressing ethical conduct) and shift the focus to Article 14 (Eligibility: Academic and General Requirements). That change alone may seem insignificant, but it also may raise the eyebrows of longtime observers who have viewed unethical-conduct findings as the most serious that can be made against individuals . . . and deliberate academic fraud as the epitome of unethical conduct.

New bylaws in Article 14 are extensive, with definitions distinguishing "academic misconduct" from "impermissible academic assistance" and a flowchart designed to guide the NCAA membership on when actions will constitute NCAA violations. Perhaps most significant is a provision defining "academic misconduct" to include only violations of "an *institutional policy* regarding academic honesty or integrity." That clearly puts the major responsibility on the NCAA's member institutions, which are charged under the new bylaws with having "written institutional policies and procedures regarding academic misconduct applicable to the general student body, including student-athletes." Investigation and adjudication of alleged academic misconduct is to be done pursuant to those institutional policies and procedures.

Thus, a presumption now exists that the NCAA will not become involved in academic fraud unless a student athlete is determined, through a campus adjudicatory process, to have violated university academic integrity policies. If an institution finds a violation of university rules, an NCAA academic misconduct violation also occurs if one of three elements is present: (1) involvement of an institutional *staff member* or booster in the misconduct; (2) the student athlete competed or received a scholarship based on an "erroneous declaration of eligibility" resulting from the misconduct; or (3) the "alteration or falsification of a student-athlete's transcript or academic record."

The bylaws then add another layer; even if there is no academic misconduct violation (because either the *institution* has not found it or none of the three elements above is present), the NCAA retains authority to find, as an alternative, an "impermissible academic assistance" violation. And that occurs when (1) a staff member or booster (2) provides "substantial" academic assistance to a student athlete (3) that is not "generally available" to the student body and (4) "results in the certification of [the] student-athlete's eligibility to participate in intercollegiate athletics, receive financial aid, or earn an Academic Progress Rate point."

I know, it sounds complicated . . . and believe me, it gets more complicated; I've just hit the basics. The bottom line seems to be that in determining whether academic misconduct (fraud) has occurred, a school's internal process preempts the NCAA's (even in a scenario as stark as Syracuse's, in which the university determined that a student athlete did not violate university policy because a one-year shred policy resulted in a lack of evidence), leaving the NCAA addressing primarily extra benefits—the core of impermissible academic assistance.

Whether this new legislation provides the clarity the NCAA membership has been seeking remains to be seen. The new bylaws do seem ripe for interesting interpretations. For example, when does impermissible academic assistance "result in" an improper eligibility certification? Is such improper assistance in one class immune from NCAA sanctions if the grade (or credit) in that class does not have an immediate impact on eligibility, even if it's part of a student athlete's cumulative academic record that meets grade-point or progress-toward-degree requirements?

Another question already has drawn considerable attention: When is academic assistance "substantial" enough to be impermissible? In the UNC case, for example, the university asserted in its response that many of the violations alleged against Jan Boxill, the women's basketball academic counselor, would not even be violations under the new regime. The enforcement staff's allegations stated, for example, that on numerous occasions Boxill "provided the beginning of a paper," provided "added content in the form of a conclusion," or provided a bibliography or "additional quotations to use." Such allegations approach the fine line between permissible and impermissible assistance but certainly are consistent with academic fraud findings in the past. Tutors may assist, but the student athlete ultimately is responsible for doing the work. Moving forward, will such assistance run afoul of NCAA restrictions?

NCAA officials have attempted to define when tutors provide such substantial assistance to a student athlete that it becomes impermissible. In explaining the pending legislative changes in February 2016, the NCAA published a memorandum from vice president of enforcement Jon Duncan (and republished it in May 2016 as an NCAA Educational Column). In that memo, Duncan sought to clarify precisely what he and his staff intended to pursue as NCAA violations:

> Some fear that the enforcement staff will overreach and allege violations when schools provide ordinary assistance to college athletes who need academic support. The enforcement

staff is sensitive to this concern and has no interest in discouraging appropriate and generous academic support for college athletes.

To be very clear, the enforcement staff will not pursue allegations where appropriate personnel provide . . . edits to a research paper. These and other similar supports advance the collegiate model and the educational interests of college athletes. The enforcement staff will not bring allegations in these instances.

In contrast, writing a paper for a college athlete or sharing exam answers are not acceptable supports and are not permitted.

An accompanying question-and-answer document said this in response to what "substantial assistance" means: "This determination is fact specific. Assistance such as proofreading, assisting a student with a problem on a math assignment or tutoring should not be considered substantial. Substantial assistance generally includes a considerable amount of assistance provided to the student-athlete that is of significant value to the student-athlete."

Well, that sort of begs the question, doesn't it? "Tutoring" should not be considered substantial. But what *kind* of tutoring? I can guarantee that athletics academic tutors have struggled for decades to determine when "appropriate and generous" academic support to poorly prepared student athletes crosses the line and becomes impermissible. And I'm not sure words like "considerable" and "significant" provide much of an answer to their questions.

Kathy Sulentic, the chair of the enforcement staff's academic integrity unit, took her own stab at providing concrete guidance. In response to a question about what "substantial" means, she stated, "That's sort of the million-dollar question. We're not looking for the close call. We're not looking for a paragraph added. We're not looking for heavy editing. We're looking for an entire paper has been done for someone. We're looking where someone got the answer key to an entire exam. We're looking at things that make a big difference for that class."

That kind of guidance is more helpful, but if Sulentic means what she says, it represents a significant departure from past practice. The enforcement staff and the Committee on Infractions regularly have acted in the face of conduct far short of writing an "entire paper" or providing answers to an "entire exam."

So the new academic integrity legislation certainly leaves difficult, open questions; the years ahead promise to bring some interesting debates. And the NCAA's broader discussion of academic misconduct is likely to get much deeper in the wake of the UNC decision, which finally came in October 2017.

A year earlier, in October 2016, a panel of the Division I Committee on Infractions convened a rare procedural hearing to address UNC's contention that the NCAA had no jurisdiction over the AFAM matter. The panel also addressed other procedural matters, including a statute of limitations defense and UNC's argument that the Wainstein report should not be considered evidence in the infractions committee's consideration of the case. The panel rejected the latter argument, citing a "broad admissibility standard for infractions hearings," but deferred a decision on the statute of limitations until after consideration of the "substantive allegations." In a subsequent letter to all the parties (UNC, the NCAA enforcement staff, Boxill, Crowder, and Nyang'oro), the panel seemingly put an end to UNC's jurisdictional argument: "The NCAA membership . . . has recognized an appropriate space for the infractions process to address circumstances involving an athletics department, coaching or athletics staff members, or other institutional personnel improperly influencing student-athletes' eligibility or academic performance. This is particularly true where conduct could demonstrate orchestrated efforts to inappropriately establish, preserve or obtain eligibility. Those issues cut to the core of the NCAA Collegiate Model, the notions of integrity and fair play and the purpose of the NCAA." The panel recognized, of course, that "whether any type of NCAA academic rules violations occurred is an issue to be resolved at a hearing on the merits," but it clearly decided that academic matters are within the infractions committee's jurisdiction.

The infractions committee panel's letter also highlighted continuing disarray in the NCAA's handling of academic fraud. The panel cited apparent confusion on the part of the enforcement staff and specifically requested the staff to "review whether the potential violations in this case are alleged in a fashion to best decide this case." In other words, in another rare move, the panel invited the enforcement staff to redraft its allegations against UNC. In doing so, the panel seemed to suggest that allegations of both academic misconduct and impermissible academic assistance would be in order.

The enforcement staff took the panel up on its rewrite invitation, issuing in December 2016 a *third* (second amended) notice of allegations. That notice, however, remained grounded on extra benefits, alleging impermissible academic assistance, but not academic misconduct.

UNC responded by doubling down on its positions: Okay, the infractions committee has jurisdiction to address the matter on its merits, but there *are no NCAA violations* related to the AFAM courses, "because the issue of the Courses is an academic issue." And because there are no "underlying violations" related to the courses, "there cannot be a failure to monitor or lack of institutional control violation."

Remarkably, after a long-awaited infractions hearing in August 2017, UNC won on virtually all counts. A six-member hearing panel clearly was bothered by academic improprieties in the case. In its public report issued October 13, 2017, the panel concluded that "it is more likely than not that student-athletes received fraudulent credit by the common understanding of what that term means. It is also more likely than not that UNC personnel used the courses to purposely obtain and maintain student-athletes' eligibility." In its final analysis, however, the panel felt constrained by the NCAA shift to *institutional* authority over academics: "Since 2014, the NCAA membership has acknowledged the question whether academic fraud occurred is one appropriately answered by institutions based on their own academic policies. The membership trusts academic entities to hold themselves accountable . . . and has chosen to constrain who decides what constitutes academic fraud."

The panel's deference to UNC was complicated by the institution's stance at earlier stages of the investigation. In proceedings before its accreditor, the university had accepted a characterization of the AFAM scandal as "academic fraud." And it had embraced the Wainstein report, which clearly concluded that academic misconduct was rampant. By the time of the infractions hearing, however, UNC had done a complete 180: "UNC pivoted dramatically from its position roughly three years later within the infractions process. UNC disavowed its earlier support of the findings and conclusions of [the Wainstein] report, distanced itself from earlier statements to its accreditor [characterizing its use of the term 'academic fraud' as a mistake—'merely a "typo" or oversight'] and ultimately defended its courses as a matter of academic autonomy. UNC did so even as it acknowledged that the courses did not meet, involved little, if any, faculty engagement and were frequently graded by a former curriculum secretary."

The infractions panel expressed deep skepticism, noting that it was "troubled by UNC's shifting positions." The panel also specifically found the Wainstein report "credible," even though UNC repudiated it and "identified potential factual inaccuracies" in the report. Nonetheless, the power of the NCAA membership's shift remained unshakeable: "What ultimately matters is what UNC says about the courses." And by the time of the infractions hearing, "UNC stood firmly by the courses in question . . . , indicating they did not violate policies existing at the time."

The first domino fell hard, and the rest followed. Because the NCAA membership chose to allow *institutions themselves* to determine what constitutes academic fraud and because UNC decided "to support the [AFAM] courses as legitimate" (despite an admission that such courses "would violate its *current* policies"), the infractions committee panel found itself unable to make an academic fraud finding. Similarly, the panel could not conclude "that extra benefit violations occurred," because the AFAM courses "were generally available to the student body, and non-student-athletes took the courses."

Impermissible academic assistance by Jan Boxill? Nope. Even though NCAA deference to educators does not apply with the same force in these circumstances, if a determination of impropriety "requires academic judgments," the infractions committee "must tread carefully." In the UNC case, determining whether Boxill provided impermissible academic assistance "would have required the panel to assess edits, suggestions and content down to the line-by-line and word basis. The panel was not in a position to make those core academic determinations."

And once the underlying academic allegations fell, the NCAA enforcement staff had little hope that either lack of institutional control or failure to monitor by UNC would remain standing. They did not. The panel did consider whether a "free-standing" (without underlying violations) lack of control or failure to monitor finding could be made, but it ultimately concluded that necessary "athletics touchpoints" were missing. In other words, because "regular students likely benefitted" from the AFAM courses as well as student athletes—and Debby Crowder testified at the hearing that "she provided the same degree of assistance to UNC students in need, regardless of their student-athlete status"—the panel concluded that the enforcement staff had not proven an "athletics motive" behind the sham coursework.

Ultimately, the only charges that stuck involved failure to cooperate by Crowder and Nyang'oro. For nearly three years,

Crowder refused to cooperate with investigators, but in the late stages, she submitted a "limited response" to the enforcement staff's last notice of allegations and participated in both a staff interview and the infractions hearing. Nyang'oro, on the other hand, never participated in the investigative or hearing processes. Because Crowder eventually cooperated, the committee found only a Level II violation against her and did not impose a show-cause penalty. Nyang'oro was hit with a Level I violation and a five-year show-cause. UNC itself escaped all penalties.

So there we have it. The biggest academic fraud case in NCAA history dies with a whimper. Nearly two decades of sham coursework, employed in part to bolster the academic standing of hundreds of student athletes, was reduced essentially to a nonissue for the NCAA. UNC's attorneys employed a brilliant strategy: take the NCAA membership's new deferential standard and run with it; disavow the damning Wainstein report, which UNC commissioned and embraced for years; and assert that no institutional academic policies *at the time* prohibited what had occurred in the AFAM department. Indeed, as the infractions report stated, "UNC took the firm position that the courses were permissible and UNC will continue to honor the grades."

The NCAA membership clearly got what it asked for. The legislative shift toward greater institutional responsibility left the AFAM scandal in the hands of UNC and its accreditors, not the NCAA. But was this a case of unintended consequences? It is hard to read the Wainstein report without coming to the conclusion that the many *athletics* connections to the AFAM scandal *should* have rendered it a matter of NCAA concern. Indeed, the entire AFAM scheme was motivated, at least in part, by the desire of Crowder and Nyang'oro to help student *athletes*. The Wainstein report notes that Crowder was "a very passionate" Tar Heels fan with "close personal ties" to the athletics department, "with her closest friend having been ASPSA basketball counselor Burgess McSwain and her companion being a former Tar Heels basketball player." Crowder "cited compassion as her primary driver" behind the AFAM scheme, but "there is no question that her strong love for and identification with the sports program contributed to her willingness to offer paper courses that were disproportionately taken by student-athletes." Recall the extreme disproportionality—47.4 percent of the AFAM paper-course enrollments were student athletes, who made up about 4 percent of the UNC student body. Nyang'oro's motivation similarly was a "particular interest . . . in helping struggling student-athletes to remain eligible."

Wainstein also cited continual "pressure" from academic counselors within the athletics department, including "countless emails to Crowder in which ASPSA counselors keep up a steady drumbeat of requests for paper classes and student-athlete enrollments." The report is replete with internal correspondence (such as the PowerPoint presentation and emails discussed earlier in this chapter) showing that both ASPSA tutors and coaching staff members knew that many of the AFAM courses were a sham and directed their student athletes toward them *because* they were a sham. When the football team's collective GPA dropped following Crowder's retirement to its lowest level in ten years, an academic counselor for football pleaded with Nyang'oro to continue the fraudulent courses . . . including the one that led to Nyang'oro's indictment, which had an enrollment entirely of football players.

Because of these (and many other) connections to athletics, the UNC decision leaves a sour taste. But it also reinforces the basic principle that the NCAA is a self-governing membership organization . . . and the participants in its rules-enforcement process are bound by the dictates of the membership. Let's hope that the membership has not inadvertently opened the door to even more academic fraud.

The underlying problems facing UNC were not new. A *Los Angeles Times* article in 2007 addressed "the time-honored tradition of athletes seeking easy classes" by noting the "stampede of student athletes up Figueroa Street from USC to Los Angeles Trade Tech College." Seems they had discovered a Spanish class at Trade Tech that was an easy mark. The Spanish professor told the *Times*, "I've never given an easy grade in my life. You come to my class and work, and I see you want to learn, I'll give you an A. I see some lazy ass, coming late all the time, acting like he doesn't care, I won't give him an A. I'll give him a B." Auburn was investigated in 2006 for a scheme similar to UNC's—a multitude of directed-readings courses in sociology and criminology that involved no class time and little work. Even Stanford, of all places, was embarrassed in 2011 by a report of a Courses of Interest list distributed by the Athletic Academic Resource Center. Resource center personnel defended the list, which was distributed only to student athletes, on the ground that the courses met the athletes' practice and competition schedules, but some student athletes apparently had a different take, viewing it as a list of easy classes. One student athlete was quoted as saying that the classes on the list were "always chock-full of athletes and very easy A's."

The UNC case, however, became a lightning rod for critics who view academic fraud as just one more symptom of an intercollegiate athletics world in crisis. And we haven't even discussed generous admissions standards that many big-time programs employ to bring academically weak student athletes into the institution in the first place. A 2009 Associated Press review of admissions data from most Division I football programs "identified at least 27 schools where athletes were at least 10 times more likely to benefit from special admission programs than students in the general population." The depth and breadth of the AFAM scandal clearly refocused public attention on academic fraud, and observers were watching carefully to see how the UNC case ultimately was resolved. Now that it has been resolved in a manner that appears to be soft on UNC, a reexamination of NCAA priorities surely will be in order. To quote sportswriter Dana O'Neil again, "Most people can't get their knickers in a twist over a coach making too many phone calls to a prospect or buying a recruit a cheesesteak. 'Aberrant' courses? That's an NCAA violation most people can get behind."

A final note is in order. The most serious allegations facing UNC as an institution (as opposed to allegations against individuals) were the dreaded lack of institutional control and an accompanying failure to monitor. But in virtually every infractions case, such allegations are grounded on *underlying rule violations*. For example, the NCAA enforcement staff will make allegations 1 and 2 and then allege that "the scope and nature of the violations set forth in allegations 1 and 2 demonstrate" that the institution failed to exercise institutional control over (or failed to monitor) its athletics programs.

The UNC result was consistent with general NCAA practice—the allegations regarding institutional control and failure to monitor went away, at least in part, because the underlying violations (even those relating to Jan Boxill) went away. That practice surely remains on the minds of many supporters of Penn State, which was involved in perhaps the biggest case in NCAA history—another case in which the extent of NCAA *authority* was front and center.

11

The Extent of NCAA Authority

Nothing strengthens authority so much as silence.

LEONARDO DA VINCI

One big-time athletics program will not be found in the NCAA's major infractions database. Since the creation of the database in 1953, Penn State has not been involved in a single major infractions case. Yet we all know of the NCAA leveling some of its harshest sanctions ever on Penn State. How does that happen?

Penn State has some interesting company on the very short list of "clean" programs. Only two other institutions among the sixty-five schools in the Power 5 conferences (ACC, Big 10, Big 12, PAC-12, and SEC) similarly have no major violations— Boston College and Northwestern. Stanford was on the list until the fall of 2016, when it became subject to its first major violations.

Boston College? The name should ring a bell. It was the home of one of the most infamous point-shaving scandals in NCAA history. The troubles began in the summer of 1978, when a group of professional gamblers recruited Boston College players to rig (or attempt to rig) men's basketball games. One of the gamblers was Henry Hill, an associate of New York's Lucchese organized crime family famously played by Ray Liotta in the movie *Goodfellas*. Hill opened up in a February 1981 *Sports Illustrated* cover story coauthored with *SI* sportswriter Douglas S. Looney:

I'm the Boston College basketball fixer. It was a day's pay, it was interesting and it gave me a nice feeling. If you're not a gambler, you'll never understand, but it was a rush.

Here's what I did:

I paid three Boston College basketball players during the 1978–79 season to shave points—not to blow games—in nine games between December 16, 1978 and March 1, 1979. The players were Rick Kuhn and Jim Sweeney, who were in it from the beginning, and Ernie Cobb, the star of the team, who was with us the last five games. It cost me $2,500 per player per game—except when they screwed up and I didn't give them anything or cut them back. As a complimentary service, I bet money for the players when they so requested.

We really had our ups and downs, but when the last pass had been thrown out of bounds, I had won on six of the games, lost on three, and made between $75,000 and $100,000. Not bad for 11 weeks' work. . . . And the players probably made about $10,000 each. . . .

It sounds simple. Heck, all we wanted was BC to win by less than the betting line when it was favored and to lose by more than the line when it was the underdog. So we'd always bet on the BC opponent.

By the time the federal Organized Crime Strike Force was done with its work, five men stood convicted of conspiracy to commit sports bribery and other racketeering-related crimes. Rick Kuhn received a ten-year prison sentence, later reduced to twenty-eight months after he agreed to testify in a later trial against Ernie Cobb and Peter Vario, a Lucchese mob boss who allegedly had approved the plan. Both Cobb and Vario were acquitted, despite Cobb's admission that he had accepted $1,000 from one of the convicted coconspirators. Jim Sweeney was not charged, despite also admitting to taking $500 in cash. That was probably the correct resolution, considering Sweeney cooperated, testified without immunity, and corroborated Henry Hill's testimony against a mob higher-up, one

Jimmy "the Gent" Burke. The feds had been unsuccessful in building a case against Burke for the spectacular Lufthansa heist—a daring theft of nearly $6 million in cash and jewelry at the JFK International Airport in December 1978—and other crimes. But Burke got twenty years for his role in the point-shaving case, and Sweeney "didn't get whacked" (his words, in a 2014 interview). Three other coconspirators received from four to ten years in prison. Henry Hill testified under immunity and spent many years in the U.S. Marshals' Witness Protection Program.

So Boston College does not exactly have a clean slate. Nor does Northwestern. Though not as widely known (perhaps because they were arranged by run-of-the-mill gamblers rather than wiseguys), *two* interrelated gambling scandals engulfed Northwestern in the same year. In late March 1998, in an embarrassing announcement on the eve of that year's Final Four, federal prosecutors in Chicago indicted four individuals, including two former Northwestern men's basketball players, for participating in a point-shaving scheme during the 1994–95 season. A third player was named as an unindicted coconspirator. A fifth indictment charged a former Wildcats football player, Brian Ballarini, with running an illegal gambling operation on campus around the same time.

As was often the case, the 1994–95 Wildcats were Big 10 basement dwellers, headed for a 5-22 season record. Kenneth Dion Lee, a starting guard, also happened to have a gambling habit. Beginning with small bets on college and professional sports, Lee eventually accrued a $4,000 debt to campus bookie Ballarini. According to the indictment, Ballarini, on one occasion, threatened that "violence or other criminal means would be used to harm" Lee if he didn't pay up. Under the circumstances, then, it was not difficult for gambler (and incidentally, former Notre Dame placekicker and soccer standout) Kevin Pendergast to recruit Lee into a point-shaving scheme. Pendergast also owed a substantial debt to his own bookie in Indiana. Everyone needed money, and the team was used to losing. As Lee would reflect later, would it matter so much if they lost by twenty-five points when the spread was twenty? And would anyone even notice lackluster play when a team was down so far?

Lee and Pendergast pled guilty to sports bribery, as did Lee's teammate Dewey Williams, the starting center, and one of Pendergast's gambling associates, Brian Irving. The plea agreements included admissions that on one occasion, after Lee and Williams played poorly in a thirty-point loss to Penn State (a loss significantly wider than the spread), Pendergast paid Lee $4,000 in cash "in a yellow envelope in an alley" by Buffalo Joe's, a popular restaurant near the Northwestern campus. Lee shared some of his earnings with his teammates, Williams and the unindicted coconspirator, and presumably paid down his debt to Ballarini.

In late November 1998, two days before Thanksgiving, a federal judge sentenced all four defendants—Lee, Williams, Pendergast, and Irving—to short prison terms. Pendergast got two months; the other three got one month. All four defendants had cooperated with authorities, including agreeing to help the NCAA and FBI in their antigambling education efforts, but the judge felt that at least some incarceration was essential as a deterrent to others.

The other shoe dropped on Northwestern a week later, on the afternoon of the Wildcat football team's end-of-season banquet, when federal prosecutors announced indictments against four former football players. The campus bookie, Ballarini, had pled guilty the summer before to gambling charges relating back to 1994 and had told prosecutors that he had accepted bets from football players on games in which they played. Those players all were subpoenaed to testify before a federal grand jury, and prosecutors now brought perjury charges, alleging that the players had lied to the grand jury by denying they had placed the bets. One of the players, star running back Dennis Lundy, also was accused of actual point-shaving by intentionally fumbling the ball near the goal line in a November 1994 game against Iowa. In early February 1999 Lundy admitted to just that—he had placed a bet on the Iowa game, through Ballarini, and won $400 when Northwestern lost the game by more than the point spread, in part because of the critical turnover at the goal line. Lundy had previously told the grand jury that he had sprained his wrist earlier in the Iowa game and fumbled when he "got hit on the arm real good." Videotapes of the game showed he was untouched. The other indicted players also eventually admitted to betting on Northwestern games and lying about the bets to the grand jury. When all the dust settled, eleven former Northwestern basketball and football players were implicated in point-shaving, illegal gambling, or perjury.

Despite the fact that point-shaving and players gambling on their own games strike at the very heart of sports competition, the NCAA deals with gambling issues outside the realm of a major infractions case. To be sure, NCAA bylaws specifically prohibit "sports wagering" by either student athletes or athletics department staff members. But the only sanctions specifically provided for gambling violations relate to student-athlete ineligibility. For example, for point-shaving violations or gambling on one's own team, the relevant bylaw provides, "A student-athlete who engages in activities designed to influence the outcome of an intercollegiate contest or in an effort to affect win-loss margins ("point shaving") or who participates in any sports wagering activity involving the student-athlete's institution shall permanently lose all remaining regular-season and postseason eligibility in all sports." Student athletes who engage in other types of gambling, "through the Internet, a bookmaker or a parlay card," are subject to ineligibility for a year and permanent ineligibility on a second offense.

Student athletes, then, face severe sanctions for gambling, but even in a serious case involving point-shaving, *institutions* rarely receive penalties. In December 1997, just months before the Northwestern case broke, two Arizona State men's basketball players pled guilty to conspiracy for accepting bribes to shave points in 1994. The NCAA announced that there would be no sanctions against the university, because "there is no information . . . indicating that the institution knew or should have known" of the players' actions. A dedicated agents, gambling, and amateurism staff of the NCAA (housed in enforcement services) noted after its investigation that what occurred at Arizona State "is the result of a societal problem, not just an Arizona State problem."

Point-shaving scandals in both football and men's basketball hit Toledo from 2008–11, but no major cases appear in the NCAA database. Even at the University of San Diego, where a former *assistant coach* facilitated a point-shaving scheme (with the help of a point guard who perhaps is the best ballplayer ever to play for the Toreros), the school and the NCAA agreed in 2013 on a *secondary violation* without institutional penalties.

Why the kid-glove treatment for schools involved in point-shaving or other prohibited gambling activities? In addition to gambling being a societal problem, the criminal justice system took over in all these cases—the perpetrators were charged with *crimes* and dealt with accordingly. When the underlying behavior (and rule violation) of student athletes—point-shaving, for example—constitutes a crime, the NCAA typically lets the criminal process work its course; no sense piling on with a major infractions case.

We've seen a similar scenario play out in many instances involving criminal conduct by student athletes. The University of Colorado, for example, garnered numerous headlines in the late 1980s for criminal behavior by a couple of dozen football players—rape, assault, menacing, burglary, use of stolen property, brawling, criminal trespass, disorderly conduct, drunken driving. The team was profiled in a 1989 *Sports Illustrated* article by Rick Reilly, who also commented, "Still, as bad as things have been in Boulder, Buffalo fans figure their team's troubles would barely make the 10 o'clock news in Norman, Okla." During my second year of teaching at the University of

Oklahoma in 1989, quarterback Charles Thompson appeared on the cover of *Sports Illustrated* in an orange jumpsuit after his arrest for selling cocaine. The cover story, entitled "Oklahoma: A Sordid Story—How Barry Switzer's Sooners Terrorized Their Campus," also recounted the arraignment of three players on rape charges and the shooting of another player by a teammate. More recently, allegations of a climate of sexual harassment and assault by football players at the University of Montana formed the basis of Jon Krakauer's book *Missoula*. Similar allegations reared their ugly head at Baylor University, where a high-profile president and popular head football coach lost their jobs as a result.

In none of these cases—and many more like them—did the NCAA initiate a major infractions case or impose sanctions on the involved institutions; while the underlying misconduct may have been a crime, it was not an NCAA *rule violation*. Of course, some conduct—point-shaving, for example, or drug violations—may fall in both camps. But typically, when student athletes or coaches engage in criminal behavior, the NCAA defers to the criminal justice system, even though in some instances one could make an argument that a school lacked institutional control over its athletics program.

That brings us to Penn State. This truly sordid story is all too familiar to most readers. The facts first came to light in November 2011, when Jerry Sandusky was arrested and charged with forty counts of child sexual abuse. Sandusky had been an assistant football coach for the Nittany Lions for thirty years, including twenty-three as defensive coordinator for legendary coach Joe Paterno. In 2011 Sandusky had been retired for twelve years, but he was still an active member of the Penn State community and had unfettered access to athletics facilities on campus. Sandusky was well known in the broader community as well, in part because of his involvement with the Second Mile, a charitable organization he had founded to assist troubled young boys.

Compounding the shock of Sandusky's arrest were the horrific details in a statewide grand jury's findings of fact. The grand jury graphically described years of sexual abuse of eight victims, all groomed by Sandusky through their contacts with the Second Mile. Some of the assaults allegedly had occurred in the showers of athletics department facilities on campus. On one occasion in 2000, a custodian reported to his fellow custodians that he had seen Sandusky performing oral sex on Victim 8 in the showers of the Lasch Football Building. No one reported the incident to authorities, because they feared losing their jobs. On another occasion only a few months later, a twenty-eight-year-old graduate assistant with the football program, Mike McQueary, "heard rhythmic, slapping sounds" coming from the Lasch showers about 9:30 on a Friday night. When he looked into the shower area, he "saw a naked boy, Victim 2, whose age he estimated to be ten years old, with his hands up against the wall, being subjected to anal intercourse by a naked Sandusky."

The latter incident would prove particularly troubling for university officials. Reports were made up the chain of command at the university—McQueary to his boss, head coach Joe Paterno; Paterno to Timothy Curley, the director of athletics, and to Gary Schultz, the university's senior vice president for finance and business; and ultimately to university president Graham Spanier. None of these individuals, however, reported the abuse to law enforcement or child welfare authorities, despite the fact that all of them, with the exception of McQueary, were aware of another shower incident in 1998, when Sandusky was *still employed* at Penn State as defensive coordinator of the football team. In the 1998 incident, the mother of an eleven-year-old boy (Victim 6, also involved with the Second Mile) reported to the university police department that Sandusky had touched her son inappropriately in the Lasch Building showers. Investigators interviewed Sandusky, who admitted to hugging the boy while both were naked in the shower, but he said there "wasn't anything sexual about it." The investigation was closed, even though Sandusky said he had engaged in similar behavior with other children in the past, with an admonition to Sandusky not to continue showering with children.

So beginning in 1998 Spanier, Schultz, Curley, and Paterno all were aware of at least one of Sandusky's proclivities . . . and really, what grown man *showers* with preteens?! Despite the fact that the investigation went no further in 1998, they all must have wondered what may be in Sandusky's dark heart. Schultz's notes at the time reflect his personal concerns; Sandusky's behavior was "at best inappropriate @ worst sexual improprieties . . . Critical issue—contact with genitals? . . . Is this opening of pandora's box? . . . Other children?"

Yet when McQueary's even more troublesome report came to them in 2001, Spanier, Schultz, and Curley collectively decided on a plan similar to the 1998 resolution—basically, advise Sandusky that showering with young boys (at least in university facilities) is still improper. Despite the group's initial inclination to report the incident to the state's Department of Public Welfare, Curley, "after giving it more thought and talking it over with Joe [Paterno]," proposed that he tell Sandusky showering with boys in the football locker room was a problem and offer him "professional help"; only if he did not cooperate (presumably, by continuing to engage in such showers) would the Department of Public Welfare be notified. President Spanier responded to Curley in an email that the plan was "acceptable to me. . . . The only downside for us is if the message isn't 'heard' and acted upon, and we then become vulnerable for not having reported it. But that can be assessed down the road. The approach you outline is humane and a reasonable way to proceed." Schultz agreed: "This is a more humane and upfront way to handle this. . . . We can play it by ear" as to reporting.

These exchanges occurred in February 2001. According to the grand jury's findings of fact, six months later Sandusky sexually assaulted Victim 5 in the Lasch Building showers, and he went on to assault other victims over the next several years.

A criminal investigation finally began in 2009, when Victim 1, at the time a Pennsylvania high schooler, reported to authorities that Sandusky had molested him on numerous occasions, beginning when the boy was twelve years old. A grand jury investigation began and continued before a second grand jury, which released its initial report and charging recommendations in November 2011. After posting bail following his first arrest, Sandusky was rearrested on December 7, 2011, after the grand jury issued new recommendations involving two additional victims (bringing the total charges to fifty-two).

McQueary had testified before the grand jury in December 2010, stating in graphic terms what he saw in the Penn State lockers nearly a decade earlier. (In later court testimony, he reiterated that was Sandusky "sexually molesting" Victim 2 . . . "having some type of intercourse with him.") He also testified that he told Paterno the following day what he had witnessed. A week and a half after the incident, McQueary met with Curley and Schultz and, according to the grand jury report, told the two men that "he had witnessed what he believed to be Sandusky having anal sex with a boy in the Lasch Building showers."

How on earth could that incident go unreported to authorities? McQueary and Paterno apparently believed their responsibility ended upon their reports to their superiors, and strictly as a matter of Pennsylvania *law* at the time, they may have been right. As for Curley and Schultz, they apparently engaged in careful parsing of the words of McQueary, who testified truthfully that he had not witnessed actual penetration. At a later preliminary hearing, McQueary also said he never used the words "anal intercourse" or "rape" in describing the incident to anyone. Curley and Schultz had their say before the grand jury in January 2011. Curley suggested that McQueary had given them the impression only of nonsexual "horsing around" between Sandusky and the boy. Schultz's testimony was especially odd and disturbing; he had the impression that in the course of "clowning around" in the shower, Sandusky "might have grabbed the genitals of the young boy. I had no impression that it was anything more serious than that." *What?!* Pressed by prosecutors to consider whether grabbing a young boy's genitals (while naked in the shower) might constitute criminal behavior, Schultz replied, "That's inappropriate. I don't know if it's criminal. If it's in the context of wrestling or something like that. I don't know."

The grand jury did not believe their accounts of what McQueary told them; it recommended for both Curley and Schultz charges of perjury and failure to report suspected child abuse. In announcing formal charges, Pennsylvania attorney general Linda Kelly condemned the two officials in stark terms: "Their inaction likely allowed a child predator to continue to victimize children for many, many years." For his part, President Spanier, who had been advised the week before of the pending criminal charges, issued a prepared press release, pledging his "unconditional support" of Curley and Schultz, who "operate at the highest levels of honesty, integrity and compassion. I am confident the record will show that these charges are groundless and that they conducted themselves professionally and appropriately."

Prosecutors filed no criminal charges against Paterno, whose discomfort with the whole situation was palpable. He told the grand jury that McQueary had reported Sandusky "fondling, whatever you might call it—I'm not sure what the term would be—a young boy." After the scandal broke, Paterno told the *Washington Post* that it may not have made any difference if McQueary had been more graphic in his description, "because I never heard of, of, rape and a man." Despite his difficulty articulating what occurred, Paterno understood (and, by his account, reported to Curley) that McQueary had seen Sandusky sexually violating his victim: "I don't know what you would call it. Obviously, he was doing something with the youngster. It was a sexual nature."

President Spanier testified before the grand jury a few months after the others, in April 2011. He told the grand jury that Curley and Schultz had briefed him on the shower incident, but the essence of that briefing was simply that an unnamed staff member (Spanier said McQueary was not identified to him at the time) "thought he saw (Sandusky and a boy) horsing around in the shower and he was a little uncomfortable with it, so he brought it to Mr. Curley's attention." When asked whether the horseplay could have been sexual in nature, Spanier said Curley and Schultz gave him no such indication. Furthermore, he told the grand jury that at no time did the three men discuss whether to report the incident to child welfare officials. When asked if he was aware of any prior accusations against Sandusky, Spanier responded in the negative.

All those assertions turned against Spanier. In November 2012 prosecutors charged him with eight criminal counts, including perjury, failure to report suspected child abuse, conspiracy, obstruction of justice, and child endangerment. The latter three counts also were added to the charges against Curley and Schultz, and Attorney General Kelly once again minced no words in condemning the actions of all three men: "This was a conspiracy of silence by top officials to actively conceal the truth." The accompanying grand jury report was equally harsh, noting that "the actual harm realized by this wanton failure is staggering. . . . The continued cover-up of this incident and the ongoing failure to report placed every minor child who would come into contact with Sandusky in the future in grave jeopardy of being abused." The charges against Spanier essentially alleged that Spanier knew full well in 2001 that the incident involved child sexual abuse; that the three men had specifically discussed reporting it to authorities but backed off when Curley suggested an alternative plan of action; and that Spanier had been aware of the 1998 accusations against Sandusky, which had been reported by the victim's mother to the university police.

The shocking details of the initial grand jury report in November 2011, which quickly became national headlines, must have been devastating to Penn State supporters—not the least of which were the members of the university's board of trustees. The trustees were blindsided by the news, in part because Spanier and university counsel Cynthia Baldwin reportedly downplayed the seriousness of the grand jury investigation in a report to the trustees in May 2011, just a month following Spanier's appearance before the grand jury. As noted earlier, McQueary testified before the grand jury in December 2010, followed by Schultz, Curley, and Paterno in January 2011. The board of trustees had held further meetings in July and September, but no discussion of the ongoing criminal investigation took place at either meeting.

One can imagine the anger and disgust of the trustees in early November, when news of Sandusky's arrest became public. The board responded accordingly. Within the week, Spanier, Schultz, Curley, and Paterno all were out of a job—Paterno and Spanier were fired, Curley went on administrative leave, and Schultz retired. On November 21, 2011, the board announced that former federal judge and FBI director Louis Freeh had been retained to conduct an internal investigation.

Over the next eight months, an investigative team from the law firm of Freeh, Sporkin, and Sullivan conducted hundreds of interviews and examined a multitude of documents, including email messages recovered from university hard drives, servers, and backup tapes. The documents would prove incriminating. The Freeh group publicly released its report on July 12, 2012, and in its overview, the report stated that the "most important documents" were email messages among Spanier, Schultz, and Curley in 1998 and 2001. Schultz also had kept a "Sandusky" file that included notes contemporaneous with the 1998 incident. The documents suggested that all three men, along with Coach Paterno, were aware of the 1998 incident in which the mother of Victim 6 had reported Sandusky's inappropriate behavior in the showers of the Lasch Football Building. The 2001 documents revealed the agreed-upon plan *not* to report the McQueary-witnessed abuse, as well as Spanier's comment that "the only downside for us is if the message isn't 'heard' and acted upon, and we then become vulnerable for not having reported it."

The Freeh report in July 2012 came three weeks after Sandusky had been found guilty by a jury, beyond a reasonable doubt, of forty-five counts of child sexual abuse. Thus, what *Sandusky* had done was open to little dispute. But with respect to the culpability of the other Penn State employees—Spanier, Schultz, Curley, and even Paterno—one should understand that the Freeh team was handicapped in part by the same constraints that face the NCAA enforcement staff in an infractions investigation. The Freeh, Sporkin, and Sullivan law firm is not a government entity; it has no subpoena power or other authority to *compel* witnesses to cooperate. Sandusky, Schultz, and Curley declined to submit to interviews with the Freeh investigators. The Pennsylvania attorney general requested that McQueary not be interviewed. Paterno reportedly expressed a willingness to interview, but he died of cancer in January 2012, before an interview could be conducted. Of the key involved individuals, only Spanier interviewed with Freeh's investigators, and he reiterated that he never received a report that Sandusky had engaged in child sexual abuse.

Nonetheless, the Freeh group found the documentation to be compelling and delivered a *scathing* indictment of numerous Penn State actors. Among its findings were the following:

The matter included a "total and consistent disregard by the most senior leaders at Penn State for the safety and welfare of Sandusky's child victims."

Spanier, Schultz, Curley, and Paterno "concealed Sandusky's activities from the Board of Trustees, the University community and authorities."

The four "repeatedly concealed critical facts . . . in order to avoid the consequences of bad publicity."

Their actions were "unchecked by the Board of Trustees that did not perform its oversight duties."

The actions (and inaction) of Penn State officials were influenced by a "culture of reverence for the football program . . . at all levels."

Harsh findings indeed . . . and if true, worthy of the strongest condemnation. The Paterno family later commissioned their own report, and at 238 pages, it was nearly as long as the 267-page Freeh report. This one, the Thornburgh report, was spearheaded by former U.S. attorney general Richard Thornburgh and titled *Critique of the Freeh Report: The Rush to Injustice Regarding Joe Paterno*. In an interesting clash of ex–Justice Department executives, Thornburgh concluded that Freeh's findings were "factually wrong, speculative and fundamentally flawed." Freeh responded that the Thornburgh report was "self-serving" and said he stood by his conclusion that "four of the most powerful people at Penn State failed to protect against a child sexual predator harming children for over a decade."

The Penn State case is stunning even without consideration of the NCAA's reaction. But what happened next is *truly* stunning, from an NCAA watcher's perspective. On July 23, 2012, just eleven days after the Freeh report was publicly released, NCAA president Mark Emmert and Edward Ray, chairman of the NCAA Executive Committee and Oregon State University president, held a nationally televised news conference to announce unprecedented penalties against Penn State: a $60 million fine, to be used to assist victims of child sexual abuse; a four-year ban on postseason competition in football; a sizable scholarship reduction in football over four years, reducing initial scholarships from twenty-five to fifteen per year and total scholarships from eighty-five to sixty-five per year; five years of probation; and the vacation of all wins of the Penn State football team from 1998 to 2011.

The vacation-of-wins penalty also would be reflected in the personal coaching record of Joe Paterno, who had passed away as the winningest FBS (Football Bowl Subdivision of Division I) coach in NCAA history. In one quick stroke, Paterno lost 111 wins and fell from number one to number five on the all-time win list. In 2009 I had argued one of my last appeals on behalf of the Committee on Infractions. The case involved academic fraud at Florida State University, some involving football players. The university fought a vacation-of-records penalty strenuously, primarily because Bobby Bowden, the FSU head football coach, would be losing not only twelve wins but also a neck-and-neck battle with Joe Paterno to see who would finish his coaching career with the most career wins. The vacation of wins in the Penn State matter moved Bowden decisively up to first place. As we'll see later, though, Bowden's roller-coaster ride continued, falling from his perch in 2015, when Paterno's wins were restored.

The Penn State penalties were extraordinary not only in their severity but also in the way they were imposed. Postseason bans, scholarship reductions, vacation of records, probation—all are familiar penalties imposed by the Committee on Infractions in cases involving major rule violations. Even fines are typically within the committee's arsenal of sanctions, though $60 million certainly got people's attention. The amount was selected because it approximated one year's gross revenue from the Penn State football program. But the Committee on Infractions did not impose the penalties on Penn State; indeed, the committee was not involved in the case at all. Heck, even the NCAA enforcement staff had little involvement, because the NCAA leadership used the Freeh report as the basis for the sanctions, seeing no need to conduct an independent enforcement staff investigation.

NCAA president Mark Emmert remarked after reading the Freeh report that he "was struck by how thorough the investigation was. We could not have duplicated it if we had done our investigation." I have no doubt that that is true. The enforcement staff's resources do not compare to the resources of Freeh, Sporkin, and Sullivan, who were given free rein (and paid handsomely) by Penn State to conduct as thorough an investigation as possible. The Freeh report notes at the beginning that Freeh and his team conducted "over 430 interviews" and analyzed "over 3.5 million pieces of pertinent electronic data and documents." Under those circumstances, why *shouldn't* the NCAA be able to use the fact findings of the Freeh investigation, particularly when *Penn State itself* commissioned and embraced the Freeh report? In any infractions case, the enforcement staff hopes to work cooperatively with institutional representatives, and if the institution conducts a thorough internal investigation and falls on its sword, the staff should be free to use the findings and conclusions presented by the institution. Similarly, the enforcement staff should be free to use information obtained through the criminal justice process, as it did in the Michigan basketball case. Here, NCAA officials not only had the Freeh report, but they also had testimony presented under oath in grand jury and court proceedings.

But was this an *infractions* case? No . . . and that's what makes the Penn State case so interesting from a process perspective. Not surprisingly, there is no NCAA bylaw prohibiting child sexual abuse. Nor do the bylaws address failure to report suspected child abuse, perjury, conspiracy, obstruction of justice, or child endangerment. The reason is obvious—all these actions involve *crimes*, and an NCAA manual focused on athletics and competitive equity hardly could, or should, incorporate an entire criminal code. As noted at the beginning of this chapter, criminal activity—even by student athletes, coaches, or others involved in the intercollegiate athletics enterprise—typically is left to law enforcement authorities and the criminal justice system. That is true, as we have seen, even in cases in which criminal behavior also constitutes a rule violation, such as point-shaving. For that reason, many knowledgeable observers have questioned the extent of the

NCAA's authority in the Penn State case. In other words, what business is it of *the* NCAA to address Jerry Sandusky's despicable criminal acts?

A partial answer, of course, is that the NCAA was not addressing *Sandusky's* acts, it was addressing the actions (and inaction) of Penn State leaders, who represented one of the NCAA's member institutions. And presumably, a voluntary membership organization has ample latitude to regulate the conduct of its members and their representatives. But the NCAA is still an *athletics* association; are the relevant actions of Spanier, Schultz, Curley, Paterno, and McQueary athletics related? Tangentially—some of Sandusky's assaults took place in the Lasch Football Building. And at least with respect to the 1998 shower incident, Sandusky was still an athletics department employee. Even after his retirement in 1999, Sandusky was able to use both his status as a former coach and his access to the football facilities as tools in his effort to groom children for abuse.

One also might argue that the actions and inaction of Penn State officials evidenced a lack of institutional control, which is not an unusual finding in a major infractions case. But to my knowledge, the Committee on Infractions has never found lack of institutional control without also finding *underlying* rule violations. For example, persistent recruiting violations may support an *additional* finding that the institution lacked appropriate control over one of its athletics programs. In the Penn State case, no underlying violations—at least in the traditional sense—existed to undergird a finding of lack of institutional control.

It didn't matter; NCAA leaders felt the situation at Penn State was *so* despicable that it was an affront to the association's "values." President Mark Emmert had been on the job for only a year, but he already had spoken forcefully about integrity in member institutions' activities. As noted at the beginning of chapter 8, 2011 had been a rough year for the NCAA, which was facing a torrent of bad news about rule violators. In August 2011 the NCAA released a public statement from Emmert entitled "Cheating Will Not Be Tolerated." He had met with a specially convened group of university presidents earlier that month, and they were fed up. In get-tough language, Emmert announced that penalties for rule violators were going to get tougher; indeed, the NCAA's entire enforcement regime would be changed to make clear that the cost of breaking the rules would "[outweigh] any benefit."

Emmert, of course, was talking about *rule* violators, but when the first criminal charges at Penn State were announced only three months later, Emmert saw an opportunity to broaden his get-tough message. On November 17, 2011, twelve days after the criminal charges against Sandusky, Schultz, and Curley were announced, Emmert sent a letter to interim university president Rodney Erickson (the board of trustees had removed Spanier the week before), signaling an NCAA investigation and invoking Article 2.4 of the NCAA Constitution—The Principle of Sportsmanship and Ethical Conduct. Article 2.4 states, "For intercollegiate athletics to promote the character development of participants, to enhance the integrity of higher education and to promote civility in society, student-athletes, coaches, and all others associated with these athletics programs and events should adhere to such fundamental values as respect, fairness, civility, honesty and responsibility. These values should be manifest not only in athletics participation, but also in the broad spectrum of activities affecting the athletics program."

Erickson told Emmert that the university would be conducting its own investigation and asked that the NCAA hold off until that investigation ran its course. Four days later, Louis Freeh announced that Penn State had hired his firm to conduct an internal investigation; his high-powered status undoubtedly helped to persuade Emmert that the Freeh group would be thorough and conscientious in its investigation. Erickson agreed to share the results of the investigation with the NCAA, and between November 2011 and July 2012, when the Freeh report was publicly released, Penn State kept NCAA leaders updated on a regular basis.

One thing was clear from the Freeh report—the Freeh group's investigation was indeed thorough. It was not "complete" in the sense that all critical witnesses could be interviewed, but it was certainly as thorough as the NCAA enforcement staff could hope to conduct. Regardless of what happened next, there would be no need for an independent NCAA investigation. What else was clear from the report was that things looked bad for Penn State. The report pulled no punches in condemning both the actions of Penn State leaders and a "culture of reverence for the football program" that allowed Sandusky to perpetrate his crimes for many years.

The NCAA essentially had three choices in response to the now-completed investigation: it could (1) condemn publicly the actions of those implicated in wrongdoing and do nothing more—that is, leave the matter for the criminal justice system to resolve and leave Penn State to pick up the pieces of its shattered reputation; (2) refer the matter to the traditional rules-enforcement process, with ultimate resolution by the Committee on Infractions; or (3) reach an agreement with the university to resolve the matter outside the ordinary enforcement process but still with NCAA sanctions. NCAA leaders opted for number three. They were so outraged by what had happened that they simply could not countenance doing *nothing* in the way of sanctions. And they had to admit that the matter did not fit neatly into a traditional infractions case because of the absence of underlying rule violations. The final option, however, required *agreement* by Penn State.

Penn State officials undoubtedly had plenty of advice regarding how to address the concerns of the NCAA leadership, but one key player appears to have been Gene Marsh, whom the university hired as outside counsel around the time the Freeh report was released. Marsh, a former chair of the Division I Committee on Infractions, was now in private practice with a law firm in Birmingham, Alabama, following a long and distinguished career as a law professor and faculty athletics representative at the University of Alabama. The negotiations between Marsh and NCAA leaders—particularly NCAA president Mark Emmert and general counsel Donald Remy— are chronicled in an *ESPN: The Magazine* piece by Don Van Natta Jr. in August 2012. The article, entitled "On Death's Door: Inside the Secret Negotiations That Brought Penn State Football to the Brink of Extinction," reveals a phone call on July 17, 2012 (five days after the release of the Freeh report), between Marsh and Remy. Remy, according to Marsh, said on the call that Penn State was facing a multiyear death penalty. President Emmert had consulted with both his Executive Committee and his Division I Board of Directors; according to Van Natta's account, the majority of the board of directors (a group of university presidents) "had coalesced around a decision: Shut down Penn State's football program for four years." For Marsh, this did not sound like a true negotiation: "In federal bankruptcy court, there is a concept of a cram-down—a judge tells creditors, 'Here's the deal, this is all you are going to get, a few pennies on the dollar, and you should be happy with that.' You know, take it or leave it, because you don't really have any choice. Well, this was the NCAA equivalent of a cram-down."

That July 17 was a Tuesday. The next few days involved efforts by Marsh and other Penn State representatives to convince NCAA leaders to back off the death penalty. By the weekend, the parties had come to a resolution: the NCAA and Penn State would agree, by way of a formal consent decree, to the set of sanctions previously noted—$60 million fine, four-year postseason ban, major scholarship reductions, five years' probation, and vacation of fourteen years of wins. The sanctions would be short of the death penalty—the Nittany Lions would still be allowed to compete on the gridiron—but extraordinarily harsh and unprecedented penalties nonetheless. The NCAA would announce the resolution publicly at a nationally televised press conference on Monday, July 23.

Members of a voluntary association presumably can agree to almost anything association related, so it is tempting to bypass any serious discussion of the NCAA's authority or jurisdiction in the Penn State matter simply by acknowledging that the two parties *agreed* to the resolution. But "cram-down" and "consent" seem mutually exclusive. And make no mistake—the consent decree itself indicates, even in its title, that the resolution was "imposed" by the NCAA and "accepted" by Penn State. The sanctions section of the document also indicates that "the NCAA *imposes* the following sanctions on the University." That certainly seems to suggest that the NCAA had the upper hand. Penn State surely must have felt like a beaten pup after relentless media coverage, and President Erickson was concerned that not accepting the NCAA sanctions would "make ourselves look worse and unrepentant in the eyes of the nation."

Documentation revealed in a subsequent lawsuit against the NCAA by Pennsylvania state senator Jake Corman and state treasurer Rob McCord has proven to be interesting. The suit initially focused on whether the money from the $60 million fine could be spent entirely within the state of Pennsylvania; the NCAA initially resisted that approach but later capitulated. During the course of the litigation, the judge handling the matter expanded the suit's scope to address the legality of the overall sanctions—essentially whether the NCAA had the authority to do what it did. The discovery process in the Corman-McCord suit revealed email messages and deposition statements that led numerous commentators to suggest that the NCAA had bluffed its way to the sanctions—that is, that it essentially coerced Penn State to accept the penalties by threatening to impose a multiyear death penalty that really was not a viable option.

I don't think the NCAA leadership was bluffing. I don't doubt that many of the university presidents on the NCAA Board of Directors and NCAA Executive Committee believed, at least initially, that the death penalty was the appropriate sanction for what they viewed as outrageous behavior at Penn State. But I'm not sure those presidents had a full understanding of either the death penalty itself or how the infractions and enforcement processes really work. Fundamentally, the death penalty originated in the mid-1980s as a penalty for egregious *repeat violators*. Even in very recent years (long after the Penn State sanctions were imposed), one could go on the NCAA website and find a Frequently Asked Questions section in a discussion of the enforcement process. In that section was the question "What is the 'death penalty'?" The NCAA's answer? "The *repeat-violator* legislation ('death penalty') is applicable to an institution if, within a five-year period, the following conditions [including a major violation occurring within five years of the starting date of the penalty assessed in a prior major case] exist." Penn State was not a repeat violator; it has never had a single major infractions case!

Technically, "prohibition against an intercollegiate sports team or teams participating against outside competition for a specified period" had been listed as a disciplinary measure available to the Committee on Infractions, even outside a death penalty case. But the fact is, the committee has never seriously considered imposing the penalty on a non-repeat violator. Indeed, the fact that the Division I infractions committee has imposed the death penalty only once—on SMU in 1987—indicates that even repeat violators will escape the death penalty unless their infractions history *really* stands out.

The presumption that the death penalty is reserved for repeat violators was recognized even in the consent decree between the NCAA and Penn State. In explaining why the penalty was not imposed, despite "serious consideration and significant discussion," the decree reads, "While these circumstances certainly are severe, the suspension of competition is most warranted when the institution is a repeat violator and has failed to cooperate or take corrective action. The University has never before had NCAA major violations."

Does that mean the NCAA bluffed? Documents in the Corman-McCord litigation indicate that NCAA leaders engaged in a vigorous debate about potential Penn State penalties prior to formulation of the consent decree. Those discussions suggested that Penn State had a choice, and presumably, that choice was conveyed to Penn State officials. The first choice was to accept the harsh penalties ultimately offered up by the NCAA; by doing so, Penn State could avoid the death penalty, resolve the matter expeditiously, and move forward. The second choice was a "long, hard slog," as the NCAA general counsel put it, through a regular enforcement process that ultimately could result in the death penalty being imposed by the Committee on Infractions. Put that way, I certainly would not fault Penn State officials for wanting to put the ugliness behind them and come to a quick resolution. Even though the sanctions might deal a crushing blow to the football program in the short run, at least they would know what they were dealing with and could focus on rebuilding both the football program and the university's reputation. And in the final analysis, considering what the NCAA did with the sanctions later, I believe that resolution worked to Penn State's benefit.

But I also believe it was a false choice. First, I do not understand why it would have been a "long, hard slog" through a conventional enforcement process. The investigation was done; NCAA leaders decided as soon as the Freeh report was released that they would embrace the report, negating the need for an independent enforcement staff investigation. Presumably, the matter could have been placed on the Committee on Infractions' docket fairly quickly . . . and as noted earlier, the committee rarely, if ever, had a backlog that would delay a final decision.

More importantly, I believe the chance of the death penalty ultimately being imposed was *slim*. The committee would weigh whatever alleged rule violations were presented by the enforcement staff, but even the NCAA's vice president of enforcement (at the time, Julie Roe Lach) testified in a deposition that she "had a question . . . about the likelihood of an enforcement investigation, while potentially appropriate, actually yielding charges. . . . It wasn't an automatic that this would wind up before the Committee on Infractions." Roe Lach's doubts were well founded, because the case did not involve underlying rule violations. Lack of institutional control, perhaps founded on unethical conduct by Penn State officials, may have been a plausible charge, but it was by no means guaranteed. And "even if charges were brought," Roe Lach questioned "how the committee on infractions, acting as an independent judge and jury, would react to those charges." Again, her doubts were well founded; based on my nearly ten years of experience on the committee, I believe the committee would have been skeptical about whether there was even a viable infractions case, let alone one that would justify a death penalty.

Despite questions about the viability of the death penalty, the NCAA leadership (particularly the Executive Committee) believed it had to act boldly to reinforce the association's "values." Addressing the jurisdiction issue as well, the consent decree incorporated "the findings of the Criminal Jury and the Freeh Report" in concluding that Penn State had fallen woefully short:

> The NCAA concludes that this evidence presents an unprecedented failure of institutional integrity leading to a culture in which a football program was held in higher esteem than the values of the institution, the values of the NCAA, the values of higher education, and most disturbingly the values of human decency. The sexual abuse of children on a university campus by a former university official—and even the active concealment of that abuse—while despicable, ordinarily would not be actionable by the NCAA. Yet, in this instance, it was the fear of or deference to the omnipotent football program that enabled a sexual predator to attract and abuse his victims. Indeed, the reverence for Penn State football permeated every level of the University community. That imbalance of

power and its result are antithetical to the model of intercollegiate athletics embedded in higher education. Indeed, the culture exhibited at Penn State is an extraordinary affront to the values all members of the Association have pledged to uphold and calls for extraordinary action.

Over-the-top? The reader can be the judge . . . and while one is at it, ask whether the "culture" in Happy Valley is significantly different than it is in Ann Arbor, Baton Rouge, Chapel Hill, Gainesville, Lincoln, Norman, Tuscaloosa, or a host of other venues where big-time sports stretch commonsense notions of appropriate priorities.

My own discomfort about the consent decree centers on the precedent it sets. NCAA leaders can say what they want about the uniqueness of the case, but the fact remains that they took a case that "ordinarily would not be actionable by the NCAA" and slammed one of its members with an unprecedented set of penalties. Certainly, what happened at Penn State deserves our outrage—our visceral reaction to child sexual abuse should be one of disgust and loathing. But where do we draw the line? We've read of far too many questionable university reactions, for example, to charges of rape by student athletes. Does a "culture" of inaction in this context also warrant NCAA sanctions? If not, why not? Wouldn't it also offend our commonly held "values"?

I *wish* several things had happened in reaction to the mess at Penn State. If NCAA leaders felt so strongly that Penn State had to be punished, I wish they had imposed different penalties. Why vacate wins, for example? That penalty typically is reserved for schools that compete with ineligible players. No Penn State football players were ineligible as a result of Jerry Sandusky's actions. Scholarship reductions? Typically, a key ingredient in such a sanction is the school's competitive or recruiting advantage gained from a violation. Surely Penn State gained no such advantage from Sandusky's actions. A significant competitive advantage also often underlies a postseason ban. Such a ban also may be appropriate when involved individuals remain with the athletics program. By the time of the consent decree, however, none of the involved individuals remained at Penn State. A lack of institutional control sometimes supports a postseason ban, but the NCAA leadership carefully avoided such a finding, opting instead for a focus on values and "institutional integrity." I understand why; lack of institutional control typically relates to a school's inadequate rules-compliance program. No allegations were made regarding breakdowns in Penn State's adherence to athletics-related rules.

My point is that when the Penn State penalties *look* like infractions penalties, observers naturally question why such penalties were not imposed through the ordinary infractions process. If the case was so extraordinary that it demanded exclusion from that process, then perhaps extraordinary penalties—in kind, not just in severity—also were warranted. The $60 million fine, in my view, comes closer to fitting the bill. *That* was both extraordinary and creative . . . and surely NCAA leaders could have exercised their creativity in fashioning other sanctions.

If the Penn State resolution truly was intended to *change the culture* of reverence to big-time athletics, perhaps other creative measures could have been taken. I know this will be considered heresy or naivete by many, but how about sending a message regarding out-of-control football spending? I believe an exceptional opportunity to do things differently presented itself after Penn State—perhaps, for example, committing to paying a head football coach no more than the university president?—but an article in *Fortune* in late 2015 listed James Franklin, Penn State's head football coach, as number eight on its list of highest-paid coaches, at $4.4 million per year. Back to business as usual.

Even some small actions may have helped. A part of the sanctions against Penn State was a waiver of ordinary transfer rules—that is, "any entering or returning football student-athlete will be allowed to immediately transfer and will be eligible to immediately compete at the transfer institution, provided he is otherwise eligible." (A transfer typically has to sit out a year before competing at a new school.) One disgusting spectacle after the Penn State sanctions were announced was the speed at which other schools descended on Penn State student athletes, like vultures to road kill. Some observers described a "recruiting frenzy" on the Penn State campus in the first forty-eight hours following the announcement of the sanctions. Decrying the scene, Bill O'Brien, Paterno's immediate successor as head coach, was quoted as saying, "Our players are in our building [the Lasch Football Building] right now and they don't want to leave the building because there are coaches from other schools in the parking lot waiting to see them." Penn State's leading rusher the year before was a running back named Silas Redd, who quickly found himself as a starter on the football roster at the University of Southern California. At the time, the USC football program was only halfway through a four-year probation for major violations in the Reggie Bush case. Why not restrict free transfers to schools that were not currently on probation so that rule-breaking institutions were not enriched? Of course, the scene also could have prompted the NCAA to reexamine the rules under which student athletes could be recruited in such circumstances—beyond simply requiring notice, by both the student athlete and the recruiting institution, of an interest in discussing a transfer.

I *wish* the NCAA had not begun so quickly to *rescind* its penalties. The erosion began in September 2013, a little over a year into the sanctions, when the NCAA announced that it would begin restoring some of the scholarships that had been taken away from the Nittany Lions. A year after that, in September 2014, the NCAA restored Penn State's eligibility for postseason competition (two years early) and eliminated all remaining scholarship limitations. At the same time, in response to the Corman-McCord suit, the NCAA withdrew its objection to the

$60 million fine being directed to abuse prevention programs only in Pennsylvania, rather than to a national endowment for abuse victims. Finally, in January 2015 the NCAA gave back all fourteen years' worth of vacated Penn State wins; JoePa was back on top as the all-time-winningest major-college coach. Voila! Everything was right with the world. Former U.S. senator George Mitchell, who had been appointed as an "athletics integrity monitor" to ensure that Penn State adhered to an Athletics Integrity Agreement set forth in the consent decree, proclaimed that Penn State had made such exemplary progress that sanctions were no longer appropriate. NCAA leaders, who had selected Mitchell for the job, agreed.

Really?! This case represented such an "unprecedented failure of institutional integrity," stemming from a "culture of reverence" to an "omnipotent" football program, that it called for "extraordinary action" outside the usual infractions process . . . and the penalties begin rolling back just over a year later? The rescission actions simply provided fodder to those who had questioned the NCAA's authority to impose sanctions in the first place. They viewed the actions as an implicit acknowledgment by the NCAA that it had exceeded its authority and now was taking back the penalties to correct its mistake. Others viewed the actions as capitulation in the face of litigation. After all, the penalties began rolling back after Corman and McCord filed their lawsuit in January 2013. Pennsylvania governor Tom Corbett had brought his own suit, also in January 2013, challenging the NCAA's authority under federal antitrust laws. Even if the rescission decisions were not made in response to litigation, a *perception* that they were could lead to even more litigation designed to force concessions from the NCAA.

Still others (myself included) were more concerned about a new precedent. Does the NCAA's retreat on the Penn State penalties now open the door to penalty rescissions in the future, regardless of the egregiousness of the misconduct that led to the penalties? The Committee on Infractions, for example, has never walked back a penalty because of an institution's good behavior postsanctions. Will institutions now pressure or at least ask the NCAA to consider a penalty rollback in similar circumstances? Or will there ever be similar circumstances? NCAA leaders undoubtedly would say again that Penn State was a unique case, so one should not assume any precedential effect from any of the decisions made in the case. But even so, the quick rescission of the penalties seems to weaken the authoritativeness of NCAA decision-making.

In a perverse way, I wish Penn State had called the NCAA's bluff, if that's what it was. What would have happened if Penn State had *not* accepted the consent decree and the heavy set of sanctions imposed by the NCAA? Court documents suggest that NCAA leaders were willing to allow Penn State to proceed to the "long, hard slog" of a traditional enforcement process. If so, the Committee on Infractions ultimately may have had to decide whether the case was suitable for traditional findings and penalties. I imagine, though, that the NCAA leadership had another choice—simply to impose the death penalty, as it allegedly threatened. My guess is that if the death penalty had been imposed, we would have been treated to a full airing of the jurisdiction issue—in court, in a lawsuit that would still be going on today. In the meantime, the Nittany Lion football team would have been competing as usual, with a full complement of scholarships, a healthier budget, postseason eligibility, and a win-loss record that remained intact. Who knows how things ultimately would have turned out, so again, it probably was in Penn State's best interests to secure the sure deal and move on, as painful as it was in the short run.

Finally, I want to return to where the book begins, with the questions of accountability and responsibility raised in the St. Bonaventure case in the first chapter. I wish Penn State's board of trustees had been engaged throughout the process, beginning when McQueary, Curley, Schultz, Paterno, and Spanier were testifying before the grand jury. It is nearly unfathomable that the board was kept in the dark (or chose to remain in the dark) until criminal charges were publicly announced by the attorney general. To me, it's equally unfathomable that the full board was not engaged after the Freeh report was announced, when the consent decree was being formulated. Media reports indicate that only the board chair and her executive committee knew about the consent decree before it was announced publicly. ESPN writer Don Van Natta Jr. reported that university officials said that keeping the other board members uninformed was necessary because "the NCAA had warned Penn State that if there was a leak about proposed sanctions to the media, the discussions would end and the death penalty would be all but certain." If that is true, it sounds like either a dysfunctional board that can't be trusted to keep a secret or a true NCAA cram-down.

It is certainly true that the full board did not have a say in accepting or rejecting the consent decree. One trustee told Van Natta, "I can't believe this shit. No one told me a damn thing." Truly amazing . . . those of us on campuses respect the authority of a university president, but we also know that presidents report to boards. Was it even within President Erickson's authority to sign the consent decree on his own, without the support of his full board, and bind the university to the harsh terms—and tone—of the "agreement"? In the end, it didn't matter—the majority of a divided board ultimately supported both Erickson and the consent decree. It was time to take their medicine and move forward. And we'll have to wait to see whether the Penn State case was a one-off or whether it will impact infractions cases and NCAA penalties in the future.

In the meantime, four individuals were held accountable. Jerry Sandusky was convicted in June 2012 of forty-five counts of child sexual abuse involving ten victims and is currently serving a prison sentence of thirty to sixty years. He maintains his innocence to this day. After years of legal wrangling, the criminal cases against Curley, Schultz, and Spanier finally played out in 2017. In March of that year, Curley and Schultz each pled guilty to one misdemeanor count of child endangerment. In exchange for their pleas, prosecutors dropped all remaining charges, including felony conspiracy. The court had dismissed perjury and obstruction of justice charges against all three defendants in 2016. Spanier rejected a plea deal, went to trial, and ultimately found himself in similar circumstances. A jury convicted him of one misdemeanor count of child endangerment but acquitted him on the remaining counts, including felony conspiracy. Sentencing for all three occurred on June 2, 2017. Spanier, despite his rejection of a plea deal, actually received a lighter sentence than the others—four to twelve months, with two months in jail and the remainder under house arrest. Curley received seven to twenty-three months, with three in jail, while Schultz landed at six to twenty-three months, with two in jail.

In January 2018 the NCAA sent a letter of inquiry to Michigan State University "regarding potential NCAA rules violations related to the assaults Larry Nassar perpetrated against girls and young women, including some student-athletes at Michigan State." Nassar, a former team doctor for the U.S. women's gymnastics team, had just been sentenced to 40–175 years in prison after pleading guilty to sexually abusing seven young gymnasts. (He had previously been sentenced to sixty years as a result of child pornography convictions.) During the sentencing proceeding, more than 150 female gymnasts testified that Nassar had abused them.

The parallels to Penn State are obvious. Observers wondered what NCAA rule violations were implicated by Nassar's criminal behavior and whether the NCAA would pursue traditional sanctions against Michigan State as it did against Penn State. In late August 2018 we got our answers. The NCAA announced that it was ending its inquiry into Michigan State's involvement in the Nassar matter, because it had "not substantiated violations of NCAA legislation."

Without Penn State as a guide, that appears to be the correct result. In its earlier letter of inquiry to Michigan State, the NCAA cited Article 2.2 of the NCAA Constitution, which in general terms obligates member institutions to protect their student athletes' welfare. But that constitutional provision has not been invoked in the past to ground a *rule violation*. Neither, of course, had the similarly aspirational constitutional provision President Emmert invoked in his initial letter to Penn State—Article 2.4, The Principle of Sportsmanship and Ethical Conduct.

Perhaps the Michigan State resolution signals that Penn State is indeed a one-off and that the NCAA is reverting to its core role as an *athletics* association, leaving criminal misconduct to law enforcement authorities.

Conclusion

I was a three-sport athlete in high school and a wrestler throughout college, on a partial scholarship at a small public school that is now an NCAA Division II institution. I love college athletics, and I attribute whatever successes I've had in life, at least in part, to the discipline, dedication to goals, teamwork, and other life skills that I gained through athletics. That positive experience was part of my motivation for accepting a volunteer role on the Committee on Infractions. And an enriching opportunity it was. Even though I had a close-up view of the dark side of college athletics, I also had the good fortune to work with some of the hardest-working, most dedicated individuals I've ever known—fellow committee members, NCAA staff members, representatives of schools and coaches involved in infractions cases, and a host of others whose common denominators were a love of the game and a commitment to fair competition.

My college athletics experience in the early and mid-1970s seems almost quaint in comparison to today's standards. My teammates and I studied the course bulletins carefully each semester and registered for classes on our own; we went to class, like everyone else, until mid- to late afternoon; we then practiced until 5:30 or 6:00 before heading back to our dorms or other homes for dinner; and we studied after dinner, without the help of special tutors. On weekends—and the occasional weeknight—we'd compete; if that competition involved travel, we'd ride in cars, typically hundreds of miles and often with our makeup schoolwork on our laps. Remarkably, most of the university's coaches (including my head wrestling coach and the head football coach, who later became athletics director) held doctorate degrees and full faculty positions. Coaches didn't have to have someone checking to see if we were attending class; they often *had* us in class.

While undoubtedly things have changed (I doubt, for example, that many coaches today, at any level, hold PhDs or EdDs and teach regular loads), it's important to recognize that many more college athletics programs resemble mine of the seventies than they do the programs of the Power 5 institutions, which provide most people their impression of college athletics today. More than 1,100 colleges and universities compose the NCAA, but few compete before national TV audiences or have the $100-million-per-year budgets that some of the big-timers now do. Another 250 schools serving sixty-five thousand student athletes compose the NAIA—National Association of Intercollegiate Athletics—the nation's other major athletics association, to which mostly smaller schools belong.

More student athletes, for example, compete at the Division III level of the NCAA than in Division I. The NCAA website describes Division III this way: "Academics are the primary focus for Division III student-athletes. The division minimizes the conflicts between athletics and academics and helps student-athletes progress toward graduation through shorter practice and playing seasons and regional competition that reduces time away from academic studies. Participants are integrated on campus and treated like all other members of the student body, keeping them focused on being a student first."

Sounds almost idyllic, doesn't it? But one must recognize that these schools are as much a part of the NCAA as the Alabamas, Michigans, or Oklahomas. So proposals to blow up the NCAA model must take into account all the potential repercussions. While our focus tends toward the high-profile programs, the Power 5 institutions represent roughly 6 percent of the membership. The other 94 percent rely on the resources of the NCAA—including ninety national championships in twenty-four sports across the three divisions—to provide quality athletics experiences to their student athletes.

What does the Power 5 experience look like? A December 2015 article in the *Washington Post* began this way: "The people in charge of Clemson University's athletic department have not settled on a design for the miniature golf course they are building for their football team, but they know it will have just nine holes, not 18. That will leave room for the sand volleyball courts, laser tag, movie theater, bowling lanes, barber shop and other amenities planned in the $55 million complex that South Carolina's second-largest public university is building exclusively for its football players."

A couple of states away, Auburn unveiled the new high-definition video screen in its football stadium—just under eleven thousand square feet, at a cost of nearly $14 million, despite a reported $17 million athletics department deficit the year before. Thirty-six head football coaches, according to a 2016 *USA Today* survey, made over $3 million per year; Jim Harbaugh of Michigan topped the list at over $9 million. But Alabama would have none of that—a later report indicated that Nick Saban, with the aid of a signing bonus for a contract extension, would move to $11.125 million for the 2017–18 season. In 2018 at least eighty-two head coaches made $1 million or more, and an LSU *assistant* coach made $2.5 million. Salaries of the top fifteen highest-paid coaches whose teams were represented in the 2018 men's basketball tournament started at $2.7 million, escalating to nearly $9 million for Duke's Mike Krzyzewski. (Guess what . . . that's not what they made at schools like Iona, Lipscomb, South Dakota State, or Texas Southern—maybe another reason to root for the underdog in the tourney.) In 2016 the NCAA extended its TV contract with CBS and Turner Broadcasting for the tourney for eight years, at a cost of $8.8 *billion*.

These are just a few examples of the *money* involved in big-time college athletics. And one cannot consider the world of infractions without considering money. The greater the financial rewards, the greater the incentive to skirt the rules—it's as simple as that.

The NCAA rules-enforcement process has been the target of critics for decades, in part because it is perceived as ineffective. Perhaps it is. After all, new major cases pop up *all the time* . . . and it seems sometimes that the next big case somehow outmatches the previous one in terms of just how low, or even tawdry, we can go. (Yes, I'm looking at you, Louisville. While we were trying to process the massive academic fraud at UNC, you hit us with "striptease dances" and "sex acts" for high school recruits?!)

NCAA leaders took on a major reform effort in 2012–13 to take away the risk-reward analysis that many rule breakers seemingly engaged in: Do the potential rewards (for example, greater job security and even higher salaries resulting from more wins) outweigh the risk that I'm going to be caught breaking this particular rule? In announcing a new penalty matrix, President Ed Ray of Oregon State University, who chaired an enforcement working group focused on harsher and more consistent penalties, noted the group's major objective: "that people who were doing the 'risk-reward' calculation would think twice whether it was in their interests to engage in bad behavior."

Think twice? Maybe. Refrain from the risk-reward analysis? Doubtful. Refrain from bad behavior? Well, I guess we can hope . . . but we are probably kidding ourselves if we think a new multilevel violation structure, more efficient enforcement process, or more clarity from penalty guidelines will result in substantially fewer or less serious violations. This is particularly so when the financial arms race continues unabated.

But that doesn't mean we shouldn't try. Indeed, that's all we can do. And if overhauling (or even simply tweaking) the enforcement system makes cheaters more accountable, it's worth the effort. I'm particularly encouraged by the recent legislation on head coach responsibility; *that*, in my judgment, has the potential to be a game changer. Suspending a head coach for the actions of subordinates carries significant new weight, and hopefully, even the threat of such a sanction will encourage stricter monitoring by head coaches and greater promotion of that elusive atmosphere of compliance.

I am not as optimistic about some of the other changes in the enforcement structure. I expressed some of my reservations in chapter 9, and I won't repeat them here. I *hope* the penalty guidelines will achieve the desired (or at least perceived?) consistency in penalties . . . though I reject the narrative that inconsistency was a major problem in the old regime. I know personally how hard the Committee on Infractions worked to be consistent during my tenure.

It is encouraging, perhaps, to see harsher penalties outlined in the new penalty matrix (a three- or four-year postseason ban, for example, which *really* would have an effect on recruiting), but it remains to be seen how often such a penalty will be imposed. Hopefully, cases with the most-serious aggravating factors, which warrant the most-severe sanctions, will be few and far between.

The enforcement working group noted that postseason bans and scholarship reductions seemed to be the sanctions that worried institutions the most, but those penalties have been employed for decades, with little apparent deterrent effect . . . or even much of an effect on the schools that were sanctioned. Alabama's two-year postseason ban in 2002, for example, proved to be little more than a bump in the Crimson Tide's road to utter dominance in football.

So we'll see if the recent NCAA reforms have an appreciable effect on the number and severity of infractions cases. As we wait to see if progress is being made, the NCAA enforcement staff and various volunteer committees will continue their efforts to hold rule breakers accountable. Their jobs are hard enough without the incessant criticism and hyperbole that characterizes much of modern sports journalism. Does it help Taylor Branch's case, for example, to repeat the assertion of a disgruntled lawyer that *all* the NCAA's enforcement actions "are random and selective"?

As I suggested in the introduction, criticism of the NCAA comes with the territory, but one of my goals with this book is to encourage *informed* and thoughtful analysis of infractions cases and enforcement processes. And it doesn't take an insider's knowledge . . . all it typically takes is a complete and careful reading of public infractions reports. I hope I've piqued your interest in learning more. Have at it.

As this book was entering final editing and publication phases, the college athletics world was reeling from yet another bombshell, this time in men's basketball. In September 2017 the U.S. attorney for the Southern District of New York announced federal indictments against ten individuals, including four assistant men's basketball coaches (at Arizona, Auburn, Oklahoma State, and Southern Cal), two Adidas employees, an agent, a financial advisor, a program director for a youth AAU (grassroots) basketball program, and even the owner of a high-end clothing store who served as a middleman, introducing well-dressed college coaches to agents and financial advisors. Allegations of bribery, wire fraud, and conspiracy included charges that the college coaches accepted bribes to steer NBA prospects to certain agents and financial advisors and that Adidas representatives paid large sums to high school players and their families to steer the players to Adidas-sponsored colleges and eventually to induce the players to sign with Adidas when they turned pro.

In response to the scandal, NCAA president Mark Emmert and his Division I Boards of Directors and Governors appointed a Commission on College Basketball, headed by former U.S. secretary of state Condoleezza Rice and including such luminaries as former NBA stars Grant Hill and David Robinson. The commission's charge was to examine and make recommendations regarding three aspects of Division I men's basketball: (1) the relationship between the NCAA and "outside entities," including apparel companies, grassroots basketball, and agents; (2) the NCAA's relationship with the NBA, focused on one-and-done athletes who attend college for one year because of the NBA's minimum-age rule of being nineteen years old; and (3) the relationship between the NCAA national office and its member institutions, "to promote transparency and accountability."

For the purposes of this book, the last charge is particularly meaningful, because it involves an examination of the NCAA's current rules-enforcement processes, including "whether the collaborative model provides the investigative tools, cultural incentives and structures to ensure exploitation and corruption cannot hide in college sports."

In April 2018 the commission submitted its report and recommendations, which were not limited to men's basketball. The report states, "The NCAA's investigative and enforcement processes require a complete overhaul. Complex cases must be thoroughly investigated, and resolved by neutral professional adjudicators, with authority to impose punishment that will have a significant deterrent effect.... Volunteers who are members of fellow NCAA member institutions should not resolve cases. Instead, a panel of professional adjudicators, appointed for a term of years, must make final and binding decisions and must have the authority to impose substantial punishments." Among the substantial punishments the commission recommended were *five-year* postseason bans and *lifetime* bans from college coaching in egregious cases.

Almost immediately after its release, the NCAA leadership (President Emmert and the chairs of his board of directors and board of governors) endorsed the commission's entire report. The boards appointed numerous working groups to work on the details, and a short four months later, in August 2018, the NCAA issued a lengthy statement entitled *Committed to Change*. The statement announced a variety of measures to implement the commission's recommendations, including some that could have a significant impact on the rules-enforcement process.

The NCAA leadership embraced the commission's notion that "complex" cases should be resolved through a modified procedure. In my experience on the infractions committee, very few cases were complex. Some involved egregious or extensive violations, but little is complex, for example, about institutional representatives making cash payments to recruits. In its new formulation, however, the NCAA includes the following as potentially complex cases: "those involving major policy issues related to core NCAA values; investigations with stale or incomplete facts; cases with adversarial posturing or a refusal to cooperate; cases with breaches of confidentiality; and when increased stakes, including potential penalties or other pressures, are driving institutional decision-making." As the Rice commission recommended, potential penalties now can include postseason bans of up to five years and lifetime bans from college coaching.

Schools, the infractions committee, or the enforcement staff can request that a case be classified as complex, and a new "infractions referral committee" will determine if the case fits the bill. Cases deemed complex will be eligible for a new "independent alternative resolution" process that includes a "complex case unit" to investigate allegations and an "independent college sports adjudication panel" to determine whether violations occurred and to impose penalties. The complex case unit will include both external investigators and members of the NCAA enforcement staff. The adjudication panel will consist of fifteen members "with legal, higher education and/or sports backgrounds who are not affiliated with NCAA member schools or conferences"; subpanels of five will decide each case. These new processes and structures will be effective August 1, 2019.

So change is afoot again, and we'll have to wait to see whether this new round of reforms has an appreciable effect on the number and severity of major infractions cases. The Rice commission recommended the use of independent investigators "empowered to require the cooperation of witnesses and the production of documents, including financial information, from NCAA member institutions and their employees and contractors, with significant penalties for non-cooperation." With all due respect, current NCAA bylaws already require full cooperation from member institutions and their employees, and failure to cooperate always has been a significant factor in the infractions committee's assessment of penalties. A problem does exist, of course, for witnesses who are *not* institutional employees or students, such as boosters, *fired* coaches, and student athletes who have graduated or left the institution for other reasons. Lack of subpoena power makes it impossible for enforcement staff to force cooperation from such individuals, and that problem will persist, regardless of how independent the new investigative body is.

The NCAA did clarify another important point in its recent statement—the new bodies charged with investigating and adjudicating complex cases "can accept findings and use information and positions taken in other administrative proceedings, including from a court of law." In October 2018 a federal court jury found the first three criminal defendants in the college basketball scandal—two Adidas employees and an agent—guilty of wire fraud and conspiracy. Expect the NCAA's new complex case unit to use the information developed during that criminal investigation, and others to follow, as it builds its own major infractions cases against bad actors in college basketball.

Notes

Introduction

1 "How can you people": Nathan Darrell Ford, email message to NCAA Committee on Infractions, December 13, 2000, on file with author.

1 The case involved violations: NCAA, *Southern Methodist University Public Infractions Report*, December 13, 2000, https://web3.ncaa.org/lsdbi /search/miCaseView/report?id=102170.

5 "Cruelly, but typically": Taylor Branch, "The Shame of College Sports," *Atlantic*, October 2011.

5 "I stand corrected": Joe Nocera, "N.C.A.A.'s 'Justice' System," *New York Times*, January 6, 2012.

5 "Like the Mafia": Buzz Bissinger, "Heisman Hypocrisy," *Daily Beast*, December 12, 2010.

6 U.S. congressman Bobby Rush: "Congressman Rush Compares NCAA to Mafia," *University Business*, November 3, 2011.

6 Award-winning journalist: Frank Deford, "The NCAA: Is Membership Worth It?" NPR.org, April 11, 2012.

6 "It's easy to cast": Jim Wang, "Will You Get Audited by the IRS?" *U.S. News and World Report*, February 29, 2012, https://money.usnews.com /money/blogs/my-money/2012/02/29/will-you-get-audited-by-the-irs.

7 "At first I thought": John Henderson, "Neuheisel Can Go Home Again," *Denver Post*, April 18, 2008.

7 Leading their team: See "Derrick Rose," NBA, nba.com/players/derrick /rose/201565.

8 One of the allegations: NCAA, *University of Memphis Public Infractions Report*, August 20, 2009, https://web3.ncaa.org/lsdbi/search/miCaseView /report?id=102315.

8 The University of Memphis appealed: NCAA, *University of Memphis Public Infractions Appeals Committee Report*, March 22, 2010, https:// web3.ncaa.org/lsdbi/search/miCaseView/report?id=102528.

8 Not surprisingly: The following comments were posted on Associated Press, "NCAA: Memphis Must Vacate Wins," *ESPN Conversations*, March 22, 2010, http://www.espn.com/mens-college-basketball/news/story?id

=5018281: jzielinski515, March 22, 2010; Allan28479, March 22, 2010; Rayking19, March 22, 2010; JAR242, March 22, 2010; on file with author.

8 "Total bull from the NCAA": Methos4h, March 22, 2010, comment on Associated Press, "NCAA: Memphis Must Vacate Wins," on file with author.

8 The italicized reference: Dick Vitale, "Self, Calipari May Again Be in Finale," *USA Today*, November 5, 2009.

9 In the Memphis case: NCAA, *University of Memphis Public Infractions Report*.

1. The Fallout

11 NCAA bylaws permit: *2018–2019 NCAA Division I Manual* (Indianapolis: NCAA, 2018), bylaw 14.5.4.6.5; all citations to the NCAA *Division I Manual* refer to this version unless otherwise stated.

12 The men's basketball coaching staff: NCAA, *St. Bonaventure University Public Infractions Report*, February 19, 2004, https://web3.ncaa.org/lsdbi/search/miCaseView/report?id=102216.

12 The hiring was considered a coup: "Jan van Breda Kolff," NBA Coaches, nba.com/coachfile/jan_van_breda_kolff.

13 He spoke to Kort: NCAA, *St. Bonaventure Public Infractions Report*.

13 NCAA bylaws also make presidents: NCAA *Division I Manual*, bylaw 2.1.1.

13 "I believe we have a problem": NCAA, *St. Bonaventure Public Infractions Report*.

14 According to Swan's account: William E. Swan, "The Real March Madness: Anatomy of an Athletics Scandal," *Trusteeship*, July–August 2003.

15 In mid-February 2003: NCAA, *St. Bonaventure Public Infractions Report*.

15 The day would have been saved: NCAA, *St. Bonaventure Public Infractions Report*.

16 Five days later: Swan, "Real March Madness."

16 Van Breda Kolff claimed: "Van Breda Kolff Denies Wrongdoing, Responsibility in St. Bonaventure Scandal," *Business Wire*, April 29, 2003; Associated Press, "Van Breda Kolff Gains Closure after Player Scandal," ESPN, April 19, 2005, http://www.espn.com/mens-college-basketball/news/story?id=2041246.

16 As the NCAA Committee: NCAA, *St. Bonaventure Public Infractions Report*.

17 The special review committee report: Jill Lieber, "St. Bonaventure Scandal Leaves Death in Its Wake," *USA Today*, November 17, 2003.

17 Swan, by all accounts: Lieber, "St. Bonaventure Scandal."

18 Bill Swan stated early: Swan, "Real March Madness."

18 "Every time Bill Swan": Lieber, "St. Bonaventure Scandal."

18 "I am so sorry": Lieber, "St. Bonaventure Scandal."

19 To his credit: NCAA, *St. Bonaventure Public Infractions Report*.

20 "This decision point": Swan, "Real March Madness."

20 As the Committee on Infractions put it: NCAA, *St. Bonaventure Public Infractions Report.*

21 "The institution's president": NCAA *Division I Manual*, bylaw 2.1.1.

21 In August 2011: C. Thomas McMillen, "Accountability on the Quad," *New York Times*, September 1, 2011.

21 The Freeh report: Freeh Sporkin and Sullivan, *Report of the Special Investigative Counsel Regarding the Actions of The Pennsylvania State University Related to the Child Sexual Abuse Committed by Gerald A. Sandusky*, July 12, 2012, http://www.washingtonpost.com/wp-srv/sports /penn-state-freeh-report/REPORT_FINAL_071212.pdf; subsequently referred to as the Freeh report.

21 According to Anne D. Neal: Richard Pérez-Peña, "In Report, Failures throughout Penn State," *New York Times*, July 12, 2012.

22 President Ray insisted: Colleen Curry, "Penn State Hit with $60 Million Fine, but Football Team Avoids 'Death Penalty,'" ABC News, July 23, 2012, https://abcnews.go.com/US/penn-state-hit-60-million-fine -avoids-death/story?id=16835444.

22 Within two weeks: Paul V. Kelly and Gregg E. Clifton of Jackson Lewis (representing Penn State trustee Ryan J. McCombie) to Wendy Walters, staff liaison to NCAA Infractions Appeals Committee, August 6, 2012, on file with author.

22 In an *ESPN: The Magazine* article: Don Van Natta Jr., "On Death's Door," *ESPN: The Magazine*, August 20, 2012.

23 "I knew it was essential": Swan, "Real March Madness."

23 At the very least: Swan, "Real March Madness."

23 the Committee on Infractions cited him: NCAA, *St. Bonaventure Public Infractions Report.*

24 In its report in that case: NCAA, *Jacksonville University Public Infractions Report*, August 30, 2001, https://web3.ncaa.org/lsdbi/search/miCaseView /report?id=102184.

24 "The committee . . . firmly believes": NCAA, *St. Bonaventure Public Infractions Report.*

24 In a particularly strong statement: NCAA, *Former Head Men's Basketball Coach, University of Minnesota, Twin Cities Public Infractions Appeals Committee Report*, April 6, 2001, https://web3.ncaa.org/lsdbi/search /miCaseView/report?id=102475.

25 The appeals committee seized the opportunity: NCAA, *Former Head Men's Basketball Coach, University of Minnesota.*

26 The reforms resulted from: Gary Brown, "DI Board of Directors Approves Overhauled Enforcement Structure," NCAA, last updated October 30, 2012, https://amp.ncaa.com/amp/news/ncaa/article/2012-10-30/di -board-directors-approves-overhauled-enforcement-structure.

26 the new legislation *presumes*: NCAA *Division I Manual*, bylaws 11.1.1.1, 19.9.5.5.

26 The Committee on Infractions leveled: CBS and Associated Press, "Syracuse Coach Jim Boeheim Suspended for School Violations," CBS News, March 6, 2015, https://www.cbsnews.com/news/syracuse-coach -jim-boeheim-suspended-9-games-for-schools-academic-drug-other -violations/; NCAA, *Syracuse University Public Infractions Decision*, March 6, 2015, https://web3.ncaa.org/lsdbi/search/miCaseView/report ?id=102447.

2. Hangin' Offenses

27 The remarkable words above: David Whitford, *A Payroll to Meet: A Story of Greed, Corruption, and Football at SMU* (1989; repr., Lincoln: University of Nebraska Press, 2013), 130, 133.

28 SMU leads the country: These statistics were obtained from the NCAA Major Infractions–Legal Services Database at https://web3.ncaa.org /lsdbi/.

28 In 1958 the NCAA found: NCAA, *Southern Methodist University Public Infractions Report*, April 21, 1958, https://web3.ncaa.org/lsdbi/search /miCaseView/report?id=101704.

28 Auburn was hit: NCAA, Auburn University summary (no public report available), April 21, 1958.

29 A booster also was involved: NCAA, *Southern Methodist University Public Infractions Report*, April 12, 1965, https://web3.ncaa.org/lsdbi/search /miCaseView/report?id=101938.

29 "nothing short of abysmal": NCAA, *Southern Methodist University Public Infractions Report*, February 25, 1987, https://web3.ncaa.org/lsdbi /search/miCaseView/report?id=101734.

29 The 1974 case: NCAA, *Southern Methodist University Public Infractions Report*, August 26, 1974, https://web3.ncaa.org/lsdbi/search/miCaseView /report?id=101973.

29 That came to an end: NCAA v. Board of Regents of the University of Oklahoma, 468 U.S. 85 (1984).

29 Less than a year: NCAA, *Southern Methodist University Public Infractions Report*, January 21, 1976, https://web3.ncaa.org/lsdbi/search/miCaseView /report?id=101993.

30 The same month: Whitford, *A Payroll to Meet*, 15–18.

30 Meyer was flashy: Whitford, *A Payroll to Meet*, 19–37.

31 Buddecke later would become: Whitford, *A Payroll to Meet*, 37–39.

31 Under NCAA rules: NCAA *Division I Manual*, bylaw 13.6.2.

31 SMU, undoubtedly: Whitford, *A Payroll to Meet*, 39–40.

31 Soon things ratcheted up: Whitford, *A Payroll to Meet*, 42–47.

32 When it came to: Whitford, *A Payroll to Meet*, 44–45.

32 And to top things off: NCAA, *Southern Methodist University Public Infractions Report*, June 10, 1981, https://web3.ncaa.org/lsdbi/search /miCaseView/report?id=102050.

33 "particularly concerned": NCAA, *Southern Methodist University Public Infractions Report*, June 10, 1981.

33 The sanctions did not slow: Whitford, *A Payroll to Meet*, 93–94.

33 Ten SMU players: Whitford, *A Payroll to Meet*, 93–94.

34 The Mustangs soared again: Whitford, *A Payroll to Meet*, 97–98, 104, 114.

34 SMU hired Bobby Collins: Whitford, *A Payroll to Meet*, 105–6.

34 Studs indeed: Whitford, *A Payroll to Meet*, 101, 107–8.

35 On the summit agenda: Whitford, *A Payroll to Meet*, 109–10.

36 "It doesn't take Einstein": Whitford, *A Payroll to Meet*, 115–16.

36 Needless to say: Whitford, *A Payroll to Meet*, 116.

36 Cash may have had something: Whitford, *A Payroll to Meet*, 117.

36 The chickens started coming home: Whitford, *A Payroll to Meet*, 118–19.

37 Despite the distractions: Whitford, *A Payroll to Meet*, 131.

37 The university hired outside counsel: Whitford, *A Payroll to Meet*, 118, 126–27.

37 Assistant coach Bootsie Larsen: Whitford, *A Payroll to Meet*, 151, 153, 156; Walter Byers, *Unsportsmanlike Conduct* (Ann Arbor: University of Michigan Press, 1995), 27.

37 The attorney reported: Whitford, *A Payroll to Meet*, 127.

38 Who else mattered?: Whitford, *A Payroll to Meet*, 127–29.

38 No longer in the governor's office: Whitford, *A Payroll to Meet*, 128–29.

39 It was now time: Whitford, *A Payroll to Meet*, 129–30.

39 Compliance is the responsibility: NCAA *Division I Manual*, bylaws 2.8.1, 19.2.

40 As the NCAA investigation: Whitford, *A Payroll to Meet*, 132–35.

40 Toward the end: Whitford, *A Payroll to Meet*, 135; NCAA, *Southern Methodist University Public Infractions Report*, August 16, 1985, https://web3 .ncaa.org/lsdbi/search/miCaseView/report?id=102125.

41 A prized recruit: Whitford, *A Payroll to Meet*, 131–32: NCAA, *Southern Methodist University Public Infractions Report*, August 16, 1985.

41 The Stopperich violations: Whitford, *A Payroll to Meet*, 136–37.

41 Blount clearly displayed: Whitford, *A Payroll to Meet*, 137–38.

42 "During the period of probation": NCAA, *Southern Methodist University Public Infractions Report*, August 16, 1985.

42 SMU president Donald Shields: Whitford, *A Payroll to Meet*, 138–41.

43 The infractions hearing took place: Whitford, *A Payroll to Meet*, 143–44.

43 The committee released its report: NCAA, *Southern Methodist University Public Infractions Report*, August 16, 1985.

43 The Mustangs scratched out: "SMU Year-by-Year Records/Rankings," mcubed.net, last updated January 9, 2018, http://www.mcubed.net/ncaaf /teams/smu.shtml.

43 SMU's "history of involvement": NCAA, *Southern Methodist University Public Infractions Report*, August 16, 1985.

43 At a special convention: Rodney K. Smith, "The National Collegiate Athletic Association's Death Penalty: How Educators Punish Themselves and Others," *Indiana Law Journal* 62, no. 4 (1987): 985–1059, 1010.

44 The repeat-violator legislation: Smith, "National Collegiate Athletic Association's Death Penalty," 1010.

44 The concept instead is subsumed: NCAA *Division I Manual*, bylaw 19.9.3.

45 In August 1985: Whitford, *A Payroll to Meet*, 151.

45 A harsh reality: Whitford, *A Payroll to Meet*, 151–52.

45 In a high-stakes gamble: Whitford, *A Payroll to Meet*, 151–53.

46 David Stanley, however: Whitford, *A Payroll to Meet*, 157–58.

46 With his frustrations piling up: Whitford, *A Payroll to Meet*, 158.

46 Stanley's response: Whitford, *A Payroll to Meet*, 160, 163–65.

47 Prior to the broadcast: Whitford, *A Payroll to Meet*, 161.

47 Bill Clements was not present: Whitford, *A Payroll to Meet*, 162, 166.

47 By today's standards: NCAA, *Southern Methodist University Public Infractions Report*, February 25, 1987.

47 After the November 12 television broadcast: Whitford, *A Payroll to Meet*, 184, 187.

48 In the end: Whitford, *A Payroll to Meet*, 188, 192–93.

48 Hitch and head coach Bobby Collins: Whitford, *A Payroll to Meet*, 181–82.

49 The Committee on Infractions scheduled: Whitford, *A Payroll to Meet*, 193–95.

50 Unlike the infractions hearing: Whitford, *A Payroll to Meet*, 195.

50 Accounts of the SMU infractions hearing: Whitford, *A Payroll to Meet*, 195.

51 The entire recitation: NCAA, *Southern Methodist University Public Infractions Report*, February 25, 1987.

51 While the Committee on Infractions accepted: NCAA, *Southern Methodist University Public Infractions Report*, February 25, 1987.

52 The committee went on: NCAA, *Southern Methodist University Public Infractions Report*, February 25, 1987.

53 The committee, for example, also took: NCAA, *Southern Methodist University Public Infractions Report*, February 25, 1987.

53 Bill Clements, for example: Whitford, *A Payroll to Meet*, 209.

53 In fact, the committee imposed: NCAA, *Southern Methodist University Public Infractions Report*, February 25, 1987.

53 SMU administrators had been humiliated: Whitford, *A Payroll to Meet*, 200.

53 SMU football climbed back: "SMU Year-by-Year Records/Rankings."

54 Alabama, for example: "Alabama Year-by-Year Records/Rankings," mcubed.net, last updated January 9, 2018, http://www.mcubed.net /ncaaf/teams/al.shtml.

54 In the final AP poll: "AP Releases Final Top 25 College Football Poll," *Scout*, January 10, 2017, www.scout.com/story/1744604-ap-releases -final-top-25-cfb-poll.

54 The death penalty against SMU: "SMU Year-by-Year Records/Rankings."

54 Ford, you will recall: NCAA, *Southern Methodist University Public Infractions Report*, December 13, 2000.

55 In 2011, however: NCAA, *Southern Methodist University Public Infractions Report*, March 10, 2011, https://web3.ncaa.org/lsdbi/search/miCaseView /report?id=102372.

56 A Brown-coached UCLA team: NCAA, *University of California, Los Angeles, Public Infractions Report*, December 8, 1981, https://web3.ncaa.org /lsdbi/search/miCaseView/report?id=102054.

56 Later that year: NCAA, *University of Kansas Public Infractions Report*, November 1, 1988, https://web3.ncaa.org/lsdbi/search/miCaseView /report?id=101756.

56 During the 2014–15 season: "Southern Methodist Mustangs School History," Sports Reference, https://www.sports-reference.com/cbb/schools /southern-methodist.

56 Three months later: NCAA, *Southern Methodist University Public Infractions Decision*, September 29, 2015, https://web3.ncaa.org/lsdbi/search /miCaseView/report?id=102554.

57 Brown resigned: Scott Gleeson, "Larry Brown Steps Down at SMU; Tim Jankovich to Take Over," *USA Today*, July 8, 2016.

57 Following the imposition: Associated Press, "NCAA Memo Details Booster Payments, Other Infractions," ESPN, August 2, 2003, http://static.espn .go.com/ncb/news/2003/0802/1588938.html.

3. Unethical Conduct

59 1993 deaths of seventy-five people: Clyde Haberman, "Memories of Waco Siege Continue to Fuel Right-Wing Groups," *New York Times*, July 12, 2015.

59 "Waco horror": J. B. Smith, "'Waco Horror' at 100: Why Jesse Washington's Lynching Still Matters," *Waco Tribune-Herald*, May 15, 1916.

59 In 1953 a tornado: Andy Warren, "Waco Tornado: 64 Years after 1953's F-5 Twister," *Houston Chronicle*, May 10, 2017.

59 It remains the eleventh-deadliest: "The 25 Deadliest U.S. Tornadoes," Storm Prediction Center, National Oceanic and Atmospheric Administration, spc.noaa.gov/faq/tornado/killers.html.

59 Twin Peaks shootout: Tommy Witherspoon, "Two Years after Shootout, Twin Peaks Resolutions Remain Elusive," *Waco Tribune-Herald*, May 16, 2017.

60 George W. Bush established: The Western White House, whitehouse .georgewbush.org/western/home.asp.

60 Joanna and Chip Gaines: Magnolia, magnoliamarket.com.

60 the women won a national title: Associated Press, "Baylor Women Win Title, Cap Historic 40-0 Run," CBS News, April 4, 2012, https://www .cbsnews.com/news/baylor-women-win-title-cap-historic-40-0-run/.

60 the football program had won: "Baylor Year-by-Year Records/Rankings," mcubed.net, last updated January 9, 2018, http://www.mcubed .net/ncaaf/teams/baylor.shtml.

60 On July 25: Mike Wise, "College Basketball; Death and Deception," *New York Times*, August 28, 2003.

60 Dennehy had gone missing: ESPN News Service, "Key Dates in Dennehy Disappearance," ESPN, July 28, 2003, http://static.espn.go.com/ncb /news/2003/0721/1583886.html.

61 On July 21: NCAA, *Baylor University Public Infractions Report*, June 23, 2005, https://web3.ncaa.org/lsdbi/search/miCaseView/report?id=102265.

61 Unethical conduct is the most serious: NCAA *Division I Manual*, bylaw 10.1; NCAA, *Baylor University Public Infractions Report*, June 23, 2005.

62 As one former player: Brad Townsend, "Flashback: Who's the Real Dave Bliss? Loyal, Honorable Coach or Vindictive Egomaniac?" *Dallas Morning News*, August 24, 2003.

62 Star center Jon Koncak: Danny Robbins, "Koncak Says He Was Paid at SMU," *Fort Worth Star-Telegram*, August 5, 2003.

62 The *Star-Telegram* had obtained: Associated Press, "NCAA Memo Details Booster Payments, Other Infractions," ESPN, August 2, 2003, http://static .espn.go.com/ncb/news/2003/0802/1588938.html.

63 The assailant was Carlton Dotson: ESPN News Service, "Key Dates in Dennehy Disappearance."

63 An odd set of facts: Wise, "Death and Deception."

64 Dotson ultimately pled guilty: Mike Wise, "A Mother's Tortured Journey toward the Truth," *Washington Post*, June 22, 2008.

64 The ship first left dock: NCAA, *Baylor University Public Infractions Report*, June 23, 2005.

64 And so, with the help: NCAA, *Baylor University Public Infractions Report*, June 23, 2005.

65 With respect to Herring: NCAA, *Baylor University Public Infractions Report*, June 23, 2005.

66 And what of those money orders: NCAA, *Baylor University Public Infractions Report*, June 23, 2005.

66 One individual who did agree: NCAA, *Baylor University Public Infractions Report*, June 23, 2005.

66 During 2002 and 2003: NCAA, *Baylor University Public Infractions Report*, June 23, 2005.

67 "rampant drug use": NCAA, *Baylor University Public Infractions Report*, June 23, 2005.

68 "It doesn't have to be": Wise, "Death and Deception."

68 Doug Ash: Stephen Hawkins, "Baylor Coaches Stick Together; Bliss, Ash Are Nation's Longest-Serving Duo," *Oklahoman*, February 9, 2003.

68 "a high school play": Terrance Harris, "Baylor Escapes the Death Penalty," *Houston Chronicle*, June 24, 2005.

68 This was after Rouse: Dana O'Neil, "Rouse in Oblivion Five Years after Baylor Scandal," ESPN, May 6, 2008, http://www.espn.com/mens-college -basketball/columns/story?columnist=oneil_dana&id=3371852.

69 Rouse claimed: Melissa Horton, ed., "OTL Abar Rouse," produced by Art Berko, June 2, 2013, ESPN video, 8:35, https://vimeo.com/67665278.

69 "What we've got to create": Christian Red, "Caught on Tape: Lie about Drugs; Bliss Told Players, Coaches to Say Dennehy Was Dealer," *New York Daily News*, August 17, 2003.

69 "All they've got to remember": "Excerpts from Bliss Tapes," *USA Today*, August 18, 2003.

69 According to Rouse: O'Neil, "Rouse in Oblivion."

70 The day after Dennehy's funeral: NCAA, *Baylor University Public Infractions Report*, June 23, 2005.

70 To Baylor's credit: NCAA, *Baylor University Public Infractions Report*, June 23, 2005.

71 Baylor's self-imposed penalties: NCAA, *Baylor University Public Infractions Report*, June 23, 2005.

71 "serious and widespread": NCAA, *Baylor University Public Infractions Report*, June 23, 2005.

71 Moreover, this was Baylor's third: NCAA, *Baylor University Public Infractions Report*, June 23, 2005.

72 For example, Dennehy: NCAA, *Baylor University Public Infractions Report*, June 23, 2005.

72 Again, to its credit: NCAA, *Baylor University Public Infractions Report*, June 23, 2005.

73 "clean record and good reputation": NCAA, *Baylor University Public Infractions Report*, June 23, 2005.

73 In August 2003: Barry Horn, "Ex-aide: Bliss an 'Angry Man,'" *Dallas Morning News*, August 19, 2003, http://209.157.64.200/focus/f-news/966606/ posts.

73 Perhaps Lord Acton: Lord Acton to Archbishop Mandell Creighton, April 5, 1887, in *Lectures on Modern History by the Late Right Hon. John Emerich Edward First Baron Acton*, ed. John Neville Figgis and Reginald Vere Laurence (London: Macmillan, 1906), http://oll.libertyfund .org/titles/acton-acton-creighton-correspondence#lf1524_label_010.

74 "We walked up to the edge": "Baylor Barely Avoids 'Death Penalty,'" *Knight-Ridder Newspapers*, June 24, 2005; Harris, "Baylor Escapes the Death Penalty."

75 In what has come closest: NCAA, *Baylor University Public Infractions Report*, June 23, 2005.

75 Baylor, however, stepped up: NCAA, *Baylor University Public Infractions Report*, June 23, 2005; "Baylor Barely Avoids 'Death Penalty.'"

76 In the language of the legislation: NCAA *Division I Manual*, bylaw 19.9.5.4.

77 The language of the penalties: NCAA, *Baylor University Public Infractions Report*, June 23, 2005.

78 Another high-profile example: Rana L. Cash, "Oregon Gets No Postseason Ban, Chip Kelly Hit with Show-Cause Penalty," *Sporting News*, June 26, 2013.

79 Dave Bliss, for example: Berry Tramel, "Dave Bliss Returning to College Basketball 12 Years after Scandal at Baylor," *Oklahoman*, April 6, 2015.

79 In the Baylor case: NCAA, *Baylor University Public Infractions Report*, June 23, 2005.

79 In my experience: NCAA, *New Mexico State University Public Infractions Report*, June 20, 2001, https://web3.ncaa.org/lsdbi/search/miCaseView/report?id=102182.

79 Assistant coaches Doug Ash and Brian O'Neill: Harris, "Baylor Escapes the Death Penalty"; NCAA, *Baylor University Public Infractions Report*, June 23, 2005.

79 Doug Ash became: "Detroit Pistons Staff & Executives," Real GM, basketball.realgm.com/nba/teams/Detroit-Pistons/8/staff-members.

79 Brian O'Neill returned: Associated Press, "Richardson Appoints Executive Director of Sports Authority," *Albuquerque Journal*, February 5, 2008.

80 Rodney Belcher initially coached: Matt Welch, "Longtime Assistant Rodney Belcher Named Head Coach of Plano Senior Girls Basketball," *Plano Star Courier*, March 24, 2014.

80 Within six months: Danny Robbins, "Bliss Finds More Controversy in High School Hoops," Associated Press, May 7, 2011.

80 Rather than accept: Clay Falls, "Allen Academy Moving Forward after Parting Ways with TAPPS," KBTX, November 29, 2010, https://www.kbtx.com/home/headlines/Allen_Academy_Moving_Forward_After_Parting_Ways_With_TAPPS_111017929.html.

81 In April 2015: Tramel, "Dave Bliss Returning to College Basketball."

81 Rouse weathered the initial scandal: O'Neil, "Rouse in Oblivion."

82 Rouse has stated: O'Neil, "Rouse in Oblivion."

82 On the heels of the Baylor scandal: Horton, "OTL Abar Rouse."

83 When pressed on why: O'Neil, "Rouse in Oblivion."

83 Fortunately, Rouse seems to be: "Abar Rouse, Former Baylor Asst. Coach," *Sporting Life with Jeremy Schapp*, March 31, 1997, https://www.espn.com/espnradio/play?id=19043660.

84 In a 2009 interview: Natalia Jones, "Forgiveness Is Bliss: Former Baylor Basketball Coach Talks of Triumphs and Tragedies," *Gainesville Register*, September 18, 2009.

84 "He regrets it deeply": "Baylor Barely Avoids 'Death Penalty.'"

84 "I have a full understanding": Horton, "OTL Abar Rouse."

85 On Friday, March 31: Des Bieler, "Ex-Baylor Coach Dave Bliss Resigns after Airing of Documentary about Murdered Player," *Washington Post*, April 3, 2017.

85 In December 2008: NCAA, *Baylor University Public Infractions Report*, April 11, 2012, https://web3.ncaa.org/lsdbi/search/miCaseView/report?id=102353.

86 One of his text messages: NCAA, *Baylor University Public Infractions Report*, April 11, 2012.

86 An interesting fact: NCAA, *Baylor University Public Infractions Report*, April 11, 2012.

4. The Infractions

87 The case involved Howard: NCAA, *Howard University Public Infractions Report*, November 27, 2001, https://web3.ncaa.org/lsdbi/search/miCaseView/report?id=102186.

88 As Cardale Jones: Teddy Greenstein, "Cardale Jones, Known for Ill-Advised Tweet, Takes Stage for Ohio State," *Chicago Tribune*, December 1, 2014.

88 As the Howard case unfolded: NCAA, *Howard University Public Infractions Report*, November 27, 2001.

89 When the committee issued: NCAA, *Howard University Public Infractions Report*, November 27, 2001.

89 The allegations in that case: NCAA, *University of Minnesota, Twin Cities, Public Infractions Report*, October 24, 2000, https://web3.ncaa.org/lsdbi/search/miCaseView/report?id=102169.

89 The infractions report: NCAA, *University of Minnesota, Twin Cities, Public Infractions Report*, October 24, 2000.

90 The NCAA *Division I Manual*: NCAA *Division I Manual*.

91 The Fog Index: Robert Gunning, *The Technique of Clear Writing* (New York: McGraw-Hill, 1952); see also "The Gunning's Fog Index (or FOG) Readability Formula," Reading Formulas, http://www.readabilityformulas.com/gunning-fog-readability-formula.php.

91 One sobering moment: NCAA, *University of California, Berkeley, Public Infractions Report*, June 26, 2002, https://web3.ncaa.org/lsdbi/search/miCaseView/report?id=102235.

92 Later in my tenure: NCAA, *Florida State University Public Infractions Report*, March 6, 2009, https://web3.ncaa.org/lsdbi/search/miCaseView/report?id=102310.

92 Jon Duncan: Ralph Russo, "AP Interview: Head of NCAA Enforcement Says Academic Misconduct on Rise," Associated Press, January 28, 2015.

93 In a February 2007 report: NCAA, *McNeese State University Public Infrac-tions Report*, February 8, 2007, https://web3.ncaa.org/lsdbi/search/miCaseView/report?id=102290.

94 Enforcement chief Duncan: Russo, "AP Interview."

94 The APR initiative: NCAA, "Division I Committee on Academics," http://www.ncaa.org/governance/committees/division-i-committee-academics.

94 The APR formulas: NCAA, "Frequently Asked Questions about Academic Progress Rate (APR)," http://www.ncaa.org/about/resources/research/frequently-asked-questions-about-academic-progress-rate-apr.

94 While none of the UNC coaches: Kenneth L. Wainstein, A. Joseph Jay III, and Colleen Depman Kukowski, *Investigation of Irregular Classes in the Department of African and Afro-American Studies at the University of North Carolina at Chapel Hill* (New York: Cadwalader, Wickersham, and Taft, October 16, 2014), 94, available at https://carolinacommitment.unc.edu/files/2014/10/UNC-FINAL-REPORT.pdf; subsequently referred to as the Wainstein UNC report.

95 In 2013 Jon Duncan: Russo, "AP Interview."

95 That legislation creates: NCAA *Division I Manual*, bylaw 11.1.1.1.

96 The legislation also includes: NCAA *Division Manual*, bylaw 19.9.5.5, fig-ure 19-1.

96 In a panel presentation: John Infante, "Head Coach Responsibil-ity a Potential Gamechanger," Athnet, June 13, 2013, https://www.athleticscholarships.net/2013/06/13/head-coach-responsibility-a-potential-gamechanger.htm.

96 In another high-profile: NCAA, *Syracuse University Public Infractions Decision*, March 6, 2015.

96 The University of Connecticut: Paul Myerberg, "How a Postseason APR Ban Fueled UConn's Run to a Title," *USA Today*, April 8, 2014.

97 During that period: This summary is compiled from a review of major infractions cases in the NCAA Major Infractions–Legal Services Database.

100 David Price: Brad Wolverton, "NCAA Says Infractions Cases Will Reach Record High This Year," *Chronicle of Higher Education*, September 28, 2007.

100 In a 2011 tongue-in-cheek: Andy Staples, "Cheating for Dummies: Your Guide to Smarter NCAA Rule-Breaking," *Sports Illustrated*, July 5, 2011, https://www.si.com/more-sports/2011/07/05/cheating-dummies.

101 Marvin Austin tweeted: NCAA, *University of North Carolina, Chapel Hill, Public Infractions Report*, March 12, 2012, https://web3.ncaa.org/lsdbi/search/miCaseView/report?id=102358.

101 Head football coach Tressel's: Kim Bhasin and Dashiell Bennett, "Jim Tressel's Exclamation-Point Filled Emails Show Him Ignoring Major Violations by His Players," *Business Insider*, March 9, 2011.

101　It was impermissible: NCAA, *University of Tennessee, Knoxville, Public Infractions Report*, August 24, 2011, https://web3.ncaa.org/lsdbi/search /miCaseView/report?id=102351.

101　The criminal case against: Ray Sanchez and Julian Cummings, "Former Penn State President Spanier Gets Jail Time in Sandusky Case," CNN, June 2, 2017, https://www.cnn.com/2017/06/02/us/penn-state -administrators-sentenced/index.html.

101　The North Carolina case: NCAA, *University of North Carolina, Chapel Hill, Public Infractions Report*, March 12, 2012.

102　The breadth and depth: Kelly Parsons, "On Heels of Davis' Firing, Dick Baddour Announces Resignation," *Daily Tar Heel*, July 29, 2011.

102　The Tennessee case first came to light: Pete Thamel and Thayer Evans, "N.C.A.A. Puts Tennessee's Recruiting under Scrutiny," *New York Times*, December 9, 2009.

102　Two days after: Andy Staples, "Photo Reveals Vols Recruits Had Contact with Hostesses at Game," *Sports Illustrated*, December 11, 2009, https://www.si.com/more-sports/2009/12/11/tennessee-recruiting.

102　In the end: NCAA, *University of Tennessee, Knoxville, Public Infractions Report*, August 24, 2011.

103　NCAA bylaws prohibited: *NCAA Division I Manual*, bylaw 13.4.1.2 (pre-2014 version); bylaw 13.4.1.5 now allows text messages.

103　"I was so excited": Kelly Whiteside, "Tennessee Football Tweets Bring NCAA Whistle-Blowing," *USA Today*, May 21, 2009.

103　When Duke compliance officials: Dave Seminara, "A Recruit's Friend, a Team's Fan and a Headache for Colleges," *New York Times*, April 17, 2011.

104　In 2007 the Committee on Infractions: NCAA, *Temple University Public Infractions Report*, May 10, 2007, https://web3.ncaa.org/lsdbi/search /miCaseView/report?id=102297.

105　A major violation: *NCAA Division I Manual*, bylaw 19.02.2.1 (pre-2013 version); bylaw 19.1 now sets forth current "violation structure."

106　shortly after his appointment: Associated Press, "Mark Emmert Wants Stiffer Punishments," ESPN, May 11, 2011, http://www.espn.com/espnw /news-commentary/article/6522478/ncaa-president-mark-emmert -says-time-get-tough-rule-breakers.

106　the NCAA Board of Directors: *NCAA Division I Manual*, bylaw 19.1, figure 19-1.

107　Another goal: NCAA, *Working Group on Collegiate Model—Enforcement*, final EWG report, October 2012, 10, http://www.ncaa.org/sites/default /files/Report_Final_101112.pdf.

107　Indeed, the examples: NCAA, "Proposed New Violation Structure," initial draft on file with author.

107　A Level III "breach of conduct": *NCAA Division I Manual*, bylaw 19.1.3.

108 "current secondary violations": NCAA, *Working Group*, 25.

108 That conclusion is reinforced: NCAA, "Proposed New Violation Structure."

109 Level I violations: NCAA *Division I Manual*, bylaw 19.1.

5. Parasites

111 The blood was "everywhere": Woody Baird, "Alabama Booster Killed after Bloody Struggle at Memphis Home," Associated Press, April 12, 2006.

111 During an illustrious career: Bruce Weber, "James F. Neal, Litigated Historic Cases, Dies at 81," *New York Times*, October 22, 2010; Stephen Miller, "Watergate Prosecutor Neal Dies," *Wall Street Journal*, October 23, 2010.

112 In 2005 Neal defended: Mark Schlabach, "Alabama Booster Convicted," *Washington Post*, February 3, 2005.

112 Young reportedly had told friends: Dave Curtis, "The Odd Life and Death of Logan Young," *Orlando Sentinel*, April 23, 2006.

112 Two years earlier: Associated Press, "Convicted Bama Booster Found Dead at His Home," ESPN, April 12, 2006, http://sports.espn.go.com/ncf/news/story?id=2405013.

112 A housekeeper employed: Curtis, "Odd Life and Death."

112 Sgt. Vince Higgins: James Joyner, "Logan Young, Key Figure in Alabama Scandal, Murdered," *Outside the Beltway*, April 11, 2006; Associated Press, "Convicted Bama Booster."

112 An Associated Press report: Associated Press, "Death of Alabama Booster Young Ruled an Accident," *USA Today*, April 13, 2006.

113 Certainly Young's death: Curtis, "Odd Life and Death."

114 Over the years: NCAA, *University of Alabama, Tuscaloosa, Public Infractions Report*, February 1, 2002, https://web3.ncaa.org/lsdbi/search/miCaseView/report?id=102231.

114 In 1999 Young: NCAA, *University of Alabama, Tuscaloosa, Public Infractions Report*, February 1, 2002; Woody Baird, "No Prison Time for Lynn Lang: Ex-coach Won't Have to Forfeit Bribe Money," *Decatur Daily*, February 9, 2005, http://archive.decaturdaily.com/decaturdaily/sports/050209/lang.shtml.

114 Both Lang and Kirk: NCAA, *University of Alabama, Tuscaloosa, Public Infractions Report*, February 1, 2002.

115 After spring ball ended: NCAA, *University of Alabama, Tuscaloosa, Public Infractions Report*, February 1, 2002.

115 within months of his arrival: NCAA, *University of Alabama, Tuscaloosa, Public Infractions Report*, February 1, 2002.

115 Lynn Lang's gross salary: NCAA, *University of Alabama, Tuscaloosa, Public Infractions Report*, February 1, 2002.

116 Thus began a period: NCAA, *University of Alabama, Tuscaloosa, Public Infractions Report*, February 1, 2002.

116 Kirk arranged for Lang's SUV: NCAA, *University of Alabama, Tuscaloosa, Public Infractions Report*, February 1, 2002.

116 One big caveat: NCAA, *University of Alabama, Tuscaloosa, Public Infractions Report*, February 1, 2002.

116 National Letter of Intent Day: NCAA, *University of Alabama, Tuscaloosa, Public Infractions Report*, February 1, 2002.

117 Lang testified under oath: "Ex-Prep Coach: Seven Schools Offered Money for Player," *USA Today*, January 26, 2005.

117 Coaches from Georgia and Memphis: Baird, "No Prison Time."

117 Lang did not cooperate: NCAA, *University of Alabama, Tuscaloosa, Public Infractions Report*, February 1, 2002.

117 The general statute of limitations: NCAA *Division I Manual*, bylaw 19.5.11.

117 In any event: NCAA, *University of Alabama, Tuscaloosa, Public Infractions Report*, February 1, 2002.

117 When May rolled around: NCAA, *University of Alabama, Tuscaloosa, Public Infractions Report*, February 1, 2002.

118 Kirk also complained: NCAA, *University of Alabama, Tuscaloosa, Public Infractions Report*, February 1, 2002.

118 Eventually, Kirk also spoke: NCAA, *University of Alabama, Tuscaloosa, Public Infractions Report*, February 1, 2002.

118 One ordinarily thinks: William L. Anderson, "Federal Crimes and the Destruction of Law: Prosecutors' Abuse of the RICO and Fraud Statutes Is Threatening the Nation's Economy," *Regulation*, Winter 2009–10.

120 In exchange for his cooperation: Associated Press, "Sentence Delivered in Recruit Scandal," *New York Times*, December 18, 2002.

120 That evidence ultimately was presented: NCAA, *University of Alabama, Tuscaloosa, Public Infractions Report*, February 1, 2002.

121 Investigators later learned: NCAA, *University of Alabama, Tuscaloosa, Public Infractions Report*, February 1, 2002.

122 NCAA bylaws prohibit: NCAA *Division I Manual*, bylaw 19.7.7.3.1.

122 In the Alabama case: NCAA, *University of Alabama, Tuscaloosa, Public Infractions Appeals Committee Report*, September 17, 2002, https://web3.ncaa.org/lsdbi/search/miCaseView/report?id=102485.

122 Among those statements: NCAA, *University of Alabama, Tuscaloosa, Public Infractions Report*, February 1, 2002.

122 According to statements of fact: NCAA, *University of Alabama, Tuscaloosa, Public Infractions Report*, February 1, 2002.

123 in February 1996: NCAA, *University of Alabama, Tuscaloosa, Public Infractions Report*, February 1, 2002.

123 The allegations relating to the recruitment: NCAA, *University of Alabama, Tuscaloosa, Public Infractions Report*, February 1, 2002.

124 That is precisely the language: NCAA, *University of Alabama, Tuscaloosa, Public Infractions Report*, February 1, 2002.

124 The bar for finding an NCAA violation: NCAA *Division I Manual*, bylaw 19.7.8.3.

125 "While rogue athletics representatives": NCAA, *University of Alabama, Tuscaloosa, Public Infractions Report*, February 1, 2002.

126 "The actions and attitudes": NCAA, *University of Alabama, Tuscaloosa, Public Infractions Report*, February 1, 2002.

126 In its coup de grace: NCAA, *University of Alabama, Tuscaloosa, Public Infractions Report*, February 1, 2002.

126 "There is no doubt": NCAA, *University of Alabama, Tuscaloosa, Public Infractions Report*, February 1, 2002.

128 Most notably, the committee imposed: NCAA, *University of Alabama, Tuscaloosa, Public Infractions Report*, February 1, 2002.

128 In August 1995: NCAA, *University of Alabama, Tuscaloosa, Public Infractions Report*, August 2, 1995, https://web3.ncaa.org/lsdbi/search/miCaseView/report?id=101914.

129 In January 1998: NCAA, *University of Alabama Public Infractions Report*, February 9, 1999, https://web3.ncaa.org/lsdbi/search/miCaseView/report?id=102201.

130 The report pulled no punches: NCAA, *University of Alabama, Tuscaloosa, Public Infractions Report*, February 1, 2002.

130 The chair of the committee: John Zenor, "NCAA Rolls Crimson Tide for Violations," *USA Today*, February 1, 2002.

131 The infractions report suggested: NCAA, *University of Alabama, Tuscaloosa, Public Infractions Report*, February 1, 2002.

131 the University of Alabama announced: Zenor, "NCAA Rolls Crimson Tide."

6. The Rats You Are

133 Just before Christmas: Steve Henson, "Another Desert Storm," *Los Angeles Times*, December 22, 2000.

133 On December 12: NCAA, *University of Nevada, Las Vegas, Public Infractions Report*, December 12, 2000, https://web3.ncaa.org/lsdbi/search/miCaseView/report?id=102192.

134 The university "reassigned": Steve Addy, "With Bayno Era Over, Coach Moves On with No Regrets," *Las Vegas Sun*, March 15, 2001.

134 Bayno had a few strikes: Henson, "Another Desert Storm"; NCAA, *University of Nevada, Las Vegas, Public Infractions Report*, December 12, 2000.

134 The infractions committee also concluded: NCAA, *University of Nevada, Las Vegas, Public Infractions Report*, December 12, 2000.

134 Bayno's attorneys: Henson, "Another Desert Storm."

135 "Finally, given the added fact": NCAA, *University of Nevada, Las Vegas, Public Infractions Report*, December 12, 2000.

135 Longtime head coach: "Jerry Tarkanian Timeline," *Fresno Bee*, February 11, 2015; Associated Press, "Photos Create New Trouble at U.N.L.V.," *New York Times*, May 27, 1991.

135 His successor, Rollie Massimino: Alexander Wolff, "Divorce, Vegas Style: UNLV Gave Embattled Basketball Coach Rollie Massimino His Walking Papers but Not before Paying Him a Fat Cash Settlement," *Sports Illustrated*, October 24, 1994.

136 A return to the glory years: Associated Press, "Grgurich Steps Down at UNLV; Coach Couldn't Overcome Scars Left Over from Tarkanian Era," *Spokesman-Review*, March 4, 1995.

136 Because of the lengthy litigation: NCAA, *University of Nevada, Las Vegas, Public Infractions Report*, December 12, 2000.

136 The crowning blow: Seth Davis, "UNLV Scandal: Rebel with a Lost Cause," *Sports Illustrated*, December 25, 2000.

136 The trial in federal court: Morris News Service, "Atlanta Club's Trial Draws Southern Eyes," *Augusta Chronicle*, June 4, 2001.

137 In the trial's early stages: Morris News Service, "Atlanta Club's Trial."

137 Nonetheless, Bayno challenged: Addy, "With Bayno Era Over."

138 UNLV's president announced: Henson, "Another Desert Storm."

138 Tark the Shark: "Jerry Tarkanian," Sports Reference, https://www.sports-reference.com/cbb/coaches/jerry-tarkanian-1.html; "Jerry Tarkanian Timeline."

138 The story begins: "Jerry Tarkanian and the NCAA: Chronology of Events," last updated October 2009, http://www.oocities.org/the_fall_of_the_tide/jerrytarkanian.html; NCAA, *Long Beach State University Public Infractions Report*, January 6, 1974, https://web3.ncaa.org/lsdbi/search/miCaseView/report?id=101972.

139 In 1976 the NCAA investigated: "Jerry Tarkanian and the NCAA"; NCAA, *University of Nevada, Las Vegas, Public Infractions Report*, August 26, 1977, https://web3.ncaa.org/lsdbi/search/miCaseView/report?id=102010.

139 Tarkanian filed a lawsuit: "Jerry Tarkanian and the NCAA."

140 Following the 2002 Alabama: Doug Secrest, "Jury Rules NCAA Must Pay Alabama Football Booster $5 Million," *Birmingham News*, November 30, 2007.

140 the circuit judge threw out: Ray Keller v. National Collegiate Athletic Association, No. 2004–28-JHG (38th Cir. 2008).

140 Ultimately the parties resolved: "Jerry Tarkanian and the NCAA."

140 In 1978 a U.S. congressman: "Jerry Tarkanian and the NCAA."

141 The U.S. Supreme Court's: NCAA v. Tarkanian, 488 U.S. 179 (1988).

141 The committee was high powered: NCAA, *Report and Recommendations of the Special Committee to Review the NCAA Enforcement and Infractions Process* (Lee report), October 28, 1991, on file with author; Michael Janofsky, "N.C.A.A.'s Panel Recommends Updated Rules for Investigations," *New York Times*, October 29, 1991.

141 Among the Lee report recommendations: NCAA, *Report and Recommendations of the Special Committee.*

142 The appeals committee emphasized: NCAA, *Report of the University of Nevada, Las Vegas Public Infractions Appeals Committee*, February 16, 2001, https://web3.ncaa.org/lsdbi/search/miCaseView/report?id=102469.

143 I received a thoughtful email message: Alan W. Hester, email message to the author, October 3, 2001, on file with author.

144 "the NCAA is so mad": Eric Prisbell, "Former UNLV Coach Jerry Tarkanian Dies at 84," *USA Today*, February 11, 2015.

145 Fortunately, Charles J. Cooper: "Charles J. Cooper," Cooper and Kirk, PLLC, http://cooperkirk.com/lawyers/charles-j-cooper; Debra Cassens Weiss, "Meet Charles Cooper, the Lawyer Who Will Support Prop 8 in Arguments Today," *ABA Journal*, March 26, 2013.

145 Also at the ready: "Robert T. Cunningham," Cunningham Bounds, LLC, http://www.cunninghambounds.com/who-we-are/our-people/lawyers/bio/robert-cunningham.

146 For the Alabama appeal: Aimée Groth, "The Record Setter," *2010 Alabama Super Lawyers*, May 2010, https://www.superlawyers.com/alabama/article/the-record-setter/d9f5db86-9c8f-4a27-aed3-403aedd324a8.html.

147 In its later report: NCAA, *University of Alabama, Tuscaloosa, Public Infractions Appeals Committee Report*, September 17, 2002.

147 "You guys are 'screwed up'": Dewayne McCann, email message to the author, February 11, 2002, on file with author.

148 "Unfortunately, the main thing": Groth, "Record Setter."

149 During the decade: This summary is compiled from a review of major infractions cases in the NCAA Major Infractions–Legal Services Database.

149 Under NCAA bylaws: *NCAA Division I Manual*, bylaw 19.10.1.2-(a).

150 Appellants won some relief: These summaries are compiled from the NCAA Major Infractions–Legal Services Database.

151 Duff spoke with numerous stakeholders: James C. Duff, *Report and Recommendations of Counsel to the NCAA Special Internal Review Committee*, June 12, 2006, on file with author.

151 "A penalty prescribed by the hearing panel": *NCAA Division I Manual*, bylaw 19.10.1.1.

152 The Committee on Infractions' postseason ban: NCAA, *University of Alabama, Tuscaloosa, Public Infractions Report*, February 1, 2002.

152 a headline in one Alabama newspaper: "Running Backs Kept Alabama Offense on a Roll," *Honolulu Advertiser*, December 1, 2002.

152 Hawaii was a top-twenty-five team: "Alabama vs. Hawaii Game Summary," *USA Today*, November 30, 2002.

153 After the game: "Running Backs Kept Alabama."

153 The Tide lost to Hawaii: "2003 Alabama Crimson Tide Schedule and Results," Sports Reference, https://www.sports-reference.com/cfb/schools/alabama/2003-schedule.html.

153 In no time: "Alabama Crimson Tide School History," Sports Reference, https://www.sports-reference.com/cfb/schools/alabama.

153 "Moreover, during the two years": NCAA, *University of Southern California Public Infractions Report*, June 10, 2010, https://web3.ncaa.org /lsdbi/search/miCaseView/report?id=102369.

154 The committee report summarized: NCAA, *University of Alabama, Tuscaloosa, Public Infractions Report*, June 11, 2009, https://web3.ncaa.org /lsdbi/search/miCaseView/report?id=102314.

154 "extensive recent history": NCAA, *University of Alabama, Tuscaloosa, Public Infractions Report*, June 11, 2009.

154 the Infractions Appeals Committee denied relief: NCAA, *University of Alabama, Tuscaloosa, Public Infractions Appeals Committee Report*, March 23, 2010, https://web3.ncaa.org/lsdbi/search/miCaseView/report?id=102518.

7. Cooperation

155 MacMurray College: NCAA, *MacMurray College Public Infractions Report*, May 4, 2005, https://web3.ncaa.org/lsdbi/search/miCaseView/report ?id=102214.

155 Morehouse College: NCAA, *Morehouse College Public Infractions Report*, November 5, 2003, https://web3.ncaa.org/lsdbi/search/miCaseView /report?id=102208.

155 two other Division I programs: NCAA, *University of Kentucky Public Infractions Report*, January 10, 1953, https://web3.ncaa.org/lsdbi/search /miCaseView/report?id=101754; NCAA, *University of Southwestern Louisiana, Public Infractions Report*, August 4, 1973 (listed in database under current institution name, University of Louisiana at Lafayette), https:// web3.ncaa.org/lsdbi/search/miCaseView/report?id=101966.

156 In David Whitford's book: Whitford, *A Payroll to Meet*, 40.

156 In 1986: NCAA, *Texas Christian University Public Infractions Report*, May 9, 1986, https://web3.ncaa.org/lsdbi/search/miCaseView/report ?id=102141.

156 the infractions committee explicitly lauded: NCAA, *Texas Christian University Public Infractions Report*, May 9, 1986.

157 Bylaw 19.2.3 states: NCAA *Division I Manual*, bylaw 19.2.3.

159 Under the bylaws: NCAA *Division I Manual*, bylaw 19.9.4-(f).

160 Ed Martin had died: Associated Press, "Ed Martin, Key Figure in Michigan Basketball Scandal, Is Dead at 69," *New York Times*, February 18, 2003.

160 The Michigan infractions case: Michael Hirsley, "A Week after Michigan Crash, Questions Linger," *Chicago Tribune*, February 25, 1996.

161 Taylor was a sophomore: Associated Press, "Michigan Players Involved in Accident," *Los Angeles Times*, February 18, 1996.

161 Robert "Tractor" Traylor: Jim Cnockaert, "Accident's Effects Still Felt Six Year Later," *Ann Arbor News*, March 22, 2002.

161 Mitch Albom labeled: Mitch Albom, *Fab Five: Basketball, Trash Talk, the American Dream* (New York: Warner Books, 1993), 4–5.

161 And who owned that new Ford: Hirsley, "Week after Michigan Crash."

162 He had told them: Associated Press, "Michigan Players Involved in Accident."

162 That they disregarded: Michael Hirsley, "NCAA Minimizes Crash at Michigan," *Chicago Tribune*, February 20, 1996.

162 The SUV was coleased: Hirsley, "Week after Michigan Crash."

162 The Michigan sports information office: Hirsley, "NCAA Minimizes Crash."

163 they went "a couple miles farther": "Ed Martin Revealed: His Long and Infamous Road into Michigan Basketball History," *Michigan Daily*, May 11, 2003; Cnockaert, "Accident's Effects Still Felt."

163 Ed Martin was a retired Detroit autoworker: Larry Lage, "Michigan Booster Charged with Paying Players," *USA Today*, March 21, 2002.

163 As Gregory Lord: David Shepardson, "Webber Plea to Scuttle Federal Trial," *USA Today*, July 14, 2003.

164 Martin was invariably described: J. Brady McCullough, "Ed Martin Pleads Guilty to Money Laundering Conspiracy Charge," *Michigan Daily*, May 27, 2002; Joe Smith, "'Fab Five' Legacy Tainted," *Michigan Daily*, March 25, 2002.

164 "meals, clothing, money": NCAA, *University of Michigan Public Infractions Report*, May 8, 2003, https://web3.ncaa.org/lsdbi/search/miCaseView /report?id=102249.

164 Martin also went way back: Geoff Larcom, "Former U-M Assistant Testifies in Martin Case," *Ann Arbor News*, October 19, 2000.

165 So Ed Martin had close connections: NCAA, *University of Michigan Public Infractions Report*, May 8, 2003.

165 Fisher, the infractions committee would say: NCAA, *University of Michigan Public Infractions Report*, May 8, 2003.

165 Rumors swirled about Martin: "NCAA Gives Michigan Good News," *Detroit Free Press*, December 19, 1997.

166 "This is a most unique case": "U-M Announces Findings of Men's Basketball Investigation," University of Michigan Athletics, October 9, 1997, https://mgoblue.com/news/1997/10/9/u_m_announces_findings_of _men_s_basketball_investigation.aspx.

166 he was out as head coach: Associated Press, "Michigan Fires Fisher," *New York Times*, October 12, 1997.

167 The report indicated that Fisher: "Ed Martin Revealed"; Associated Press, "Michigan Fires Fisher."

167 the NCAA announced in December: "NCAA Gives Michigan Good News."

167 On April 28, 1999: Associated Press, "FBI Investigates UM Booster," CBS News, May 14, 1999.

168 "Martin ran a numbers operation": "UM Gambling Scandal," *Bettors World*, March 22, 2002, http://bettorsworld.com/ForumOLD/archive/index.php/t-10162.html.

168 The seized records: Associated Press, "FBI Investigates UM Booster."

168 Martin long had been known: "Ed Martin Revealed."

168 he effectively disassociated Martin: Cnockaert, "Accident's Effects Still Felt."

168 *Free Press* had noted: Associated Press, "FBI Investigates UM Booster."

169 enough for Martin to sign: Associated Press, "Banned Booster to Reveal Ties," *Augusta Chronicle*, April 8, 2000.

169 in May 2000: "Former Michigan Booster, Son Back Out of Deal," *Philadelphia Inquirer*, May 5, 2000.

169 Nearly two years later: Lage, "Michigan Booster Charged."

169 Son Carlton already was incarcerated: John Easterbrook, "Booster Busted for Paying Players," CBS News, March 21, 2002.

169 the indictment alleged: Lage, "Michigan Booster Charged."

170 Rose later would admit: Associated Press, "Jalen Rose: Booster Gave Me 'Pocket Money,'" *USA Today*, May 30, 2002.

170 Martin had told others: NCAA, *University of Michigan Public Infractions Report*, May 8, 2003.

170 Later reports suggested: Caitlin Nish, "Webber Avoids Jail, Pleading Guilty on a Contempt Charge," *New York Times*, July 15, 2003.

170 In May 2002: J. Brady McCullough, "Martin Pleads Guilty, Will Disclose Everything," *Michigan Daily*, May 30, 2002.

171 University of Michigan officials reacted: J. Brady McCullough, "'U' Will Not Focus on Players or Loans," *Michigan Daily*, May 30, 2002.

171 Over the next few months: Julie Peterson, "U-M Announces Conclusion of Ed Martin Investigation, Self-Imposes Sanctions," *University of Michigan News Service/University Record Online*, November 11, 2002.

172 The Committee on Infractions released: NCAA, *University of Michigan Public Infractions Report*, May 8, 2003.

173 But the NCAA bylaws provide: NCAA *Division I Manual*, bylaw 19.5.11.

173 "While some of the violations": NCAA, *University of Michigan Public Infractions Report*, May 8, 2003.

174 the infractions committee focused its attention: NCAA, *University of Michigan Public Infractions Report*, May 8, 2003.

174 "The fact that the athletics representative": NCAA, *University of Michigan Public Infractions Report*, May 8, 2003.

175 "There are individuals": NCAA, *University of Michigan Public Infractions Report*, May 8, 2003.

175 George Raveling: Cnockaert, "Accident's Effects Still Felt."

175 the basketball staff treated Martin: NCAA, *University of Michigan Public Infractions Report*, May 8, 2003.

175 The committee detailed the relationship: NCAA, *University of Michigan Public Infractions Report*, May 8, 2003.

175 The committee commended the university: NCAA, *University of Michigan Public Infractions Report*, May 8, 2003.

176 "Despite this mitigation": NCAA, *University of Michigan Public Infractions Report*, May 8, 2003.

176 The committee added a second year: NCAA, *University of Michigan Public Infractions Report*, May 8, 2003.

177 "The additional postseason ban": Steve Weiberg, "NCAA Expands Michigan's Penalties," *USA Today*, May 8, 2003.

177 NCAA transfer rules: *NCAA Division I Manual*, bylaw 14.7.2-(c).

178 A body of NCAA case law: NCAA, *University of Mississippi Public Infractions Appeals Committee Report*, May 1, 1995, https://web3.ncaa.org/lsdbi /search/miCaseView/report?id=102462.

179 In his public comments: Pete Thamel, "Revisiting the Fab Five at the Final Four," *New York Times*, April 2, 2009.

179 Nonetheless, the Infractions Appeals Committee: NCAA, *University of Michigan Public Infractions Appeals Committee Report*, September 25, 2003, https://web3.ncaa.org/lsdbi/search/miCaseView/report?id=102494.

180 According to the infractions report: NCAA, *University of Michigan Public Infractions Report*, May 8, 2003.

182 "analysis of the mitigating factor": NCAA, *Howard University Public Infractions Report*, November 27, 2001.

182 the subcommittee, with the support: Subcommittee report on file with author.

183 the NCAA bylaws now speak: *NCAA Division I Manual*, bylaw 19.9.4-(f).

184 In September 2002: Roscoe Nance, "Kings Star Webber Indicted," *USA Today*, September 10, 2002.

184 Prosecutors announced: Gennaro A. Filice IV, "Weber Sees Favorable Rulings," *Michigan Daily*, July 13, 2003.

185 Webber pled guilty: Shepardson, "Webber Plea to Scuttle Federal Trial."

185 The judge deferred sentencing: Michael McCarthy and Jodi Upton, "NBA Star Webber Makes Effort—and Makes Difference," *USA Today*, May 4, 2006.

185 "Go Blue": J. Brady McCullough, "Three of Four 'U' Players Did Not Pay Back Martin," *Michigan Daily*, May 30, 2002.

8. The Investigators

187 "No team inspired": Ryan McGee, "The Most Scandalous Year Ever in College Sports . . . Until Next Year," *ESPN Insider*, May 30, 2011.

188 Nevin Shapiro: Jay Weaver and Manny Navarro, "Nevin Shapiro's Two Roles: Miami Hurricanes Sugar Daddy, Pseudo Agent," *Miami Herald*, December 2, 2012.

189 Nevin Shapiro, though: Dan Wetzel, "Who Is Nevin Shapiro?" Yahoo! Sports, August 16, 2011, https://www.yahoo.com/news/nevin-shapiro -214400440--spt.html.

189 Indeed, his cooperation: Associated Press, "NCAA Investigator Wrote Letter on Nevin Shapiro's Behalf," *USA Today*, March 6, 2013.

189 Investigators, for example: Kenneth L. Wainstein, A. Joseph Jay III, Thomas M. Guerin, Colleen D. Kukowski, Keith M. Gerver, and Samantha A. Dreilinger, *Report on the NCAA's Engagement of a Source's Counsel and Use of the Bankruptcy Process in its University of Miami Investigation*, February 17, 2013, 12; subsequently referred to as the Wainstein report.

189 Shapiro's attorney: Wainstein report, 12–14.

190 Perez's assistance: Wainstein report, 13, 15.

190 Najjar followed up: Wainstein report, 14–15.

191 Hosty found: Wainstein report, 15–16.

192 After reviewing the matter: Wainstein report, 17.

192 Unwilling to accept no: Wainstein report, 17–18.

192 Najjar was undeterred: Wainstein report, 19–20.

193 Perez's work on behalf: Wainstein report, 21–24.

193 Lach, surely a bit stunned: Wainstein report, 24.

193 After an internal review: Wainstein report, 25.

194 Perez's proposal: Wainstein report, 18.

194 On the other hand: Wainstein report, 30.

195 Mark Emmert preached: Mark Emmert, "Cheating Will Not Be Tolerated," *USA Today*, August 31, 2011.

195 a report published by Yahoo! Sports: Charles Robinson, "Renegade Miami Football Booster Spells Out Illicit Benefits to Players," Yahoo! Sports, August 16, 2011, https://sports.yahoo.com/news/renegade-miami-football -booster-spells-213700753--spt.html.

195 observers began calling: Michael Marot, "Miami Hurricanes Football: NCAA 'Death Penalty' Could Be Option," *Huffington Post*, August 19, 2011.

196 On January 23: ESPN News Service, "NCAA Finds Issue with Investigation," ESPN, January 23, 2013, http://www.espn.com/college-sports/story /_/id/8872992/ncaa-reveals-found-improper-conduct-investigation -miami-hurricanes; Steve Eder, "N.C.A.A. Admits Mishandling Miami Inquiry," *New York Times*, January 24, 2013.

196 His demonstration: Eder, "N.C.A.A. Admits Mishandling."

196 "The facts do not establish": Wainstein report, 4.

196 The report did: Wainstein report, 4–5.

197 Finally, the Wainstein report: Wainstein report, 5.

197 Interestingly, the report: Wainstein report, 36–37.

197 In that light: Scott Gleeson, "Miami President Donna Shalala Responds to NCAA's 'Flawed' Investigation," *USA Today*, February 18, 2013.

197   As a result of the findings: Steve Eder, "N.C.A.A. Ousts Its Chief Officer for Enforcement," *New York Times*, February 19, 2013.

197   A former college basketball player: Wainstein report, 9, 43; Eder, "N.C.A.A. Ousts."

198   To replace Lach: Dennis Dodd, "NCAA Interim Enforcement Director Gets Permanent Title," CBS Sports, April 14, 2014, https://www.cbssports .com/college-football/news/ncaa-interim-enforcement-director-gets -permanent-title/.

198   One ESPN writer: Dana O'Neil, "NCAA Its Own Worst Enemy—Again," ESPN, January 23, 2013, http://www.espn.com/blog/collegebasketballnation /post/_/id/73698/ncaa-its-own-worst-enemy-again.

200   "In granting this mission": Wainstein report, 38.

201   "He doesn't need a reason": Erick Smith, "Lawyer Says Terrelle Pryor Will Not Talk to NCAA about Ohio State," *USA Today*, June 9, 2011.

201   The enforcement staff faces: Dan Wolken, "Departures Sap Strength of NCAA Enforcement," *USA Today*, June 13, 2013.

201   Unfortunately for Grantstein: Baxter Holmes, "Overheard Conversation Suggests NCAA Prejudged Shabazz Muhammad Case," *Los Angeles Times*, November 14, 2012.

202   About this same time: Holmes, "Overheard Conversation."

202   "Abby" was described: Holmes, "Overheard Conversation."

202   Granstein was fired: Gary Parrish, "NCAA Fires Investigator Who Han- dled Shabazz Muhammad Case," CBS Sports, December 21, 2012, https:// www.cbssports.com/college-basketball/news/ncaa-fires-investigator-who -handled-shabazz-muhammad-case/.

202   Muhammad's eligibility was quickly restored: Eric Prisbell, "NCAA Rein- states Shabazz Muhammad," *USA Today*, November 16, 2012.

203   Not surprisingly: Dana O'Neil, "Muhammad Case Really about NCAA," ESPN, November 16, 2012, http://www.espn.com/mens-college-basketball /story/_/id/8640624/shabazz-muhammad-case-shows-how-ncaa-system -work-men-college-basketball.

203   Muhammad's attorneys: Holmes, "Overheard Conversation."

203   As one commentator: O'Neil, "Muhammad Case"; NCAA, *NCAA Division I Student-Athlete Reinstatement Guidelines*, last revised May 2018, https://www .ncaa.org/sites/default/files/May2018DISAR_Guidelines_20180723.pdf.

204   "puts a far brighter light": Holmes, "Overheard Conversation."

204   "loud-mouthed boyfriend": Avinash Kunnath, "NCAA Reportedly Fires Lead Investigator in Shabazz Muhammad Case," SBNation, December 20, 2012, https://www.sbnation.com/college-basketball/2012/12/20/3790428 /shabazz-muhammad-investigation-ncaa-abigail-grantstein.

204   The soccer coach: NCAA, *West Virginia University Public Infractions Report*, May 1, 2007, https://web3.ncaa.org/lsdbi/search/miCaseView/report?id =102293.

205 The committee upbraided: NCAA, *West Virginia University Public Infractions Report*, May 1, 2007.

206 Pursuant to NCAA bylaws: NCAA *Division I Manual*, bylaw 19.5.1.

206 Before beginning an investigation: NCAA *Division I Manual*, bylaw 19.5.3.

206 The next step: NCAA *Division I Manual*, bylaw 19.7.1.

207 A similar notice of allegations: NCAA *Division I Manual*, bylaw 19.7.1.2.

207 a recent report indicated: Pat Forde, "Sources: MSU Linebacker Leo Lewis Testified at Ole Miss' NCAA Committee on Infractions Hearing," Yahoo! Sports, September 11, 2017, https://sports.yahoo.com/sources-msu-linebacker-leo-lewis-testified-ole-miss-ncaa-committee-infractions-hearing-233617799.html.

207 University representatives: NCAA *Division I Manual*, bylaw 19.7.2.

208 The enforcement staff submits: NCAA *Division I Manual*, bylaw 19.7.3.

208 The NCAA bylaws permit: NCAA *Division I Manual*, bylaw 19.6.

208 Shortly before the hearing: NCAA *Division I Manual*, bylaw 19.7.4.

208 The Committee on Infractions: NCAA *Division I Manual*, bylaws 19.7.7, 19.8.

209 A school or involved individual: NCAA *Division I Manual*, bylaw 19.10.

209 In a controversial 1988 decision: NCAA v. Tarkanian, 488 U.S. 179 (1988).

210 "much ado about nothing": Josephine Potuto, "NCAA as State Actor: Much Ado about Nothing," *Marquette Sports Law Review* 23, no. 1 (2012).

210 "They were the worst organization": Eric Prisbell, "NCAA Tries to Get Handle on Truth," *Washington Post*, February 23, 2004.

9. The Committee

211 an article by CBS Sports' Dennis Dodd: Dennis Dodd, "NCAA: Mistakes in McNair Case Shouldn't Mean Unsealing Bush File," CBS Sports, February 27, 2014, https://www.cbssports.com/college-football/news/ncaa-mistakes-in-mcnair-case-shouldnt-mean-unsealing-bush-file/.

211 "After an initial review": Tyler Conway, "USC's Pat Haden Comments on Release of Documents in McNair vs. NCAA Lawsuit," Bleacher Report, March 25, 2015, https://bleacherreport.com/articles/2409534-uscs-pat-haden-comments-on-release-of-documents-in-mcnair-vs-NCAA-lawsuit.

213 In 2011: NCAA, *University of Tennessee, Knoxville, Public Infractions Report*, August 24, 2011.

214 The NCAA Division I membership: NCAA *Division I Manual*, bylaw 4.2.

221 Under bylaws that still hold today: NCAA *Division I Manual*, bylaw 19.3.5.

221 the NCAA Board of Directors expanded: NCAA *Division I Manual*, bylaw 19.3.1.

221 The rationale for the expansion: Gary Brown, "Board Adopts Tougher, More Efficient Enforcement Program," NCAA, October 30, 2012, http://www.ncaa.org/about/resources/media-center/news/board-adopts-tougher-more-efficient-enforcement-program.

221 An accompanying NCAA press release: Brown, "Board Adopts Tougher."

222 In the ten years from January 2000 to December 2009: This summary is compiled from a review of major infractions cases in the NCAA Major Infractions–Legal Services Database.

223 Bob Bowlsby: Chris Dufresne, "Big 12 Commissioner Bob Bowlsby Says Cheating Pays in the NCAA," *Los Angeles Times*, July 22, 2014.

224 NCAA officials acknowledged: Brown, "Board Adopts Tougher."

225 In 2004: NCAA, *University of Southern California Public Infractions Report*, June 10, 2010, https://web3.ncaa.org/lsdbi/search/miCaseView /report?id=102369.

226 In 2001: NCAA, *University of Southern California Public Infractions Report*, August 23, 2001, https://web3.ncaa.org/lsdbi/search/miCaseView/report ?id=102183.

226 On April 21: NCAA, *University of Southern California Public Infractions Report*, June 10, 2010.

226 The Committee on Infractions: NCAA, *University of Southern California Public Infractions Report*, June 10, 2010.

227 Nonetheless, the penalties were harsher: NCAA, *University of Southern California Public Infractions Report*, June 10, 2010.

227 including USC's infractions history: NCAA, *University of Southern California Public Infractions Report*, June 10, 2010.

227 "It's become an accepted fact": Ted Miller, "What We Learned in the Pac-12: Week 14," ESPN, December 4, 2011, http://www.espn.com/blog /pac12/post?id=31040&_slug_=what-we-learned-in-the-pac-12-week -14&redirected=true.

228 "high-profile players": Bob Condotta, "USC Hit with Severe NCAA Penalties, Including Two-Year Bowl Ban," *Seattle Times*, June 10, 2010.

228 So he became instant fodder: John Taylor, "Larry Scott on Paul Dee: 'Irony and Hypocrisy Don't . . . Go Far Enough,'" NBC Sports, August 18, 2011, https://collegefootballtalk.nbcsports.com/2011/08/18/larry-scott -on-paul-dee-irony-and-hypocrisy-dont-go-far-enough/.

228 Another part: ESPN News Service, "NCAA Delivers Postseason Football Ban," ESPN, June 10, 2010, http://www.espn.com/los-angeles/ncf /news/story?id=5272615; NCAA, *University of Southern California Public Infractions Report*, June 10, 2010.

229 As one of the committee members: Roscoe Howard, email message to NCAA Committee on Infractions, March 2, 2010, available at "NCAA's Previously Sealed Documents," *Los Angeles Times*, March 24, 2015, 63, http://documents.latimes.com/ncaa-mcnair-documents/.

229 one committee member wryly noted: Roscoe Howard, email message to Committee on Infractions, March 2, 2010.

230 The NCAA attorneys: Dodd, "NCAA: Mistakes in McNair Case."

231 including at least one former committee member: Gene A. Marsh, "A Call for Dissent and Further Independence in the NCAA Infrac-

tions Process," *Cardozo Arts and Entertainment Law Journal* 26 (2009): 710–17.

231 After committee members' email messages: Michael Lev, "Court Documents Suggest NCAA Bias in Case against USC, Reggie Bush, Todd McNair," *Orange County Register*, March 24, 2015.

231 Criticism also has been directed: Lev, "Court Documents Suggest NCAA Bias."

232 Critics have characterized the emails: Lev, "Court Documents Suggest NCAA Bias."

232 critics claimed that the committee: Lev, "Court Documents Suggest NCAA Bias."

233 "a lying, morally bankrupt criminal": Shep Cooper, email message to Rodney Uphoff, February 22, 2010, quoted in Nathan Fenno, "Full Record in Defamation Suit by Todd McNair against NCAA Is Made Public," *Los Angeles Times*, July 15, 2015, http://www.latimes.com/sports/usc/la-sp -usc-ncaa-mcnair-20150716-story.html.

233 In the end: Nathan Fenno, "Former USC Football Assistant Todd McNair Loses Case against NCAA," *Los Angeles Times*, May 21, 2018.

234 "I am becoming increasingly uneasy": Eleanor Myers, email message to NCAA Committee on Infractions, March 4, 2010, available at "NCAA's Previously Sealed Documents," 68.

10. *Student* Athletes?

235 Many in the know: John U. Bacon, "Syracuse-UNC in Final Four Exposes NCAA's Lack of Principle," ThePostGame, April 1, 2016, http://www .thepostgame.com/daily-take/201604/final-four-syracuse-north-carolina -corruption-scandal-academics-ncaa.

235 Syracuse wasn't even eligible: NCAA, *Syracuse University Public Infractions Decision*, March 6, 2015.

235 North Carolina, in the meantime: Bacon, "Syracuse-UNC in Final Four."

236 major sanctions imposed: NCAA, *Syracuse University Public Infractions Decision*, March 6, 2015.

236 Boeheim characterized: David Waldstein, "Seeded 10th, Syracuse Is One of the Last Four Left," *New York Times*, March 27, 2016.

236 The public report: NCAA, *Syracuse University Public Infractions Decision*, March 6, 2015.

237 One episode in particular: NCAA, *Syracuse University Public Infractions Decision*, March 6, 2015.

237 The Orange had started the season: "2011–12 Syracuse Orange Schedule and Results," Sports Reference, https://www.sports-reference.com /cbb/schools/syracuse/2012-schedule.html.

237 On January 25: NCAA, *Syracuse University Public Infractions Decision*, March 6, 2015.

238 Melo and the director: NCAA, *Syracuse University Public Infractions Decision*, March 6, 2015.

238 the Orange squeaked out: "2011–12 Syracuse Orange Schedule."

238 On Tuesday: NCAA, *Syracuse University Public Infractions Decision*, March 6, 2015.

238 "St. John's . . . was outrebounded": Mark Viera, "With Depth and a Zone, Syracuse Rolls Over St. John's," *New York Times*, February 4, 2012.

239 In late February 2012: NCAA, *Syracuse University Public Infractions Decision*, March 6, 2015.

239 Two days before: Pete Thamel, "Top-Seeded Orange Lose Key Player on Defense," *New York Times*, March 13, 2012.

240 A PowerPoint presentation: Wainstein UNC report, 1, 16–22.

240 Another slide: Wainstein UNC report, 22–23.

241 Prior to the PowerPoint: Wainstein UNC report, 21–22.

241 Yet when Dr. Julius Nyang'oro: Wainstein UNC report, 15–17.

242 When curricular changes: Wainstein UNC report, 17–18.

243 In 2005 or 2006 a UNC administrator: Wainstein UNC report, 5, 21.

243 So red flags existed: Wainstein UNC report, 18, 24.

243 The media accounts: Wainstein UNC report, 24.

244 A later independent investigation: Wainstein UNC report, 3, 33–36.

244 The investigative report noted: Wainstein UNC report, 3–4.

244 Ten of the fifteen players: Dan Kane, "2005 UNC Basketball Champs: 2 semesters, 35 Bogus 'Paper' Classes," *News and Observer*, November 8, 2014.

244 An email exchange: Wainstein UNC report, 40.

245 These documents: Wainstein UNC report, 24–30.

245 In February 2014: Wainstein UNC report, 2.

245 Wainstein brought superb credentials: "Kenneth L. Wainstein," Davis, Polk and Wardwell, LLP, https://davispolk.com/professionals/ken-wainstein.

246 His report: Wainstein UNC report, 2.

246 The NCAA enforcement staff: Wainstein UNC report, 25, 29–30.

246 A dogged investigative reporter: Sarah Lyall, "Reporter Digging into Scandal Hits a University's Raw Nerve," *New York Times*, April 26, 2014.

246 For example, the *Times*: Sarah Lyall, "A's for Athletes, but Charges of Fraud at North Carolina," *New York Times*, December 31, 2013.

246 UNC hired Wainstein: Wainstein UNC report, 7–8.

246 Yes, the broad parameters: Wainstein, UNC report, 27–28.

247 the NCAA enforcement staff sent: Dana O'Neil, "NCAA's Latest Notice to UNC Takes an Unexpected Turn," ESPN, April 25, 2016, http://www.espn .com/mens-college-basketball/story/_/id/15356594/north-carolina-tar -heels-latest-ncaa-news-tough-make-sense-of.

247 the enforcement staff alleged: NCAA, *Amended Notice of Allegations to the Chancellor of the University of North Carolina, Chapel Hill*, April 25,

2016, http://carolinacommitment.unc.edu/files/2016/04/NOA_Amended
_042516_NorthCarolina.pdf.

247 In August 2016: *University of North Carolina at Chapel Hill Response
to NCAA Amended Notice of Allegations*, August 1, 2016, http://carolina
commitment.unc.edu/files/2016/08/UNC-Response-to-2016-ANOA.pdf.

248 In 2013: Ralph D. Russo, "Head of NCAA Enforcement: Academic Misconduct on Rise," Yahoo! Sports, January 28, 2015, https://sports.yahoo.com
/news/head-ncaa-enforcement-academic-misconduct-rise-225453967
--spt.html.

248 Committee on Academics: NCAA, "Division I Committee on Academics," http://web1.ncaa.org/committees/committees_roster.jsp
?CommitteeName=1ACADCOM.

249 An NCAA media release: Michelle Brutlag Hosick, "Council Clarifies
Academic Misconduct Rules," NCAA, April 15, 2014, http://www.ncaa
.org/about/resources/media-center/news/council-clarifies-academic
-misconduct-rules.

249 In mid-November: Steve Berkowitz, "NCAA's Emmert Cautions Schools
about Academic 'Mismatches,'" *USA Today*, November 15, 2015.

250 Syracuse again provides: NCAA, *Syracuse University Public Infractions
Decision*, March 6, 2015.

251 After a drawn-out procedural battle: NCAA, *Syracuse University Public
Infractions Decision*, March 6, 2015.

251 Syracuse initially appealed: NCAA, *Syracuse University Public Infractions Appeals Committee Decision*, November 25, 2015, https://web3
.ncaa.org/lsdbi/search/miCaseView/report?id=102540.

251 Extra benefits are defined as: NCAA *Division I Manual*, bylaws 16.01.1,
16.02.3.

251 A benefit is impermissible: NCAA *Division I Manual*, bylaw 16.02.3.

252 Indeed, academic support services: NCAA *Division I Manual*, bylaw
16.3.1.1.

252 In addition to his coaching duties: NCAA, *University of Georgia Public
Infractions Report*, August 5, 2004, http://web3.ncaa.org/lsdbi/search
/miCaseView/report?id=102223; Associated Press, "Coach Gave Every
Student an A," ESPN, March 3, 2004, http://www.espn.com/mens-college
-basketball/news/story?id=1750279.

252 The NCAA enforcement staff: NCAA, *University of Georgia Public Infractions Report*, August 5, 2004.

253 In the UNC case: Wainstein UNC report, 3.

253 UNC's August 2016 response: *University of North Carolina at Chapel Hill
Response to NCAA Amended Notice of Allegations*.

254 The UNC response: Robbi Pickeral, "NCAA Stays Mum on UNC Scandal,"
ESPN, August 8, 2012, http://www.espn.com/blog/collegebasketballnation
/post/_/id/62166/pickeral-ncaa-stays-mum-on-unc-scandal.

254 there were *1,871*: Wainstein UNC report, 47.

254 The Wainstein report noted: Wainstein report, 52.

255 "The athletes did the baloney": Dana O'Neil, "Get a Taste of This NCAA Baloney," ESPN, August 8, 2012, http://www.espn.com/college-sports /story/_/id/8243779/north-carolina-tar-heels-academic-scandal -exemplifies-ncaa-hypocrisy.

255 its Division I Board of Directors: Michelle Brutlag Hosick, "DI Council Adopts Academic Integrity Proposal," NCAA, April 8, 2016, http:// www.ncaa.org/about/resources/media-center/news/di-council-adopts -academic-integrity-proposal.

256 The response suggested: *University of North Carolina at Chapel Hill Response to NCAA Amended Notice of Allegations.*

256 New bylaws in Article 14: *NCAA Division I Manual*, bylaws 14.02.1, 14.02.10, 14.9.1.

257 an NCAA academic misconduct violation: *NCAA Division I Manual*, bylaw 14.9.2.

257 The bylaws then add: *NCAA Division I Manual*, bylaws 14.02.10, 14.9.2.3, figure 14-2.

258 In the UNC case: *University of North Carolina at Chapel Hill Response to NCAA Amended Notice of Allegations.*

258 the NCAA published: Jonathan F. Duncan, "Re: NCAA Division I Proposal 2015-66 (Academic Integrity)," memorandum to NCAA Division I Membership, February 12, 2016, on file with author.

259 An accompanying question-and-answer: Jonathan F. Duncan, "NCAA Division I Proposal No. 2015–66 Question and Answer Document," February 26, 2016, on file with author.

259 Kathy Sulentic: Jon Solomon, "Inside College Sports: NCAA Redefines Academic Misconduct after UNC Case," CBS Sports, September 24, 2015, https://www.cbssports.com/college-football/news/inside-college-sports -ncaa-redefines-academic-misconduct-after-unc-case/.

260 A year earlier: Committee on Infractions panel to Chancellor Carol Folt et al., November 28, 2016, https://carolinacommitment.unc.edu/files/2016 /12/November-28-2016-letter-from-Committee-on-Infractions.pdf.

260 In a subsequent letter: Committee on Infractions panel to Folt et al., November 28, 2016.

261 The panel cited apparent confusion: Committee on Infractions panel to Folt et al., November 28, 2016.

261 The enforcement staff took the panel up: NCAA, *Second Amended Notice of Allegations to the Chancellor of the University of North Carolina, Chapel Hill*, December 13, 2016, https://carolinacommitment.unc.edu/files/2016 /12/NCAA-third-notice-of-allegations.pdf.

261 UNC responded: *University of North Carolina at Chapel Hill Response to NCAA Second Amended Notice of Allegations*, May 16, 2017, https://

carolinacommitment.unc.edu/files/2017/05/UNC-Response-to-2016
-2nd-Amended-NOA-1.pdf.

261 In its public report: NCAA, *University of North Carolina at Chapel Hill Public Infractions Decision*, October 13, 2017, https://web3.ncaa.org/lsdbi /search/miCaseView/report?id=102636.

262 The panel's deference: NCAA, *University of North Carolina at Chapel Hill Public Infractions Decision*, October 13, 2017.

262 The infractions panel expressed: NCAA, *University of North Carolina at Chapel Hill Public Infractions Decision*, October 13, 2017.

263 Because the NCAA membership: NCAA, *University of North Carolina at Chapel Hill Public Infractions Decision*, October 13, 2017.

263 Impermissible academic assistance: NCAA, *University of North Carolina at Chapel Hill Public Infractions Decision*, October 13, 2017.

263 The panel did consider: NCAA, *University of North Carolina at Chapel Hill Public Infractions Decision*, October 13, 2017.

263 Ultimately, the only charges: NCAA, *University of North Carolina at Chapel Hill Public Infractions Decision*, October 13, 2017.

264 "UNC took the firm position": NCAA, *University of North Carolina at Chapel Hill Public Infractions Decision*, October 13, 2017.

264 The Wainstein report notes: Wainstein UNC report, 44.

265 Wainstein also cited: Wainstein UNC report, 44.

265 When the football team's: Wainstein UNC report, 23–24.

265 A *Los Angeles Times* article: Lance Pugmire and Gary Klein, "Summertime, and the Grading Is Easy," *Los Angeles Times*, February 2, 2007.

266 Auburn was investigated: Pete Thamel, "N.C.A.A. and SEC Await Auburn's Inquiry on Suspect Courses," *New York Times*, July 18, 2006.

266 Even Stanford: Amy Julia Harris and Ryan Mac, "Stanford Drops List of 'Easy' Classes for Athletes," *San Francisco Chronicle*, March 9, 2011.

266 A 2009 Associated Press review: Alan Scher Zagier, "Admission Breaks for Athletes Widespread," *Post and Courier*, December 31, 2009.

266 "Most people can't get their knickers": O'Neil, "Get a Taste of This."

11. The Extent of NCAA Authority

269 The troubles began: Eric Schmitt, "Rick Kuhn Recalls Point-Shaving Case," *New York Times*, June 26, 1985.

269 One of the gamblers: Tom Van Riper, "ESPN Looks Back on Boston College Point Shaving Scandal—And a Player Speaks Out," *Forbes*, October 1, 2014.

270 "I'm the Boston College basketball fixer": Henry Hill with Douglas S. Looney, "How I Put the Fix In," *Sports Illustrated*, February 16, 1981.

270 By the time: Schmitt, "Rick Kuhn Recalls."

270 Both Cobb and Vario: Joseph P. Fried, "Cobb Not Guilty in Point-Shaving Trial," *New York Times*, March 24, 1984.

270 Jim Sweeney: Van Riper, "ESPN Looks Back."

271 In late March 1998: Pam Belluck, "College Basketball; Ex-Northwestern Players Charged in Point-Shaving," *New York Times*, March 27, 1998.

271 As was often the case: Matt O'Connor, "Lee Blames Point-Shaving at NU on 'Stress, Anxiety,'" *Chicago Tribune*, December 24, 1998.

271 According to the indictment: Belluck, "Ex-Northwestern Players Charged."

271 Under the circumstances: Matt O'Connor, "Pendergast Pleads Guilty in NU Basketball Fix," *Chicago Tribune*, April 10, 1998; O'Connor, "Lee Blames Point-Shaving."

272 The plea agreements included: Wayne Coffey, "The Fixer: Why Notre Dame Kicker Dumped His Life Away," *New York Daily News*, May 10, 1998; Matt O'Connor, "NU's Lee Pleads Guilty in Hoops Fix," *Chicago Tribune*, April 21, 1998.

272 In late November: Matt O'Connor, "4 Sentenced in Gambling Plot at NU," *Chicago Tribune*, November 25, 1998.

272 The other shoe dropped: Bill Dedman, "College Football; 4 Are Indicted in Northwestern Football Scandal," *New York Times*, December 4, 1998.

273 In early February 1999: Matt O'Connor, "Lundy Pleads Guilty in Point-Shaving Case," *Chicago Tribune*, February 6, 1999.

273 When all the dust settled: "Former Wildcats Cornerback Dwight Brown Pleads Guilty in Gambling Case," *Las Vegas Sun*, December 22, 1999.

273 NCAA bylaws specifically prohibit: NCAA *Division I Manual*, bylaw 10.3.

273 In December 1997: Associated Press, "Point-Shaving Scandal Hits Arizona State," *Los Angeles Times*, December 6, 1997.

274 Point-shaving scandals: Zach Silka, "Ex-Rocket Admits to Fumbling for $500," *Toledo Blade*, August 26, 2011.

274 Even at the University of San Diego: "San Diego Avoids NCAA Sanctions in Game-Fixing Case," *Examiner*, August 13, 2013.

274 The University of Colorado: Rick Reilly, "What Price Glory?" *Sports Illustrated*, February 27, 1989.

275 quarterback Charles Thompson: Rick Telander, "You Reap What You Sow," *Sports Illustrated*, February 27, 1989.

275 allegations of a climate: Jon Krakauer, *Missoula: Rape and the Justice System in a College Town* (New York: Anchor Books, 2015).

275 Similar allegations: Associated Press, "Ken Starr Leaves Baylor after Complaints It Mishandled Sex Assault Inquiry," *New York Times*, August 19, 2016.

275 The facts first came to light: Mark Viera, "Former Coach at Penn State Is Charged with Abuse," *New York Times*, November 5, 2011.

276 Compounding the shock: *Grand Jury Findings of Fact, 33rd Statewide Investigating Grand Jury*, November 4, 2011, 1, 6–7, 21–22, http://www.washingtonpost.com/wp-srv/sports/documents/sandusky-grand-jury

-report11052011.html; subsequently referred to as the Sandusky grand jury report.

276 Reports were made: Freeh report, 66–76.

276 In the 1998 incident: Freeh report, 41–52.

277 Schultz's notes: Freeh report, 47.

277 According to the grand jury's: Sandusky grand jury report; Pennsylvania Attorney General's Office, *Second Jerry Sandusky Grand Jury Presentment*, December 7, 2011, https://www.archive.org/details/271503 -sandusky-presentment2-12-7-2011.

278 A criminal investigation finally began: Kevin Johnson, "'Victim 1' Triggered Investigation of Jerry Sandusky," *USA Today*, November 11, 2011.

278 After posting bail: "Sandusky Arrested; New Child Sex Charges Filed," CNN, December 7, 2011, https://www.cnn.com/2011/12/07/justice/penn -state-scandal/index.html.

278 A week and a half: Sandusky grand jury report, 7.

278 McQueary, who testified truthfully: Teri Thompson and Christian Red, "Mike McQueary Testifies in Graphic Detail about '02 Sexual Assault of Young Boy in Penn State Locker Room by Jerry Sandusky," *New York Daily News*, December 17, 2011.

278 Schultz's testimony: Commonwealth of Pennsylvania v. Timothy Mark Curley and Gary Charles Schultz, CP-22-MD-1374-2011, CP-22-MD-1375-2011 (December 16, 2011), 224, 232–33, available at "Curley Schultz Hearing Transcript," by OpDeathEaters, https://www.scribd .com/document/260890885/Curley-Schultz-hearing-transcript.

279 In announcing formal charges: Pete Thamel, "State Officials Blast Penn State in Sandusky Case," *New York Times*, November 7, 2011.

279 For his part: "Statement from President Spanier," *Penn State News*, November 5, 2011, http://www.news.psu.edu/story/153819/2011/11/05 /statement-president-spanier.

279 He told the grand jury: "Transcript: Joe Paterno's Grand Jury Testimony," CBS Chicago, June 12, 2012, https://chicago.cbslocal.com/2012 /06/12/transcript-joe-paternos-grand-jury-testimony/.

279 After the scandal broke: Sally Jenkins, "Joe Paterno's First Interview since the Penn State–Sandusky Scandal," *Washington Post*, January 14, 2012.

279 "I don't know what you would call it": "Transcript: Joe Paterno's Grand Jury Testimony."

280 President Spanier testified: Commonwealth of Pennsylvania, Thirty-Third Statewide Investigating Grand Jury, *Transcript of Proceedings of Grand Jury (Graham Spanier)* (April 13, 2011), 15, 21–22, 25–26, available at "Graham Spanier Grand Jury Testimony from April 13, 2011," uploaded by PennLive, https://www.scribd.com/document/192201096 /Graham-Spanier-grand-jury-testimony-from-April-13–2011.

280 In November 2012: Associated Press, "Graham Spanier Formally Charged," ESPN, November 1, 2012, http://www.espn.com/college-football /story/_/id/8579116/graham-spanier-charged-jerry-sandusky-case.

281 The trustees were blindsided: Freeh report, 87–89, 102.

281 Within the week: ESPN News Service, "Joe Paterno, Graham Spanier Removed," ESPN, November 9, 2011, http://www.espn.com/college-football /story/_/id/7214380/joe-paterno-president-graham-spanier-penn-state.

281 On November 21: Associated Press, "Penn St. Hires Louis Freeh to Investigate," ESPN, November 22, 2011, http://www.espn.com/college-football /story/_/id/7264524/penn-state-nittany-lions-hire-ex-fbi-director-louis -freeh-investigation.

281 Over the next eight months: Freeh report, 8–9, 11.

282 Sandusky, Schultz, and Curley: Freeh report, 12, 73.

282 Among its findings: Freeh report, 14–17.

283 The Paterno family: Ken Belson, "Paterno Family Challenges Accusation of Cover-Up," New York Times, February 10, 2013.

283 On July 23: Steve Yanda, "Penn State Football Punished by NCAA over Sandusky Scandal," Washington Post, July 23, 2012.

284 The vacation-of-wins penalty: CBS and Associated Press, "Bobby Bowden Becomes FBS All-Time Wins Leader after Joe Paterno's Wins Vacated," CBS News, https://www.cbsnews.com/news/bobby-bowden-becomes -fbs-all-time-wins-leader-after-joe-paternos-wins-vacated/.

284 NCAA president Mark Emmert: Don Van Natta Jr., "On Death's Door: Inside the Secret Negotiations That Brought Penn State Football to the Brink of Extinction," ESPN: The Magazine, August 20, 2012.

285 The Freeh report notes: Freeh report, 9.

287 In August 2011: Mark Emmert, "Cheating Will Not Be Tolerated," USA Today, August 31, 2011.

287 On November 17: Van Natta, "On Death's Door."

287 "For intercollegiate athletics": NCAA Division I Manual, bylaw 2.4.

287 Erickson told Emmert: Van Natta, "On Death's Door."

288 Penn State officials undoubtedly: Van Natta, "On Death's Door."

289 That July 17 was a Tuesday: Van Natta, "On Death's Door."

290 the consent decree itself: Binding Consent Decree Imposed by the National Collegiate Athletic Association and Accepted by the Pennsylvania State University, July 23, 2012, 1, 5, available at "Penn State's NCAA Sanctions," http:// www.washingtonpost.com/wp-srv/sports/ncaa-sanctions-penn-state.html.

290 President Erickson was concerned: Rodney Erickson, email message to Gene Marsh et al., July 20, 2012, http://i.usatoday.net/sports /investigations-and-enterprise/2014-12-04-penn-state-exhibits-1-5.pdf.

290 Documentation revealed: Jeré Longman, "A Boost from the State Capitol: How a Legislator Helped Penn State Escape Penalties," New York Times, February 5, 2015.

290 led numerous commentators to suggest: Frank Fitzpatrick and Erin McCarthy, "E-mails Reveal NCAA's Attempt to 'Bluff' Penn State on Sanctions," *Philadelphia Inquirer*, November 5, 2014; Matt Bonesteel, "In E-mails, NCAA Admitted It Bluffed Penn State into Accepting Jerry Sandusky Sanctions," *Washington Post*, November 5, 2014.

291 The presumption that the death penalty: *Binding Consent Decree*, 4.

292 "long, hard slog": Dustin Hockensmith, "NCAA Releases Its Own Emails, Calls Penn State Interactions 'Courteous and Professional,'" PennLive, November 14, 2014, https://www.pennlive.com/midstate/index.ssf/2014 /11/ncaa_releases_its_own_emails_c.html.

292 even the NCAA's vice president: NCAA, "Documents Clarify Penn State Consent Decree: NCAA Sets Record Straight on Agreement," November 14, 2014, http://www.ncaa.org/about/resources/media-center/news /documents-clarify-penn-state-consent-decree.

293 "The NCAA concludes": *Binding Consent Decree*, 4.

295 an article in *Fortune*: Erik Sherman, "The Highest Paid College Football Coaches in 2015," *Fortune*, December 12, 2015.

295 A part of the sanctions: *Binding Consent Decree*, 6.

296 Some observers described: Joe Schad and Don Van Natta Jr., "Source: Silas Redd Thinking USC," ESPN, July 26, 2012, http://www.espn.com /college-football/story/_/id/8199175/penn-state-nittany-lions-silas-redd -meeting-usc-trojans-coach-Lane-Kiffin.

296 The erosion began: "NCAA to Restore Penn St. Scholarships," Fox Sports, September 24, 2013, https://www.foxsports.com/college-football/story /ncaa-gradually-restore-penn-state-football-scholarships-lost-jerry -sandusky-scandal-092413.

296 A year after that: Steve Eder and Marc Tracy, "N.C.A.A. Rolls Back Punishment of Penn State," *New York Times*, September 9, 2014.

297 Finally, in January 2015: ESPN News Service, "Joe Paterno Is Now Winningest Coach," ESPN, January 16, 2015, http://www.espn.com/blog/bigten /post/_/id/114470/paterno-to-be-winningest-coach-again.

297 Former U.S. senator: Eder and Tracy, "N.C.A.A. Rolls Back Punishment."

297 Pennsylvania governor Tom Corbett: Mark Scolforo, "Pennsylvania Governor Sues NCAA for Sandusky Sanctions," *Oregonian*, January 3, 2013.

299 Media reports indicate: Van Natta, "On Death's Door."

299 "I can't believe this shit": Van Natta, "On Death's Door."

299 Jerry Sandusky was convicted: Tim Rohan, "Sandusky Gets 30 to 60 Years for Sexual Abuse," *New York Times*, October 9, 2012.

299 In March of that year: Angela Couloumbis, Jeremy Roebuck, and Susan Snyder, "Two Ex-PSU Officials Plead Guilty to Child Endangerment in Sandusky Case," *Pittsburgh Post-Gazette*, March 13, 2017.

300 A jury convicted him: Will Hobson, "Former Penn State President Graham Spanier Convicted of Child Endangerment," *Washington Post*, March 24, 2017.

300 Sentencing for all three: Will Hobson, "Former Penn State President Graham Spanier Sentenced to Jail for Child Endangerment in Jerry Sandusky Abuse Case," *Washington Post*, June 2, 2017.

300 In January 2018: NCAA, "Letter of Inquiry Sent to Michigan State," January 24, 2018, www.ncaa.org/about/resources/media-center/news/letter-inquiry-sent-Michigan-State.

300 Nassar, a former team doctor: Scott Cacciola and Victor Mather, "Larry Nassar Sentencing: 'I Just Signed Your Death Warrant,'" *New York Times*, January 24, 2018.

300 The NCAA announced: Brendan Quinn, "Analysis: At Michigan State, the NCAA Closes the Door on Two Inquiries, Paves New Ground for MSU, and Itself," *Athletic*, August 30, 2018, http://theathletic.com/497175/2018/08/30/analysis-at-michigan-state-the-ncaa-closes-the-door-on-two-inquiries-paves-new-ground-for-msu-and-itself/.

Conclusion

304 The NCAA website describes: NCAA, "NCAA Division III," www.ncaa.org/about?division=d3.

305 A December 2015 article: Will Hobson and Steven Rich, "The Latest Extravagances in the College Sports Arms Race? Laser Tag and Mini Golf," *Washington Post*, December 21, 2015.

305 Auburn unveiled: Will Hobson and Steven Rich, "Playing in the Red: College Athletic Departments Are Taking In More Money Than Ever—and Spending It Just as Fast," *Washington Post*, November 23, 2015.

305 Thirty-six head football coaches: ESPN News Service, "Michigan's Jim Harbaugh Leads College Football Coaches in Salary," ESPN, October 26, 2016, http://www.espn.com/college-football/story/_/id/17892134/michigan-wolverines-coach-jim-harbaugh-salary-tops-list-college-football-coaches.

305 a later report indicated: Steve Berkowitz, "Nick Saban to Be Paid $11.125 Million This Season after Alabama Contract Extension," *USA Today*, May 2, 2017.

305 In 2018: Richard Johnson, "A History of Skyrocketing College Football Coach Salaries, from Walter Camp to Nick Saban," SBNation, October 4, 2018, https://www.sbnation.com/college-football/2018/6/4/17390394/college-football-coach-salaries-history-highest.

305 Salaries of the top fifteen: Courtney Connley, "These Are the 15 Highest-Paid Coaches in March Madness," CNBC, March 15, 2018, https://www.cnbc.com/2018/03/15/the-15-highest-paid-coaches-in-2018-march-madness.html.

305 In 2016: Associated Press, "NCAA Tournament Deal with CBS, Turner Extended through 2032," ESPN, April 12, 2016, http://www.espn.com

/mens-college-basketball/story/_/id/15190549/ncaa-tournament-deal
-cbs-turner-extended-2032.

306 "striptease dances" and "sex acts": NCAA, *University of Louisville Public Infractions Decision*, June 15, 2017, https://web3.ncaa.org/lsdbi/search /miCaseView/report?id=102682.

306 In announcing a new penalty matrix: Gary Brown, "Violator Beware: Penalties in New Enforcement Structure Pack a Punch," NCAA, January 9, 2013, http://www.ncaa.org/about/resources/media-center/news /violator-beware-penalties-new-enforcement-structure-pack-punch.

308 *all* the NCAA's enforcement actions: Branch, "Shame of College Sports."

308 In September 2017: Scott Gleeson and A. J. Perez, "FBI Arrests Four College Basketball Assistants on Charges of Fraud," *USA Today*, September 26, 2017; Marc Tracy, "Investigation Nets Charges of Illegality in Recruiting," *New York Times*, September 27, 2017; Ben Cohen, "A High-End Clothier Is Key in Probe," *Wall Street Journal*, October 5, 2017.

308 In response to the scandal: "Statement from President Mark Emmert on the Formation of a Commission on College Basketball," NCAA, October 11, 2017, http://www.ncaa.org/about/resources/media-center/news /statement-president-mark-emmert-formation-commission-college -basketball.

309 For the purposes of this book: "Statement from President Mark Emmert."

309 The report states: Commission on College Basketball, *Report and Recommendations to Address the Issues Facing Collegiate Basketball*, April 2018, 9–10.

309 Almost immediately: "Joint Statement on Commission on College Basketball," NCAA, April 25, 2018, http://www.ncaa.org/about/resources /media-center/news/joint-statement-commission-college-basketball.

309 the NCAA issued: "Committed to Change," NCAA, http://www.ncaa.org /about/committed-change.

310 the Rice commission recommended: Commission on College Basketball, *Report and Recommendations*, 9.

310 Schools, the infractions committee: "Committed to Change."

311 the new bodies: "Committed to Change."

311 In October 2018: Marc Tracy, "Three Found Guilty in N.C.A.A. Basketball Recruiting Scheme," *New York Times*, October 24, 2018.

Index